D0065366

The Complete Guide to

COLLECTING ART

THE
COMPLETE GUIDE
TO COLLECTING ART

Lee Rosenbaum

Alfred A. Knopf   New York   1982

THIS IS A BORZOI BOOK
PUBLISHED BY ALFRED A. KNOPF, INC.
Copyright © 1982 by Lee Rosenbaum
All rights reserved under International and
Pan-American Copyright Conventions. Published
in the United States by Alfred A. Knopf, Inc.,
New York, and simultaneously in Canada by
Random House of Canada Limited, Toronto.
Distributed by Random House, Inc., New York.

Owing to limitations of space, all
acknowledgments of permission to reprint
previously published material, and to use
illustrations, will be found
following the index.

Library of Congress Cataloging in Publication Data
Rosenbaum, Lee.
The complete guide to collecting art.
Bibliography: p.
Includes index.
1. Art—collectors and collecting. I. Title.
N5200.R66 1982   707'.5   82-47837
ISBN 0-394-51347-9   AACR2
ISBN 0-394-71104-1 (pbk.)

Manufactured in the United States of America
FIRST EDITION

To Don

CONTENTS

CONTENTS

Contents

ACKNOWLEDGMENTS

To all the collectors, dealers, auction-house officials, museum officials, conservators, lawyers, tax experts and insurance experts who have been so generous with their time and knowledge in interviews for this book (and in previous interviews during my ten years as an art writer), I would like to express my sincerest thanks. Special mention must go to those who gave extraordinary help: Philippe de Montebello, director of the Metropolitan Museum of Art, and his special assistant, Carol Moon Cardon, supervised the compilation of a bibliography of art reference sources for new collectors. Elizabeth Baker, editor of *Art in America* magazine, read and commented on the two chapters about buying and selling through dealers and about buying contemporary art. Lawrence Majewski, cochairman of the Conservation Center of New York University's Institute of Fine Arts and a special consultant to the Metropolitan Museum of Art, read and commented on the sections about conservation. Ralph Lerner, a New York City tax attorney who has served as chairman of several seminars on art law sponsored by the Practising Law Institute, read and commented on the tax chapter and helped bring it up to date with recent changes in the tax law.

Other experts reviewed smaller portions of the manuscript: Ashton Hawkins, vice-president, secretary and counsel of the Metropolitan Museum, reviewed the section on the obstacles to international movement of art objects; David Nash, director of fine arts sales at Sotheby Parke Bernet, New York, reviewed certain auction-related passages; Huntington Block, the Washington, D.C., broker who specializes in fine-arts insurance, reviewed the sections related to insurance and security.

I would also like to thank my editor, Nancy Nicholas, and my agent, Maxine Groffsky, for their confidence in me and their willingness to allow me complete freedom in writing my first book.

Finally, I would like to thank my first line of criticism and support: my husband, Donald, and my parents, Alexander and Shirley Flasterstein, who not only read and commented on the manuscript but also gave me the time I needed to complete it after Paul was born.

L.R.

FOREWORD

Many people buy art, but few feel completely comfortable about it. For all but the most experienced collectors, the pleasure of buying a painting, sculpture, drawing, print or photograph is usually mixed with at least a twinge of fear or doubt—misgivings over a piece's authenticity, quality or price, and suspicions that dealers, auction-house officials, or more knowledgeable collectors may be secretly laughing (or even sneering) at one's ineptitude. Misgivings often extend beyond the purchase of art to questions about the proper maintenance, insurance and security for a collection, and questions about the most advantageous way to dispose of one's holdings—whether by sale, donation, gift or bequest.

The art world's intimidating aura of mystery and exclusiveness frequently prevents new buyers from ever acquiring the knowledge and experience they need to gain more self-assurance in their encounters with art and art professionals. This book seeks to dispel the aura that discourages would-be collectors from entering galleries, deters new collectors from asking hard questions, and prevents experienced collectors from getting the best possible advice and service. Even the most brilliant buyer may be an inept conserver, insurer, seller or tax strategist. And even a well-connected patron of galleries and museums probably cannot boast the range of contacts—from top collectors like Paul Mellon and Norton Simon to little-known conservators, tax experts and insurance brokers—whose knowledge and insights have gone into the preparation of this book.

For the chapters on buying and selling art, I have sought the views of top dealers, museum officials, auction-house experts and collectors. The section on caring for your collection is compiled from the observations of expert conservators, insurers and security specialists. The tax chapter is drawn from the collective wisdom of respected art-tax lawyers and accountants as well as the ever-skeptical IRS officials who regularly tear apart art collectors' tax returns. And while the main theme of this book is "art for love, not money," it also includes a detailed rundown of some of the latest strategies used by those who pursue art as an investment.

This book will not make you a brilliant art collector; only the love of art and devotion to its study can do that. But if you already have (or want to develop) the love and the knowledge, the book should provide the nuts-and-bolts information needed to put those gifts to the most intelligent and successful use.

The Complete Guide to

COLLECTING ART

Chapter 1

WHAT TO COLLECT?

You have just arrived at the opening of a well-known dealer's latest exhibition when, across a crowded gallery, you spot the masterpiece of your dreams: it's beautiful, it's available, and it's love at first sight. But in art collecting, as in other passionate pursuits, first impressions cannot always be trusted. Museum directors, curators, dealers and experienced collectors often find that their first impressions do hold up under rigorous analysis, but even they can make mistakes. The less experienced you are, the more skeptical you should be of first impressions if you are serious about building a collection that you will still be proud to own as your sophistication grows. "To me, the sign of a good collection is that the collection as a whole has a level that is kept," says art historian John Rewald, who has advised some of this country's top collectors of Impressionist and Post-Impressionist paintings. "If I walk into a house and I see one or two good pieces and a dozen inferior ones, that's not a collection; that's a haphazard conglomeration."

Few new collectors begin by worrying about what kind of conglomeration their collections will eventually become. Your original reasons for wanting to buy art may not have been very exalted or complicated: you wanted something eye-catching to hang over the sofa, you wanted the social cachet that accrues to those with "good taste," or you wanted to put some of your inflation-ravaged capital into tangibles. But art collecting is a dangerous hobby, and those who begin by possessing often wind up being possessed. They gather and consume all the books and articles they can find on their specialty. They find themselves accumulating more art than they can possibly keep in their own homes (or more than they can possibly afford). They place several bids at auction above the strict limit that they had set themselves just hours earlier.

True collecting—as distinguished from decorating, status-seeking or investing—is a madness; art collecting—with its strong spiritual and aesthetic power—is probably the most passionate manifestation of this mania. As your acquisitions grow, you may find the collection taking on a life of its own, with its own spirit and its own demands. Instead of buying something to fit your decor or your investment portfolio, you may pursue an object that you feel must become part of your collection —something that the collection needs to make it a more complete expression of your concept of a certain period, style or theme.

The unifying concept differs from collector to collector. Paul Mellon, chairman of the National Gallery of Art and son of the late Pittsburgh financier Andrew Mellon, thinks of his huge group of British works from the seventeenth through nineteenth centuries (much of which he has given to the Center for British Art, which he established in 1977 at Yale University) as a collection that calls attention to the fact that British art has been undervalued and underestimated. Because he has long seen this public purpose for his British collection (as distinct from his collection of Impressionists and Post-Impressionists, which is less systematic and more governed by personal taste), he has bought many works strictly because he thought they filled a niche in his collection and would be useful to Yale. (He added, though, that he won't buy a work he doesn't like, no matter how great it is.)

Similarly, collector-scholar Paul Singer sees an overriding educational value to his group of three thousand pieces of early Chinese art. He has objects in every material, and his collection shows the sequence of development in each material. The goal of Edward Carter, a trustee of the Los Angeles County Museum of Art, is to acquire just one prime example of the work of each important seventeenth-century Dutch artist who painted landscapes, seascapes, city scenes or still lifes. Having neither unlimited wall space nor unlimited funds, he sells or donates a picture when he can substitute a finer one by the same painter. The 35 or so paintings in his collection, he said, are "among the top examples in the world and their condition is generally extraordinarily high." His opinion was confirmed by the curators of three major museums—the Metropolitan Museum of Art, Boston Museum of Fine Arts and Los Angeles County Museum of Art—where a traveling exhibition of his collection was mounted in 1981–82.

Like Carter, the contemporary-art collector Richard Brown Baker seeks a certain balance and relationship among the works he owns; and for a time, at least, he tended to pursue a similar policy of getting a single work by each artist. The contemporary-art collection of Herbert and Dorothy Vogel has a more personal unifying concept: they are friendly with many artists and usually buy works by people they know. At a 1979 panel discussion on contemporary-art collecting sponsored by the New Museum in New York, Dorothy Vogel added a few more criteria: they have to be able to fit a new acquisition into their apartment, they have to be able to afford it, and they have to like it. She said they collect ten to twelve artists in depth, with works from various periods of their careers. They also keep files of articles, reviews, announcements and letters related to those artists.

Collectors who have a strong concept of what they are trying to accomplish in collecting will sometimes go to great lengths to locate and acquire works that they feel belong in their collections. Some, like Paul Mellon, hire advisors to keep them informed of works newly on the market. Some may even go after privately owned works that are not on the market; collectors who are thoroughly familiar with an artist's oeuvre may develop a "wish list" of privately owned works that they want to acquire. They are able to find out about the holdings of others through the art-world grapevine or through research in catalogues raisonnés (books that compile all known works by a given artist, often listing the previous and current owners), and they sometimes make offers to collectors who hold works they have targeted for acquisition. California collector Norton Simon, the retired industrialist, has tried this approach on occasion but says that, in his experience, it rarely works. The seller usually expects to get a great deal of money, since he is not using a dealer or other agent as middleman; the buyer expects to get a bargain for the same reason. They therefore find it difficult or impossible to agree on a price.

First Reactions

Few beginning collectors have such grand designs. The impulse to collect usually begins simply enough, with an attraction to certain types of art. For some collectors, this attraction is powerful and may even be associated with strong physical symptoms: "I listen to my stomach and the back of my neck," said Ben Heller, a prominent dealer and collector of contemporary American art and ancient and primitive art, who is best known for his $2-million sale of Jackson Pollock's *Blue Poles* to the Australian National Gallery in 1973. "When I see something I like, I feel a visceral excitement. I'm all agitated. Some people are very cool." Paul Singer does his best to appear unexcited so the dealer won't jack up the price, but he actually reacts "in the same way as if I saw a beautiful woman: my heart beats faster and my mouth goes dry." A psychiatrist as well as a collector and scholar of early Chinese art,

Singer views collecting as "a highly erotic act, totally akin to lovemaking. The act of buying an object is done in secrecy with a slight feeling of shame at indulging yourself to this extent in an act of eroticism. Any dealer worth his salt knows that there should be no interruption while a collector looks at an object: it is a moment of great intimacy." Norbert Schimmel, a trustee emeritus of the Metropolitan Museum of Art and a major collector of ancient art from Egypt and other countries around the Mediterranean, has a less romantic but equally intense way of describing his feelings for a desired object: "It's like dope," he said. "I can't sleep until I buy it." Schimmel added that "when you hesitate, you shouldn't buy. If an object doesn't have the 'oomph' and hit you between the eyes, don't buy it. I have regretted all the times when I was influenced by somebody to buy something." Singer has regretted the opposite—being influenced to dispose of something as a fake when his instincts told him it was right. He showed the object to a dealer whose judgment he valued highly and the dealer said it was wrong. Upset because he was convinced the object was right, Singer got rid of it and later found out it had been bought by the Boston Museum of Fine Arts.

There are times, though, when even the most intuitively sensitive collector is happy to disregard first impressions: when he gradually learns to understand and love something that at first sight was strange and off-putting. In his article "Notes on the Formation of My Collection" (*Art International*, Sept. 20, 1961), contemporary-art collector Richard Brown Baker confessed that he felt "a strong revulsion to the first Kline oil that I ever saw." Revulsion turned to attraction with increased exposure, and Baker went on to buy (from New York dealer Sidney Janis in 1956) a large, important Franz Kline abstraction, *Wanamaker Block,* which was subsequently exhibited around the world and, five years after its purchase, had become the most widely known picture in Baker's collection. In a recent interview for this book, Baker said that when he likes a work of art, he doesn't start analyzing why; he just asks its price.

Another important collector of contemporary art, Eugene Schwartz, tries to be more methodical but, in the end, is just as impulsive: "I do research about the history of an artist; I get every review; I ask the opinions of other artists and knowledgeable friends; then I throw it all away and buy something I can't resist." In a field where research is even more important—Dutch seventeenth-century paintings—collector Edward Carter also gives the greatest weight to his first responses. "I rely on my intuitive reactions to pictures," he said. "Then I look for empirical evidence to justify my intuitive feelings. My initial reaction is not always confirmed, but in most cases it is."

Franz Kline, *Wanamaker Block*

If the inexperienced collector suffers all the classic symptoms of art-love—tense neck, churning stomach, dry mouth, palpitating heart, inability to sleep and even a few calm moments of aesthetic pleasure —should he, like these seasoned collectors, obey the impulse to buy? Probably not. The collectors quoted here are already experts; their trust in first reactions is based on years spent in developing an eye and a concept of what their collections should be. The first step in collecting is not buying but learning. The first thing to learn is the scope and limitations of opportunities in the field or fields that interest you. If Rembrandt masterpieces are your passion, your love will probably remain platonic. Such paintings rarely appear on the market (most are in museums) and when they do, they can command millions. On the other hand, certain fields are relatively untapped and a number of high-quality works are still up for grabs on the open market. A small sampling of relatively unexplored fields cited by experts interviewed for this book includes: Italian and Italianate landscapes of 1630–1670; Mannerist paintings (works generally characterized by distortion of the human figure and discrepancies of scale) of the period 1590–1620;

early Spanish painting (through the Baroque era); Renaissance bronze plaques; nineteenth-century Spanish painting; African art (particularly the roughly finished pieces from such areas as eastern Nigeria, Cameroon, Sudan, Upper Volta, Mali and Togo, which are less popular than well-finished objects from such areas as Zaïre, the Ivory Coast, Gabon and southwestern Nigeria); Oceanic art (particularly the rough, expressionistic pieces from Melanesia, which are less popular than pieces from Micronesia and Polynesia); early Chinese art; contemporary Chinese paintings; paintings and temple banners from India; early-nineteenth-century French lithographs; French etchings of 1820–1880; nineteenth-century French drawings by lesser-known masters; American and British prints of 1900–1950; twentieth-century photographs; American sculpture; and American portraits. Other relatively inexpensive fields (although the best examples in *any* field will command high prices) include American Indian art, American folk art, old-master drawings by lesser-known artists, Japanese netsuke (miniature carvings, often of animals or people, fashioned from wood, ivory, metal or other materials and used in the eighteenth and nineteenth centuries as toggles on Japanese robes), and contemporary art by lesser-known artists. If you choose a field that has long been popular—French Impressionism and Post-Impressionism, for example—you will need millions of dollars to amass a high-quality collection, assuming that you can find enough works on the market. "For the last ten or fifteen years, I haven't been buying French pictures," said Paul Mellon, a man who can afford to spend the requisite millions for Impressionist and Post-Impressionist works, "because I don't think the quality is as good as what was coming up before. . . . Very fine paintings are probably worth every cent you are willing to give. But prices of mediocre and bad paintings have gone up in almost the same proportion. I think people are paying more than they should."

Judging Price

Prices for works in certain fashionable or faddish fields may be disproportionately high in relation to works by undisputed masters: "I can sell works by Russell and Remington at prices comparable to Goya and Rembrandt," observed New York dealer Clyde Newhouse at a 1976 World Art Market Conference in New York, sponsored by *The ARTnewsletter* and the New School. Noting that the Russell and Remington prices were symptomatic of a runaway boom in American art with Western themes, Newhouse commented that "these prices would be ludicrous in terms of what else they could buy in the art market." Similar pricing oddities, he said, could be found in comparing works of contemporary artists and old masters: "A good Rauschenberg drawing would cost as much as a Tiepolo. It's all a question of demand and fashion." At another art-market conference sponsored in 1980 by *ARTnews* and *Antiques World* magazines and *The ARTnewsletter,* New York dealer Eugene Thaw made the same point: "The value of a good Harnett is about the equivalent of a Chardin; a good Rauschenberg is about the same as a Fragonard; a Klimt is about the same as a Goya; a good painting by Remington costs the same as a Rogier van der Weyden. . . . The fact that both a Klimt and a Goya can now bring $1 million may mean that in today's climate of taste, more collectors or museums need or want a Klimt than a Goya."

Speaking on the same panel with Thaw, David Bathurst, president of the New York branch of Christie's auction house, suggested that collectors should "start with a shopping list of artists you like the most. Start at the top and work your way down to the artist whose best painting you can afford if it comes on the market. Don't buy a minor painting or a cursory sketch by a major artist unless it really appeals to you. Don't, for example, buy one of the many horrid sketches that Renoir did and never intended to be sold. From an investment point of view, these pink sneezes are like lead balloons."

A tour of galleries and a perusal of auction catalogues and price lists will begin to give you an idea of which areas and artists are within your price range. Prints, drawings and photographs are the most affordable fields, with good examples available for a few hundred or a few thousand dollars. A similar outlay will also buy you a painting by a lesser-known contemporary artist. Antiquities and primitive art are generally lower-priced than old-master to modern paintings of comparable quality (if quality comparisons of such dissimilar works can be made). In general, the less-explored areas of collecting are less expensive than traditional fields but are also more subject to sudden price inflation due to faddism and sudden price declines due to adverse economic conditions. Once you zero in on an area that is both appealing and affordable, you should also make sure that the major sources of such art are accessible to you. While it is possible (with the help of catalogues, photographs and descriptions) to buy from galleries and auction houses without first traveling to see the works in person (more on this in Chapters 2 and 3), most experts agree that serious collectors should try to make at least occasional trips to art-market centers like New York or London. If you can't do this, you can still collect by relying on the best galleries in your region and by leaning on the advice of trusted experts who do get to the major art centers.

In deciding what to collect and how to collect it, "you've got to do a lot of hard work," according to Christopher Burge, director of fine arts at Christie's, New York. He noted that a collector must serve an apprenticeship, learning about a field just as if he were going to write a book about it. He should read as much as possible about his chosen field or fields, so that he will not make his first forays into the market- place as an obviously ignorant buyer. "Art collecting is a never-ending learning," observed Norbert Schimmel. "When I bought my first Etrus- can piece, I hadn't the slightest idea about the history of the Etruscans, so I bought books." (See the bibliography for a list of useful beginning reference sources in various fields, compiled for this book by members of the curatorial staff of the Metropolitan Museum of Art.) In addition to books and journals that analyze the history and aesthetics of your chosen field(s), your readings should include recent price lists. Eugene Thaw suggests that new collectors, before they venture into the market, should amass a year's worth of auction catalogues in their fields of interest and carefully study the accompanying price lists (which are sent after the sale to catalogue subscribers). Some art libraries also collect catalogues and prices lists. Prices at auction, where art is publicly traded, are the closest art-market equivalents to stock-market quota- tions; they can give you some insight into price levels and market trends. Thaw believes that new collectors should attend auctions sev- eral times before buying, to get a feeling for prices. Also available are newsletters that publish art-market prices and analyses, and books that compile lists of auction prices for a given year; some of these books are specialized (covering prints, American art or some other specific cate- gory), while others run the gamut from antiquities to contemporary art. (See the listings under "Market Newsletters and Periodicals" and "Price Guides" in the "General" section of the bibliography.)

Prices lists are only a starting point in getting a feel for market values. There can be a great difference of opinion over what a given work of art should cost, and the best way to avoid being overcharged is to comparison-shop. This is relatively easy in the case of works that are not unique, such as prints and photographs. If different copies of the same image are widely available, you can get a relatively secure idea of fair market value by looking up the most recent auction prices and checking the prices at various galleries. In the case of one-of-a-kind works such as paintings, you must try to find out what various sellers are getting for comparable works. (This means that you must know enough about quality and condition to know which works *are* comparable.)

Once you have done this homework, you may still occasionally decide to "overpay." If a price seems out of line to you, you may want to ask the seller why the work he is offering is so much more expensive than others you have seen on the market. He may convince you of the greater desirability of his offering, and you may learn something new about quality judgments. "When you see a first-rate object," says collector Schimmel, "you should pay through the nose to get it, because in four weeks you will forget how much you paid. You really only overpay for second-class material." Sidney Janis, a dealer in modern and contemporary art, cautions that in judging prices "the collector has to learn to forget the prices quoted to him two or three years ago. If he doesn't forget them and he feels he has to get something today at a price he knew about previously, he will collect only second-best things." The rarer and more desirable an object is, the more difficult it is to say what constitutes a "fair" price. (Further price-related issues, including the size of dealers' markups, comparative prices at auctions and galleries, and techniques of market analysis, will be discussed in later chapters.)

Judging Quality

The ability to make price judgments presupposes an ability to make quality judgments. Developing an eye for quality is the new collector's most difficult and important task. "The prime question for any collector," according to Ralph Colin, administrative vice-president and counsel of the Art Dealers Association of America and an important collector of modern masters, "is not, 'Do I like the picture?' but, 'Do I like it in comparison to other things? Is it better than all the other things I've seen?' I would not buy anything without going to other galleries and seeing what's on the market. I might see things I like better." New York dealer Richard Feigen made this point to singer-actress Barbra Streisand when she dashed into his gallery one day, eager to spend her money on a work by Henri Matisse. "In your abject ignorance of the market, I don't want to sell this to you," Feigen says he told Streisand. "I gave her the names of three other dealers to go to and told her, 'Once you've checked around, if you still want this one you can have it.' " Streisand comparison-shopped, returned to Feigen and finally bought his Matisse.

"A collector should have some frame of reference," noted John Walsh, Jr., paintings curator at the Boston Museum of Fine Arts. "The more great and important works you see, the better. That is not to say that there are not crimes of passion that the collector may commit out of sheer love and be very right. The first reaction ought to be emotional

—some real impact through the senses, whether it's great excitement, instant attraction or revulsion. But after the initial encounter and reaction comes the act of classifying and comparing. You should walk away from the art work for as long as you dare, try to clear your head, and come back and check whether your reaction was really based on anything solid that can be repeated." Similarly, Christopher Burge of Christie's observed that "in the beginning, you don't know which work of art to pick; they all look pretty good. If you've seen one, it's the best you've seen. If you've seen two, one will be better than the other. The more you see, the more you can make comparisons."

In addition to looking at as much art as possible, the new collector should ask as many questions as possible. Many dealers and auction-house specialists, and some museum professionals and experienced collectors, are happy to help new collectors who show a sincere and serious desire to learn. You should not hesitate to ask them the most basic questions about quality:

• Which of several works by a particular artist do they consider to be the best, and why?
• How do they think a particular work that you are considering for purchase ranks in the artist's oeuvre?
• How does the artist rank among others from his period and school?
• How is (was) he regarded by artists and critics who are (were) his contemporaries?
• Where can you see other works by the artist (i.e., at which specific galleries and museums)?
• Has the artist's work been widely bought by museums?
• What are the best reference sources on this artist's work? Is there any published material on the specific work you are interested in?

(The same types of questions can be asked about antiquities, primitive art and other works for which the artist is unknown, by asking for comparisons with other works from the same region and period.)

The experts all stress that collectors should develop a complete knowledge of an artist's production and his standing among his peers before venturing to buy any work. If you are interested in Picasso, for example, "you ought to know his periods and which are better because the paintings were executed in a better way or the drawing was more beautiful," according to New York dealer Stephen Hahn. Picasso's best Cubist works are generally considered his most desirable and can bring millions of dollars when they make their rare appearances on the market; works executed late in his prolific life are generally considered less masterful in conception and execution and have much more difficulty finding buyers. In his review in the *New York Times* (Feb. 13, 1980) of a Picasso retrospective at the Walker Art Center in Minneapolis, art critic Hilton Kramer said that Picasso's work of the late 1930s began to exhibit an "awful facility, amounting at times to an incontinent garrulousness, that came more and more to dominate the work of his last years. . . . We search in vain for the kind of deepening vision that is so conspicuous, and so moving, in the late works of Cézanne and Matisse, for example."

Just as a painting is not necessarily great because it was executed by a big-name artist, so a work of antiquity is not necessarily desirable because it is very old. "A beginner should not buy what he doesn't like because he is impressed by age," warns Norbert Schimmel. "There is a difference between an archaeological object and a work of art. When I began collecting, I brought a piece to John Cooney [an Egyptologist who was then a curator at the Brooklyn Museum and later became curator of ancient art at the Cleveland Museum of Art] and he said, 'It is absolutely genuine, but *so* boring!' I am no longer impressed by age. The most important thing for me is that the workmanship and quality must be good. A beginner has to learn to say no."

In addition to looking at art and listening to the quality judgments of others, a collector can learn to judge the quality of potential purchases by acquiring several works that he knows are first-rate and then seeing how possible additions to his collection would stand up in such company. Speaking on the phone recently to a collector who was uncertain whether to buy a particular work from another contemporary art dealer, New York dealer André Emmerich invoked what he calls the "reverse Gresham's law." Whereas the economic law is that "bad money drives out good money," the rule in art collecting, according to Emmerich, is: "Good art drives out bad art. Bring into your home at least a few works of indisputably great quality. Then put new things next to the objects that you know are very good, and see how they hold up." (It should be noted that this can be done with works offered by dealers, who will often let collectors bring works home on approval before buying, but it cannot be done with auction-house offerings, except by making mental comparisons.)

The most difficult challenges to a collector's judgment are posed by works for which there are no, or few, established standards of quality. Dealer-collector Ben Heller noted that, for the most part, people are not "free to see" when they are confronted with offbeat works of ancient or contemporary art that don't fit into their preconceived notions of what such art should look like. He says that he keeps his eye for quality alive by testing it on the newest art, where standards of excellence are varied and constantly changing, and ancient and primitive art, where there is "no signature yardstick. . . . Our culture pays through the nose for the security of the signature, and unsigned works generally have lesser market value," he noted. Confronting an unsigned work, he said, forces the collector to respond to it on its own merits. "There is no canon other than the work itself."

New areas of collecting also pose special problems, because critics, scholars and collectors are just beginning to come to grips with questions of quality. "We have yet to cultivate a significant number of photography historians and photography critics," noted Charles Traub, former director of Light Gallery in New York, which represents many young photographers. "Without those guidelines, the new collecting public is in a little bit of a quandary. As a dealer, I may say that someone is a good photographer, but the collector may say, 'Of course you do. You represent him.' As dealers, we have an interest in the promotion of our own people. Because there is not yet a good group of critics, this leaves potential collectors vulnerable. The new collector must address himself to a serious investigation of the medium."

As Traub suggests, advice is only as good as the advisor, and dealers and auction-house specialists, while the most accessible of experts, are also the most self-interested. "Dealers often promote second-rate pictures as first-rate because there are so few first-rate pictures available on the market," noted art historian John Rewald. Even if your own eye is good enough to tell the difference, the scarcity of top-quality works in many fields may prevent you from putting your connoisseurship to good use. Dealers often show their most favored works to their most favored customers, and the trick of art collecting, according to New York dealer Eugene Thaw, who sells works from old masters to moderns, is to get people to offer you their best. New collectors are at a serious disadvantage, in Thaw's view, because they are often offered the leftovers—works that have proved of no interest to gallery regulars. To overcome this disadvantage, Thaw suggests that the new collector pick a few firms with which he can become familiar and get a welcome when he comes, so that he can have easy access to their finds. The art world, he said, is such a small place that "if a collector makes an intelligent first purchase and behaves properly, he will immediately become part of the establishment of collectors. Dealers are always looking for collectors worth bringing along." Thaw's gallery, which rarely spends time with new collectors unless they are introduced by museum curators, scholars or other art professionals, is perhaps more exclusive than most; the availability of top-quality works to new collectors varies from dealer to dealer and from field to field. There are also examples of collectors who don't "behave properly" (i.e., in the manner most likely to ingratiate them with dealers) and yet manage to assemble magnificent collections by virtue of their connoisseurship, knowledgeable contacts or financial clout. Conversely, there are those who have excellent relationships with dealers and yet wind up with mediocre collections because they have no eye of their own and have allowed themselves to be easily led. Nevertheless, Thaw's basic premise stands: the better your relations with good dealers, the better your chances of being offered high-quality art.

So far this discussion has carefully skirted the main issue: what *is* quality in art? While many may try to describe it to you, none can make you experience it. You've heard all the standard (and sometimes conflicting) definitions: a good painting is one that has a powerful or pleasing composition, an innovative use of form or color, skillful draftsmanship, careful attention to detail, strong emotional or aesthetic appeal, etc. Perhaps the truest and least helpful definition is that a good work of art does well what it sets out to do: if it was meant to be an attractive landscape, it is, in fact, just that; if it was meant to explore new ideas about form and color, it explores them brilliantly and provocatively.

All of this is perfectly accurate, but is of little help to you when you stand in front of an art work. Appreciating art is not a verbal experience and cannot be conveyed adequately in words. Aspiring collectors may be further discouraged to learn of the belief on the part of some experts that you may never achieve the ability to distinguish good art from bad, no matter how long and hard you try. New York dealers Stephen Hahn and Klaus Perls both feel that an eye for art is like an ear for music— either you have it or you don't. "Enjoying art is a genetically programmed activity in human beings," asserts Perls. "Some people are born with a certain feeling for quality." More comforting to would-be collectors is the assertion of contemporary-art dealer Sidney Janis that "if you look and look, eventually you will begin to see."

Specialization

Your ability to see and to make intelligent collecting decisions will develop more quickly if you decide to focus on one or two specialties. Paul Singer boasts that his knowledge of Chinese art up to the twelfth century is greater than that of any curator of Oriental art, because a curator must be a generalist, while Singer has focused all his attention on a relatively small area. Similarly, Los Angeles collector Edward Carter noted that he has an edge in collecting seventeenth-century Dutch painting because other collectors of old masters, being less specialized, probably aren't as intimately familiar with this work as he is. According to dealer Eugene Thaw, "the primordial error of new collectors" is collecting without limit. Collectors, he feels, should concentrate on drawings of a certain school, paintings of a certain school or a certain period, etc. Print dealer Sylvan Cole, Jr., of Associated American Artists, the New York gallery, says that a collector should try to specialize, if possible, in a period or an artist. He should collect in depth in that area, buying at least fifty prints and, ideally, nearly a hundred, according to Cole. "If you have that kind of collection, it, of itself, has clout." Becoming a specialist may also bring you some unusual buying opportunities, since dealers and even private collectors with important works to sell tend to offer them first to collectors whose interest in such objects is strong and well known. One of Paul Mellon's prize acquisitions, for example, was *Sleeping Leopard,* a painting in enamel on Wedgwood biscuit earthenware by George Stubbs. Its previous owner, a Canadian woman who had heard that Mellon loved British painting in general and Stubbs in particular, contacted him directly and negotiated the sale.

But although specialization undoubtedly increases a collector's expertise and "clout," it may also seem too limiting to people with wide-ranging tastes. "Specialization is a pitfall avoided by the true collector," maintained the late dealer Germain Seligman in his book, *Merchants of Art.* "Art is in essence universal, and to limit its scope, willfully or unconsciously, is contrary to its very spirit. The more one delves into any single aspect of civilization, the narrower one's outlook is apt to become, with attention focusing more and more on the particular, the details rather than the whole. Collecting then either follows the line of least resistance, easy because it is familiar, or develops into an obsessive ambition to be supreme in a narrow field."

Even those collectors who do specialize often find themselves buying some (or even many) works outside their chosen fields. Schimmel's New York apartment contains a number of old-master drawings and even modern works by Giacometti and Rouault. In an article about Chicago collectors Leigh and Mary Block in the September–October 1976 issue of *Art in America,* writer Francine du Plessix (Gray) noted that "the independence of their taste frequently leads them to buy works startlingly outside the Impressionist and Post-Impressionist period for which their collection is famous." Among the Blocks' acquisitions, for example, were works by Fragonard, Henri Fantin-Latour, Adolphe Monticelli, and many contemporary American and European abstract artists. "We do not buy names," the late Mary Block was quoted as saying, "and we feel no need to stay within a period."

Making Contacts

Perhaps the most useful first step in collecting is developing relationships with those who know more than you do. The art market is an informal and unstructured place, and its denizens are, for the most part, unusually generous with their time, knowledge and assistance when approached by a newcomer who shows a serious desire to learn. Many experts will provide free counsel if properly approached (more on this later) and many neophytes who spend weeks building up the courage to walk into a gallery or call up a curator are surprised to meet professionals who regard the education of new collectors as one of their primary missions. "One of our obligations is to do what we can to help private collectors," asserted John Walsh, Jr., of the Boston Museum of Fine Arts. Similarly, in a *Collector's Handbook* published in 1978 by the Cincinnati Art Museum, the museum's director, Millard Rogers, Jr., wrote, "It is our intention now and my hope for the future that the Cincinnati Art Museum will be a better, more active focus for collecting, both private and public, that collectors will seek advice and help at the Museum, and that the Museum will foster collecting in the community. We share a common goal, after all, in acquiring and preserving works of art."

Many top dealers—contrary to the image you may have of them as unapproachable, intimidating and highly mercenary—are actually delighted to share their knowledge and opinions with interested newcomers, even if no immediate sale is in sight. At a 1979 panel discussion entitled "The Interior Designer and the New York Art Market," sponsored by the Art Dealers Association of America and the American Society of Interior Designers, top contemporary-art dealer Leo Castelli commented, "We actually don't welcome anyone more than people who are interested in having our advice. It's not an imposition if somebody comes and spends hours with us and doesn't buy anything. It really doesn't matter. Our role is to educate and instruct." Similarly, in a 1979 panel discussion sponsored by the New Museum in New York, another top contemporary-art dealer, Arnold Glimcher of Pace Gallery, said, "We educate collectors. Sometimes we see somebody twenty times over three or four years before they buy anything." While, in general, testing a dealer's patience to that extent is not recommended, almost all dealers and auction-house specialists will gladly answer intelligent questions on quality, price, condition and authenticity. Provided that you weigh their counsel against their obvious interest in promoting their own offerings, you can learn a great deal from their experience and success in the art market.

Chapter 2

DEALING WITH DEALERS

Most serious collectors, when asked how they first began to develop their eye and their judgment, give the greatest credit to the guiding influence of dealers. Yet many beginning collectors, feeling fearful and vulnerable, pace timidly back and forth in front of a gallery for many minutes before daring to enter. At a seminar on how to collect paintings, sponsored by *Antiques World* magazine at the 1980 Winter Antiques Show in New York, Carl Crossman of Childs Gallery in Boston recalled that eighteen years earlier, it had taken him four or five trips around the block before he could build up enough courage to make his first entrance into the gallery that he now runs. Yet, once the would-be collector ventures inside, he usually discovers that his fears are groundless or, at least, exaggerated. No one accosts him at the door to ask why he is there, push for a sale or exact an admission fee (except in the rare case of an admission charge for a "benefit exhibition"—a show which is mounted to raise funds for a charitable purpose and which usually consists largely of works that are on loan to the gallery and are not for sale). Unless he requests help or information, the collector who walks into a gallery for the first time will probably be discreetly ignored, free to peruse the exhibition in peace and solitude. (A different situation exists at private "by appointment only" galleries, where no public exhibitions are mounted. In order to visit these galleries, the collector must arrange a specific time to meet with the dealer and should be able to specify what types of works interest him, so that the dealer can bring them out from stock.) Sometimes prices will be posted alongside the works; sometimes a printed price list will be available at the reception desk; sometimes you will have to ask the gallery attendant for the price. You will sometimes see small red circles affixed to the wall next to certain works; these designate works that have already been sold. At some galleries, the director is almost always on hand in the public exhibition area, ready to answer your questions. At others, he will be in a back room or upstairs office and you will have to ask to see him.

In galleries offering works that particularly interest you, it is always wise to get to know the person in charge, even if there are other staff members who are eager to serve. The director is almost always the most knowledgeable and experienced person in the gallery and, hence, the one who can be of greatest help in guiding your development as a collector. He is also the person who decides whether you should be granted special favors—the chance, for example, to buy a particularly desirable work before it is shown to others, or the chance to buy something at a particularly favorable price. If you feel intimidated by a gallery's hushed, dignified atmosphere, and you fear that its eminent proprietor will snub you or be unbearably condescending, try to look at the first encounter from the gallery director's point of view. His business cannot remain vital and grow unless he carefully nurtures a group of new collectors who will come to rely on and trust his judgment. He stands to gain much and lose nothing by being helpful to those who show a serious, developing interest in the art he sells.

"A beginning collector is more interesting, in a way, than an old collector," commented Clyde Newhouse of the highly respected Newhouse Galleries in New York. Speaking on the same panel with Carl Crossman at the 1980 Winter Antiques Show, Newhouse observed that dealers enjoy showing new collectors their "finds"—quality works that the dealer was able to pick up at a reasonable cost. Dealers like to give new collectors a chance to "share the good luck" of such finds, he said. "A starting collector should ask the dealer to show him quality things in a certain price range," said Newhouse. "He can get a good start with a first-rate dealer." Similarly, dealer Richard Feigen said that he too likes to give new collectors a good start. "It's easy to establish yourself as a client," he said. "It depends on your attitude. I met a young collector whom I liked very much but who had never bought anything from me. He wanted to buy a work by Joseph Cornell. I got a great Cornell that an important client wanted, but he already had some Cornells. I let the new collector have it, because he didn't have anything. I had to play God with that object." At the 1979 seminar on "The Interior Designer and the New York Art Market," Richard Solomon of Pace Gallery expressed a similar receptiveness to new collectors: "If only you knew the cartwheels we turn when people walk in off the street," he said "We try to treat everyone as if they're a potential client."

Looking at the first encounter from the dealer's point of view may, however, give rise to a second and, perhaps, more justified fear. The dealer may regard the uninformed new buyer as an easy mark—a convenient repository for inferior and/or overpriced goods. Even dealers with the highest reputation for integrity and quality will (Feigen's comments notwithstanding) often save their best offerings for established customers and will give those customers the best breaks on price. The new collector's disadvantages are compounded in dealing with less scrupulous galleries, which may try to cash in on someone's lack of knowledge by passing off fakes or reproductions as valuable originals.

Art dealers are regarded by many new and would-be collectors as shifty, dishonest and predatory. The stereotype is not entirely unjustified. The art trade is a largely unregulated business, and virtually anyone can open a gallery, selling worthless reproductions or mass-produced paintings for as much as the uninformed buyer is willing to pay. It is usually simple enough to distinguish the sellers of schlock from the serious dealers—by the quality of their offerings and by the reputation they have earned among other art professionals. But even some of the most renowned dealers in the finest masterpieces have, unfortunately, not always been above reproach. In his memoirs, *Self-Portrait with Donors,* John Walker, former director of the National Gallery of Art in Washington, recounted how the legendary British dealer in old masters, Joseph Duveen, regretting his purchase of a hard-to-sell painting by Masaccio, had it "repainted to make it prettier." (The painting, which Duveen had bought on the recommendation of his adviser, the eminent art scholar Bernard Berenson, was finally sold to Andrew Mellon for donation to the National Gallery in Washington, which Mellon founded.) Also "greatly repainted," Walker reported, were many of the "ridiculously overpriced" eighteenth-century British portraits with which Duveen "inundated the houses of American millionaires." A recent reminder of the dangers of putting complete faith in a distinguished firm's integrity was the 1979 conviction of the world-renowned seventy-eight-year-old Paris dealer of Impressionist and modern masters, Paul Pétridès, for knowingly selling stolen paintings. Considered to be one of the world's leading authorities on Utrillo, Pétridès was accused of buying and selling eighteen paintings (including a Utrillo) stolen in 1972 from a Paris businessman.

Despite such horror stories, new collectors are usually well advised to rely on the advice and expertise of sellers who have gained reputations for quality and integrity. "You have to trust the dealers you deal with, or you shouldn't deal with them," said Paul Mellon. According to art historian John Rewald, "If you go to first-rate dealers consistently, you will wind up with a good collection. The dealer will probably reserve his best pieces for you or, when he gets a good picture, he will let you know and give you an early opportunity to purchase it."

Getting Dealers' Names

The first problem for the newcomer is finding out who the trustworthy and high-quality dealers are. Friendly relations with the staff of your local museum can give you a good start: museums are often pleased to supply new collectors with the names of several reputable dealers catering to specific fields of interest. Museum shows can also tip you off to which dealers are highly regarded by a museum's staff. Galleries often lend works to major shows, and are identified as lenders on the wall labels and in the catalogues. There are also various published lists that may help you. Dealers considered preeminent in their fields were listed by Grace Glueck, a *New York Times* reporter, in her article, "The Experts' Guide to the Experts," which appeared in the November 1978 issue of *ARTnews*. In two articles in the *New York Times*, critic John Russell listed the New York print dealers he considered most worthy of attention ("A Connoisseur's Guide to the Fine Art of Print Collecting," June 22, 1979, and "The City's Prints Scene: Quality Art at High Prices," Dec. 5, 1980). In another article, Russell listed the Los Angeles art galleries that he found most rewarding ("A Tour of Los Angeles Galleries," Dec. 2, 1979). Poet-critic Carter Ratcliff, art critic for *Saturday Review* and a contributing editor of *Art in America* magazine, described and rated a number of New York galleries (mostly contemporary) in his article, "Making It in the Art World: A Climber's Guide," in the Nov. 27, 1978, issue of *New York* magazine. Another assessment of New York contemporary art galleries was provided by Alexandra Anderson and Carrie Rickey in "Up Against the Wall Street: An Investor's Guide to Galleries," *Village Voice*, Oct. 15–21, 1980. Reading reviews and more general articles is a good way to get a feel for which galleries are taken most seriously by the experts. Gallery advertisements in newspapers and magazines are *not* good sources of guidance, however. The advertising departments of many of the most prestigious publications make no quality judgments and cheerfully sell space to the most lackluster, undistinguished outfits. "You get a weird image of art by looking at the magazines," observed print dealer Sylvan Cole, Jr. "They carry ads by every fly-by-night print publisher. There has been a tremendous proliferation of new dealers, many with no expertise or credentials whatsoever." Similarly, commercial art fairs in the U.S. are usually not a good source of information for collectors seeking the names of top dealers. Such fairs are in many cases open to almost any gallery or publisher willing to pay the registration fee, regardless of quality or professional reputation.

Some of the more established dealers have tried to make it easier for collectors to identify and approach them by banding together in various professional organizations that issue free members' directories. The directories list members' names, addresses and specialties. The associations usually include only galleries that have substantial track records and that purport to uphold high professional standards. A leading group of dealers is the Art Dealers Association of America (575 Madison Ave., New York, N.Y. 10022), which was organized in 1962 and, at this writing, includes more than a hundred galleries around the country (but mainly in New York), offering works in a wide variety of fields (primarily paintings, drawings and graphics). A gallery belonging to the association must have been in operation for at least five years and must (according to ADAA's directory) "have a good reputation in its community for honesty and integrity in its dealings with the public, museums, artists and other dealers." Other gallery associations include the National Antique and Art Dealers Association of America, 59 E. 57th St., New York, N.Y. 10022; the Association of International Photography Art Dealers, Box 1119, F.D.R. Station, New York, N.Y. 10022; and the American Association of Dealers in Ancient, Oriental and Primitive Art. This last group does not issue a directory, but its president, Douglas Ewing, says that collectors can get a list of member dealers in their fields of interest by contacting him at 159 1/2 E. 94th St., New York, N.Y. 10028. Galleries in certain areas—Southern California and San Francisco, for example—have formed their own local associations.

Membership in an association does not guarantee a dealer's integrity. Marlborough Gallery in New York, which was heavily fined in court for unconscionable practices in its handling of the estate of Mark Rothko, was a member of ADAA from 1968 until the court decision was handed down in late 1975. "There are as many crooks within the Art Dealers Association as there are outside of it," claimed one iconoclastic dealer who happens to be a longtime member of the group. Conversely, lack of membership in an association should not cause you to shun a particular gallery. Many respected dealers are too new to have established the track record required for association membership, and several long-established, highly reputed ones (including Wildenstein and O. K. Harris galleries in New York and Vose Galleries in Boston, for example) either have not been invited or have chosen not to join

ADAA. Gallery associations' lists should only be used as starting points for further investigation.

There is another drawback to these lists. Members of the national associations are heavily concentrated in New York, with only a smattering of "approved" names in other parts of the country. Local art publications and personal contacts with local collectors, dealers and museum professionals should give you some idea of the most respected names in your area. But the failure of the New York–based national associations to include many out-of-towners is not entirely a case of local chauvinism—New York truly is the art capital of the country (if not the world), and most of the top galleries are located there. Good purchases of regional art can best be made in the appropriate region; if you choose a field that has a national or international market, however, you may be able to make some good finds locally but you will probably also have to devise some way of tapping sources in New York. There are several ways to accomplish this. You can use local dealers as your agents, establish your own long-distance relationships with New York dealers, or make regular trips to New York. If your own locality has at least one high-quality dealer in your field of interest who is well informed about works appearing on the market in New York and other cities, he can let you know about and arrange for you to purchase works offered elsewhere. Your local dealer will often be able to acquire works from other dealers at a discount (possibly a reduction of 20 percent) and he may pass on at least part of that discount (say 10 percent) to you. In the contemporary art field, some New York dealers (Leo Castelli, for example) have developed networks of out-of-town and foreign dealers whom they regularly supply with shows of works by gallery artists. (Castelli says that only about 5 percent of his sales are made to New Yorkers, 45 percent to others around the country and 50 percent to Europeans.) Some non–New York dealers (Richard Gray of Chicago, for example) regularly select works from a variety of top New York contemporary art galleries for display and sale in their own galleries. "I can have a greater range of works in my gallery than a New York gallery has," Gray asserted. "My problem is that people think the best material is not to be had locally but in New York."

Despite what Gray says, it is true that New York galleries are likely to keep their very best works for their galleries' own clients, and most experts agree that collectors should try to develop relationships with selected New York dealers (as well as with dealers in other parts of the country who have distinguished reputations in their fields). Once you have done this (through personal meetings or through long-distance purchases), the dealers may let you know when they acquire works that might interest you. Still, you should probably also remind them periodically of your continuing interest through visits, phone calls or letters. "I've sold paintings to some people in the Midwest whom I've never seen," said Carl Crossman of Childs Gallery of Boston, who noted that, with Bostonians among this country's earliest collectors of French Impressionists, his city "has always been a great repository of eighteenth- and nineteenth-century art." Long-distance sales, Crossman said, are typically made from photographs or color transparencies. After examining these, along with related descriptive material, the collector can have a desired work sent to him "on approval." He then has a limited amount of time to decide whether to buy it or return it to the gallery. (Even a collector who is able to visit the gallery is often allowed to take works on approval, to see how it looks in his home and, perhaps, to get advice from other experts.) The late Nelson Rockefeller frequently bought works by telephone without seeing them first, according to Sidney Janis. "During the last fifteen years of Rockefeller's collecting life, he didn't go to galleries because he was too busy, but he read every catalogue that was published." Out-of-towners, he said, can best stay informed of dealers' latest offerings by subscribing to their catalogues. (However, some dealers—particularly those who do not mount public exhibitions—do not usually issue catalogues. With such dealers, regular personal contacts are even more important.)

Sizing Up Dealers

Once you have learned the names of a number of dealers selling works in your field of interest, how can you determine which ones are most worthy of your trust? The quality of the merchandise will tell part of the story, provided you have reached the point where you are beginning to be able to judge quality. Some contemporary galleries, for example, specialize in what Carter Ratcliff, in his *New York* magazine article, called "the schlock elite"—artists with commercial and (to some eyes) decorative appeal but little serious artistic merit. (Ratcliff put artists M. C. Escher, Peter Max, LeRoy Neiman, Simbari, Fritz Scholder and Frank Gallo in this category.) It is not uncommon for galleries to advertise such names alongside those of more highly respected artists such as Picasso, Chagall and Dali. (Works stocked in such galleries by these three big-name artists are likely to be prints from their later years, when many experts feel that the quality of their work markedly declined.) "Some galleries heavily advertise the name artists in an effort to sell their no-name artists," said Sylvan Cole, Jr. "The name artists give them the umbrella of legitimacy to sell a lot of other stuff." In the case of galleries selling older art, a sales pitch that touts the work of a very obscure painter as a "guaranteed investment" should make you wary. Most serious dealers do not flaunt the investment merits of their wares, preferring to stress their artistic merits. Almost no serious dealer will presume to predict the investment potential of a little-known and as yet unappreciated artist. (He may say that he thinks the artist's work is underpriced, but he won't try to lead you to believe that this situation will change dramatically or soon.) Also be suspicious of a dealer whose asking prices seem to be considerably below what you think comparable works are fetching elsewhere. Such "bargains" are apt to be fakes, reproductions, extremely damaged works, or works that are flawed in some other crucial way. Still, New York old-masters dealer Stanley Moss noted that "you can do better sometimes at an unreliable dealer than a reliable one: He may have one good picture but he might not know it." Such "finds" occur rarely, however, and a collector has to be an expert to recognize them.

When can you trust a dealer? "When he's gotten too rich to cheat you," said Clyde Newhouse, slightly tongue-in-cheek. Similarly, Richard Feigen observed that "you should deal with a firm that has more to lose by taking advantage of you than it stands to gain by the profit of doing it. You have to find someone who is objective and not hungry, who has access to a lot of expertise and market know-how. To judge a dealer, you have to be a good judge of character. You should make it plain to him that if he makes a mistake with you, it will be the last mistake, because you will never go to him again."

No reputable dealer should object to your consulting other experts before you make a purchase, and many will let you take the object from the gallery on approval for this purpose. A dealer who has given you an oral description of what you are purchasing should be willing to set down that description in writing on the bill of sale (including, when known, the artist, title, date, medium and dimensions); if you should later discover (with convincing proof) that the true facts about the work differ significantly from this description, the dealer should be willing to give you a refund. (The written description should specify that the work is *by* the particular artist. Many a "Picasso" has been sold that was merely a copy of a work by the artist. Your bill of sale should specify that the work was executed "*by* Picasso.") Many dealers will also extend return privileges for works which have no problems of authenticity or attribution but which, for whatever personal reasons, you no longer wish to own. While dealers will probably not give you a cash refund for hard-to-sell works (such as works by little-known artists) or very expensive ones, they may allow you to trade your purchase for another comparable work in their stock (possibly only for another work by the same artist). The extent of a dealer's return policy may give you some idea of the extent to which he himself believes in and stands by the quality and desirability of what he sells.

Collector Edward Carter noted that dealers are usually less receptive to buying back pictures than to trading, which requires no cash outlay. A dealer who requested anonymity noted that trading has certain advantages for the collector as well: If a collector makes a profit when he sells a work back to a dealer, he must pay a tax on the profit. If he trades for another work, he is also legally supposed to pay tax on that transaction, but almost no one does; the transaction is simply not reported. "I'm always amazed when I hear of a case like this [one that involves art swapping]," says Thomas Hartnett, chief of the art valuation group in the Internal Revenue Service's national office. "I wonder who would have talked." (More on the tax implications of art transactions in Chapter 9.) Another advantage in trading with a dealer, according to collector Paul Mellon, is that it may be easier than selling an unwanted work at auction. If the dealer is someone with whom you have done a lot of business, he might give you a better deal than you would be likely to get at auction, Mellon observed. Trading, he said, can help the collector "get what he wants without putting up a lot of cash," but he noted that "there is not much point in trading with a dealer unless he has things that you want and you get the same relative value back."

There are circumstances when a dealer is happy to pay a substantial profit to a collector who brings back one of the dealer's works—when the work is highly desirable and can probably be resold later for a still higher price. "Three years ago someone bought a picture from us for $55,000," said Clyde Newhouse at the *Antiques World* seminar. "I paid him $135,000 for it today. I'm delighted to see him do that." Always eager to increase their stock of top-quality goods, some dealers actively solicit returns of works they have previously sold. Lawrence Fleischman of Kennedy Galleries in New York, for example, said he frequently contacts old clients to see if they are willing to sell back certain works, and he recently paid one such client a 200 percent profit on an Edward Hopper that Fleischman had sold him ten years earlier.

How Dealers Can Help

Once you have chosen to work with a few dealers who impress you with the quality of their offerings, reputations and business practices, you will want to approach them in the way most likely to bring about their greatest helpfulness and friendliness. The best dealers have no lack of potential clients for high-quality works, and they can afford to be choosy about whom to favor with their best works and best advice. "Dealers have a very psychological relationship with their clients," notes dealer Eugene Thaw. "A supply of good things is difficult to obtain and the only way to collect them is to be first in line. You need a privileged relationship with someone who supplies first-class things and you have to establish a relationship of trust with that dealer. You just can't be too difficult." Similarly, Lawrence Fleischman, who sells American art of the eighteenth to twentieth centuries, noted that there are a few great works of art that he can sell over the telephone, and his decision about whom to call "depends on who I like the best. The people I like are the ones who give a damn about art." When works are offered in gallery exhibitions, those collectors who are invited to view the show as it is being installed (before its official opening) get the first pick. Some shows are sold out even before they open. "All of us have a group of collectors who are the nucleus of our galleries," said Arnold Glimcher of Pace. Those collectors, he added, get the chance to see newly offered works before the general public does. A collector who is keenly interested in a certain type of art or a certain artist should ask the gallery staff if he might drop by during the installations of such works. He should also ask to be put on the gallery's mailing list, to be notified of openings. (In keeping with the informal atmosphere of the art trade, anyone who knows about the opening of a gallery show can usually attend, with or without invitation.)

When a collector is not within the chosen group of "friends of the gallery," he may not only find that certain works are unavailable to him; he may also find that the dealer is reluctant to give his best advice about the works that are available. In his essay in *Art International* about the formation of his collection, Richard Brown Baker recalled that when, as a new collector of contemporary art, he expressed an interest in buying a particular work by French abstract painter Georges Mathieu, dealer Samuel Kootz seemed "ever so slightly to discourage me from fixing on this one." Baker later discovered, he said, that Kootz had in fact concurred in Baker's choice as the best in the show. "I suspect, now that I have greater familiarity with New York dealers," Baker wrote, "that on this occasion, when he was launching a controversial new artist, he was not eager to see the best example go to a totally unknown purchaser. Known now as a collector, I am made aware that dealers like to place the work of artists whom they are introducing in 'good collec-tions.' . . . Dealers know that when several collectors of prominence buy an unknown artist, his work will more quickly come to the attention of other collectors. What good, they ask themselves, will it do to have the masterpiece of our latest protégé hidden in the sitting room of an Oshkosh pharmacist? The most advantageous place for it would be on the walls of the Museum of Modern Art, or, failing that, in the possession of a respected collector who will show it to sophisticated viewers. This fact of contemporary-art economics I didn't then know. It is open to abuse, and in more recent years one of many worries has been not to fall into the trap of buying mediocre paintings when they are offered before exhibition at advantageous prices to help launch some mediocre new artist."

There are many other ways in which dealers help their favorite collectors, in addition to giving them good buying opportunities at (in some instances) reduced prices. As mentioned, a prime function of dealers is to educate new collectors, and the better your relationship with a dealer, the better your education is likely to be. Contemporary-art dealer Ivan Karp of O. K. Harris Gallery in New York said that he is happy to give interested new collectors "a thirty-minute speech describing the history of modern art movements and what we think is important." (Thirty minutes from the fast-talking Karp is like ninety minutes at normal speed.) Similarly, dealer Sidney Janis said that he is happy to help educate new collectors. He added, though, that he no longer devotes much time to this because "in most cases, it's resented"; many people, he has discovered, feel that they are being condescended to when a dealer lectures them on art. "Still, if someone encourages me, I'll give them an honest opinion," said Janis. He added that all his works are available to collectors and museums on a "first come, first served basis," with no special preference given to established clients.

Some dealers will not only counsel you about works offered in their own galleries, but will give you advice about buying from other sources. When collectors ask about other galleries, Leo Castelli says he will tell them where they should go and what they should get. He will even let them know when another gallery has a work by one of his own artists that is of better quality (or more to the collector's taste) than works available at his own gallery. Dealers with whom you have established good working relationships may even examine and give you opinions about works that you have received on approval from other dealers. But Lawrence Fleischman noted that it is dangerous to go to one dealer to check another's stock. "The art business is bitter and competitive," he said. "Dealers will lie about each other." Similarly, dealer Stephen Hahn noted it is "human nature that a dealer always prefers what he has and wants to sell his own goods. I prefer that collectors don't ask me [about other dealers' stock]. But if they do, many times I advise them to buy. A number of times, though, I have said I thought something was much too expensive." Dealer André Emmerich said that he does give advice about other galleries' artists and prices, but added that when his feelings are strongly negative, he tries to indicate this subtly, so as not to impose his views on the collector: "I say to the collector, 'Are you sure? Look at it a second time.' " He added that "anything I say is suspect," because he has an interest in selling his own offerings, on the one hand, and does not wish to appear critical of a fellow dealer, on the other. Similarly, Paul Mellon noted that "dealers' advice is always a little suspect, since they are naturally trying to put their best foot forward in selling their own pictures. . . . Low-key behavior and a minimum of comments seem to keep the natural tendency of dealers to overdo somewhat in check."

In addition to advising on works offered at their own and other galleries, dealers frequently advise collectors on auction-house offerings and even bid for collectors at auction (sometimes free of charge, sometimes for a fee). Having a dealer bid for you gives you the benefit of his knowledge of appropriate price levels and bidding strategies (more on this in the next chapter). Dealers will also help collectors who wish to sell works at auction, by negotiating the terms of the consignment (including the amount of the commission that the consignor must pay the auctioneer). "If you have a pro on your side, the auction house will be more forthcoming and you will get better terms," maintained dealer Eugene Thaw. "We know their techniques."

The advice and other services that dealers give their clients are often free of charge. But if a great deal of time and work (negotiation, research, condition analysis, etc.) is involved, a fee may be requested. Fleischman said he charges $1,000 a day plus expenses for intricate advisory assignments and he gets a commission of about 5 percent of the purchase price for works that he buys for collectors at auction. Collector Paul Mellon said that dealers bidding for collectors at auction often get about 10 percent for works costing less than $10,000, 5 percent for works from $10,000 to $1 million and 1 or 2 percent for higher-priced works. "You may negotiate this before the sale," he observed. David Nash, director of fine arts sales at Sotheby Parke Bernet's New York auction house, said that some dealers take a flat fee of $500 to $1,000 for bidding on a collector's behalf, regardless of the price of the object. Eugene Thaw said that he gets a 10 percent fee when he acts as a collector's advisor on purchases or sales, but he added that, in many cases, the financial benefits that the client receives from his services equal or exceed his fee: When he negotiates consign-ments to auction, he passes along to the client any finder's fees (usually 2 percent) paid to him by the auction house, he negotiates reduced costs to the consignor for expenses such as catalogue photographs and insurance, and he pushes for the lowest possible commission rate pay-able by the consignor to the auctioneer. When he negotiates purchases from other dealers, he can often get a discount (which he says is at least 10 percent, sometimes 15 to 20 percent) that is greater than the collec-tor could negotiate himself, and he passes that discount along to his client.

How to Approach a Dealer

What kind of behavior on the part of a collector is most likely to predispose a dealer to offer his best works, his best advice and his fullest service? "You should make it plain to the dealer that you put yourself in his hands and lay the responsibility on him," said Richard Feigen. "You should say, 'I trust you, and I want to collect only great things. I want things in the greatest condition and the greatest exam-ples of the artist's work. In all candor, is this an optimum work by this artist, in optimum condition?' " The question, he said, should be put "not contentiously and not antagonistically. Otherwise, caveat emp-tor." Similarly, Ben Heller said that a collector who wants to get a dealer's best help should "throw himself on the dealer's mercy, or appeal to the dealer's venality by saying that he is going to be a big buyer. You have to find out how to get to that particular person."

Getting to a dealer, according to Feigen, means figuring out "why he is doing what he's doing. . . . The error certain collectors make," he said, "is that they don't put their finger on the pulse of the person to whom they appeal for advice. They just think about what *they* want and are not sensitive to what the other person wants. What I want is recognition of my talent." The kind of collector Feigen likes to deal with "doesn't give me art lectures, cheat me or badger me. He makes himself pleasant to deal with. . . . Certain collectors trust no one and no one trusts them. They pick brains where they can by the power of the purse. Some collectors, like Norton Simon and [the late] Joseph Hirshhorn, love to bargain. That is not a pursuit in which I take particu-lar pleasure. Some people exhaust me, and those two exhaust me. The arrogance of power and money alienates me."

In his book *Merchants of Art,* the late dealer Germain Seligman described his growing alienation from collector-publisher William Randolph Hearst: "Contrary to the majority of men of business acumen, Hearst loved to dicker, a practice of dubious value in the art world, leading rather to bargaining than to bargains. Thus, through the years I did business with William Randolph Hearst, I never derived from it the true enjoyment I felt with his great contemporaries. An art dealer's pride and satisfaction is not entirely measured by the total amount of money a client spends; it is measured also by the quality and the exceptional character of the works of art chosen. The dealer wishes to feel himself a guide and mentor, and, because he recommends and encourages the purchase of an object he considers fitting, he is willing to assume a special moral responsibility. But when, contrary to the dealer's better judgment, the client purchases less fitting items, the art dealer loses interest in the client. It becomes then, purely a business transaction, devoid of the human ties which connect the true collector and the art dealer who enjoys his profession. Financially our relations with Hearst were satisfactory, but we derived little pride from his acquisitions of a more or less decorative nature. Too often they were the leavings of a collection we had bought up in toto for the sake of a few fine pieces."

In addition to favoring collectors who respect their judgment, dealers are most receptive to those who show a serious appreciation of art and a sincere desire to learn as much as possible about it. "If I get the feeling that people really want to learn, I am perfectly happy to tell them everything I know. If they seem superficial, I clam up," said Klaus Perls. The collector who gives the dealer "some idea of what he wants, or the price range," is also appreciated, according to Carl Crossman. The collector who announces, "I would love a great marine painting, but I can spend no more than $10,000," or, "I am looking for a fine contemporary drawing for under $1,000," is much more welcome than those who say, "I want to look at everything and I'll know what I want when I see it." The latter approach, Crossman observed, "leaves the dealer out in the cold."

Similarly, Eugene Thaw commented that "a collector should tell me honestly what he's looking for and what his limits are. He should not ask to look at a $2-million van Gogh if what he's really interested in is a $50,000 Picasso drawing. It is a maddening thing when a collector wants to see everything I've got and wastes my time. If he does that, I won't show him anything next time." Thaw added that the amount of help he is willing to give collectors "depends on how much they respect and trust me and how much they are interested in the quality I stand for and the privilege of seeing great things. People who are arrogant and aloof with me don't get the best out of me." Similarly,

Stephen Hahn observed that "some people who are just starting to collect act as if they know much more about painting than I do. I have no patience with that."

An important part of building a good relationship with a dealer, according to John Walsh, Jr. of the Boston Museum of Fine Arts, is "not to abuse the gentlemanly privileges that potential clients get. . . . The art business is still a startling thing to businessmen who are used to written contracts. Expensive transactions happen with just a hand-shake. You can reserve a picture, taking it out of circulation while you think about it; some dealers are willing to put something aside for quite a while. It's a system that's easily taken advantage of and dealers resent being misled about someone's intentions." Some collectors, according to dealer Ivan Karp, go so far as to take works home "on approval" for display in their homes during social occasions. After the big party, the art comes off the walls and goes back to the dealer. Collectors who betray a dealer's trust in this manner will wear out their welcome very quickly.

Also unpopular among serious dealers is the collector who quickly looks over the dealer's offerings and then announces that he wants to buy something that will be a "good investment." Lawrence Fleischman recalled a recent encounter with a would-be purchaser who "walked into my gallery and said, 'What's the best buy you've got here?' I suggested that he go to my competitors." Similarly, Leo Castelli said that he "detests" the emphasis on art speculation, and declared that he would not sell to anyone who asks, "Is it a good investment?" This is not to say that you should not inquire whether a dealer believes that an expensive purchase will at least hold its value. But dealers feel the greatest sympathy toward those who are art-hungry, not money-hungry, and they do not like to be pressured into guaranteeing high annual rates of return. Fleischman goes so far as to prefer collectors who seek no financial rewards from their art purchases but, in fact, go into debt to acquire desired objects. "People who sacrifice to buy paintings are the dearest to my heart," he said. "I enjoy it when I take a great work of art and place it with someone who is excited about it. One collector I've been working with is a restaurant owner in the Midwest who buys beyond his income because he cares so much. I sold him a Burchfield drawing that he is wild about, and he's still paying it off. I have a client who borrowed $1 million from a bank for a group of works he wants." Other passionate but impecunious collectors manage to keep out of debt by swapping art works or even other kinds of goods or services for the objects they desire.

Discussing Price

Perhaps the most difficult and delicate aspect of dealer-collector relations is the negotiation of price and terms of payment. Pricing policies vary from gallery to gallery, and even from work to work in the same gallery. Different collectors may be quoted different prices for the same work, depending on how the dealer feels about the collector or the work at a given moment. Different dealers have different attitudes toward bargaining, and the way you approach the question of price may depend on the quirks of the particular seller. Edward Carter observed that the way you discuss prices has to do, in part, with your knowledge about a dealer's flexibility. "Some are more flexible in price than others. Some are known for taking higher markups. . . . Your price history with a dealer influences how much you want to discuss price with him. You should not be openhanded, but you should be reasonable and not squeeze for the last penny. Some people, particularly in the European markets, are notoriously high-priced. You would be unlikely to pay the first price they asked of you. If you think something is overpriced, you should say so." Carter added that there are times when he does not bargain at all. A recent example, he said, was his purchase of a painting from Clyde Newhouse that Newhouse's father had sold to someone forty or fifty years earlier. Newhouse bought the painting from the man's estate and told Carter that he didn't pay a high price for it and he had not shown it to anyone but Carter. "I did not bother to try to reduce the price he quoted me," Carter said, "because I believed him."

As Carter's comments indicate, dealers have different relationships to different art works, and a particular work's price may depend, in part, on how much the dealer had to pay for it, how long he has had it, how much difficulty he has had trying to sell it and how much he needs cash at a particular time. If he has the work on consignment, his bargaining leeway will be limited by the wishes of the consignor. "If you know that a dealer has had trouble selling something, you will probably be able to negotiate with him more successfully," noted Carter. "I am notorious for not being moved on price," said dealer Stanley Moss, "but sometimes I can be—if I am bored with a picture, if I need the money, or if I want to buy something else." Ralph Colin recalled that in June 1945, dealer Valentine Dudensing, needing cash for a summer art-buying trip abroad, sold him a Léger, a Soutine and a Miró for bargain prices. If a dealer needs capital to buy new works for his inventory, he may give you a good deal on works he wants to sell, Colin observed. On the other hand, if a work has a broad and ready market, a collector's negotiating power is very limited. "If nine out of ten paintings in a particular show have sold," observed Ben Heller, "you don't have much chance of getting a discount on the tenth."

In a letter to the *New York Times* (Nov. 9, 1975), Leo Castelli was unusually candid about how dealers set prices. "As a dealer in contemporary works of art," he wrote, "it is my right and privilege to sell them at any prices I determine and to make different prices to different prospective purchasers as I may determine in my own interest or in the interest of the artist. Various factors influence my determination—the distinction of the purchaser and his collection, the frequency with which the purchaser makes purchases from me, my personal relations and friendship with the purchaser, etc. Anyone who does not understand this attitude by a dealer is indeed naïve."

How much can you bargain off the original asking price, assuming that the dealer is in a flexible mood? Discounts of 10 percent are common and are often built into the asking price. Discounts can sometimes go as high as 25 percent, but rarely higher. Paul Singer reported that one Chinese art dealer in New York routinely slashes prices by 50 percent; "he always tells the customer that the price is half," he said. Stephen Hahn said that every collector he knows tries to bargain. His gallery has a 10 percent discount built in for everybody, with 15 to 20 percent discounts for museums. "If I know a collector is tough," said Hahn, "I tell him the net price right away." Carl Crossman said Childs Gallery has a hard and fast rule: they give a 10 percent discount on most pictures for payment in cash. "Beyond that I cannot be pushed," said Crossman. "I don't feel the price to a dealer should be less than the price to our best clients." Lawrence Fleischman said Kennedy Galleries give a 10 percent discount to museums and top clients but might add 20 percent onto the price if someone is a "slow payer." Klaus Perls said he gives a 10 percent discount to those who pay within a month; museums, dealers and agents get a maximum of 20 percent off, and dealers and agents are expected to kick back 10 percent to the buyers. In sales of contemporary art, "a little bit of negotiation" is common, according to Ivan Karp. He added that at O. K. Harris Gallery the price reduction is usually at the expense of the gallery (which takes a lower commission), rather than of the artist. (Much of the inventory of a contemporary-art gallery is on consignment from artists; the gallery generally takes a percentage commission on sales and pays the remainder to the artist.) Negotiation is possible, Karp said, if an artist is just emerging from obscurity, but may not be possible for popular works by big-name artists. For works by unknowns, "compassion should enter," Karp said. "If a painting is priced at only $900 to $1,500, it's not fair to negotiate."

The way you go about negotiating will depend, in part, on your personal style and, in part, on your sense of the most effective way to appeal to a particular dealer. A simple, typical approach, according to Clyde Newhouse, is, "That's a bit expensive for me. Can you do any better?" Stephen Hahn suggests, "I would love to buy that, but I would appreciate a better price." He added that he gives the best break to "people who are nice." Collector Norbert Schimmel noted that some people try to hide their enthusiasm to get the price down, but he added that he has not personally adopted such tactics. "When I go to a dealer, the dealer knows what he has. I cannot pretend that this is not quality. I say, 'That's a beautiful object.' " He noted, though, that collectors have an advantage over museums in negotiating with dealers, because museum decision-making and payment are often drawn out over many months, whereas "when I come in as a private collector, I make a decision like that and the dealer has his check immediately."

The negotiating technique that gets the highest praise from dealers for being both fast and effective is the Paul Mellon method. Eugene Thaw said that the "understood arrangement" with Mellon is: "Give me your best possible price and I will tell you yes or no. I will not come back with a counter-offer. If I say no, don't come back to me." Similarly, Richard Feigen suggested that a collector should say: "Look, I don't want to bargain with you. I want to do business with you and I hope to continue to do so on many occasions. I want your lowest price, and I will be very upset if I hear that you quoted someone else a price that was less than what you quoted me." A lighthearted approach ("Oh, come on. Let me have it for . . .") is also sometimes effective, Feigen said, provided that the collector doesn't persist to the point of becoming tedious.

The opposite of the Mellon method is the Hirshhorn haggle. In his biography of the late contemporary-art collector, *Hirshhorn: Medici from Brooklyn,* Barry Hyams observed that "to get the bottom price, [Hirshhorn] haggled like a rug seller." Hyams described an encounter between Hirshhorn and Harry Brooks, head of the Wildenstein Gallery, who was working for Knoedler (another major gallery in New York) when Hirshhorn came in to look around. Brooks recommended Maurice Prendergast's *Girl in Blue* at $10,000. " 'How much off?' inquired Hirshhorn. 'The usual—15 percent,' Brooks replied. 'What about the Eakins?' Brooks looked at *Miss Anna Lewis,* said $35,000, and, anticipating Hirshhorn's question, added, 'Also 15 percent.' Hirshhorn indicated three additional pieces and offered to take all five at one-third discount. A strenuous duel ensued which concluded on a compromise of 20 percent. At the day's end, Hirshhorn phoned to say his interest in the three works had waned but he still wanted the Prendergast and the Eakins—at the same discount, of course. Exhausted, Brooks surrendered."

Norton Simon is also well known for exhausting his bargaining opponents. "He makes you squirm and squeal until you say to yourself, 'This is the last time I put up with this,' " said Richard Feigen. Similarly, Stanley Moss said that Simon "needs a corpse. If I say my last price, unconditionally, is $100,000, he goes for $90,000." In his own defense, Simon (who is universally admired for the quality of his collection, if not always for his style in assembling it) said that he would not find it necessary to bargain so much if dealers "would not play games and would tell me the actual condition and history of the picture and not puff it." He said that he bargains when he feels that an art work is worth less than the dealer is asking "in relation to the condition of the picture or what the picture is." Simon frequently does his own research on potential purchases, with the help of distinguished experts.

The dangers of acquiring a reputation as a haggler are obvious. "There is no point in dickering with dealers," maintained Mellon. "They will always take that into consideration when they ask you the price. Next time, the dealer will ask more." This was confirmed by Fleischman, who said, "If I know a guy is a chiseler, I prepare the price that way." In addition, the collector who makes himself too difficult to deal with is the one "you will go to last if you have something important to sell," Feigen observed. Unimpressed by such arguments, Simon maintained that "dealers raise their asking prices anyway," whether a collector is known as a bargainer or not; the important thing is to "know what the proper values are," so that you can judge for yourself whether the dealer's asking price is fair. He added that "even those dealers who say we're difficult to deal with are quick to show us things when they get them."

Other collectors, though, are convinced that, in the long run, they will get better treatment (and maybe even better prices) if they are not overly contentious. Speaking at the New Museum seminar on collecting contemporary art, Eugene Schwartz said that he always asks for a discount, but if there is none, he buys anyway. "Most dealers need money and like it if you don't haggle too much and pay on time," he noted. "If you do that, they may give you a little preference next time." Richard Brown Baker commented that "it is not immensely important to me that I get the lowest possible price, particularly since I buy the products of striving, unestablished artists who, in most cases, need the money." He added that a collector can sometimes get a better deal by negotiating directly with the gallery owner, rather than with an assistant (who is not authorized to discount works beyond a certain point). One can sometimes improve one's bargaining position, he said, by buying two or more things at once (à la Hirshhorn). "Sometimes you can get a little painting thrown in if you buy a big one," Baker said.

A collector can also negotiate the time over which the purchase price is to be paid. "Not paying on the spot is traditional practice," observed Ivan Karp. Here again, however, practices differ from gallery to gallery. Klaus Perls said that he formerly gave people up to three years to pay, but in a buyer's market, dealers are much more flexible about payment than in a seller's market. Buyers from Perls can, at this writing, take up to a year to pay, but he makes them sign an invoice stating that title remains with the gallery until payment is completed. Most members of the Art Dealers Association now do this, Perls said, to avoid having to sue for their money later if a collector defaults. He added that dealers are reluctant to extend credit during periods of high inflation, since the money they receive a few years hence is worth far less than the money they get today. (No interest is charged on the agreed-upon purchase price, although, as noted, a dealer may offer a better price to someone who indicates he will pay immediately.)

The policy at Kennedy Galleries is to allow six months to a year for payment; the gallery rarely allows people to take works home on approval. At Sidney Janis Gallery, credit is rarely extended at all; works are allowed out on approval for about a week. Collectors who cannot get credit from dealers may still be able to finance their purchases by contacting one of the growing number of banks that are willing to extend loans using art as collateral. Art was formerly regarded by bankers as unsuitable for collateral because of the possible fluctuations in its value and the problems of determining its authenticity. But with art gaining favor as an attractive vehicle for investment, more banks are developing expertise and confidence in art-related matters. A work of art that meets the following conditions is more likely to be deemed by bankers to be suitable collateral: value, authenticity and title to the work can be reliably determined; the work can be readily marketed; a reputable appraisal and a verifiable record of provenance for the work have been obtained. Even if these conditions are met, however, the value of the art alone will probably not be regarded as sufficient basis for a loan; the bank will also give weight to the borrower's general creditworthiness.

The Big Markups

Perhaps the hardest thing for collectors to understand and accept in their relations with dealers is the usual gallery practice of charging a very hefty markup. It is common in many fields for a dealer to charge double what he paid for an object, and in some cases the markup will be substantially higher (such as when the dealer buys an object very cheaply because the seller does not realize its true worth, or when the dealer holds an object many years, for long-term appreciation). In general, markups are at their highest (100 percent or more) in fields where turnover is relatively slow and supply limited (e.g., old masters and antiquities). Stephen Hahn, who deals in the popular field of nineteenth- and twentieth-century French paintings, said that his markup is considerably lower—10 to 15 percent on expensive paintings that are sold quickly, 30 to 40 percent on less expensive paintings and those held for longer periods. Lawrence Fleischman said that his markup for American art is 20 percent for works he can turn over very quickly, 40 percent for works sold a year after he acquires them. Most of the time, you won't know what a dealer paid for an object; you may occasionally find out, however, through the art-market grapevine or from auction records. What you learn may make you angry, causing you to redouble your bargaining efforts or even to search for ways to circumvent dealers entirely (by buying at auction or directly from artists or other collectors). But further reflection (as well as experience with the uneven quality of works at auction and with the difficulty of trying to ferret out high-quality works on your own) may lead to some understanding of why dealers feel justified in charging what they do. Richard Feigen noted that collectors who buy from him get the benefit of his "thirty-nine years of experience in seeing things and knowing where high-quality works are tucked away. . . . A lot of people tend to impose on our profession pricing and profit rules that are applicable to other professions. It is true that we make a bigger percentage profit than other professions—sometimes as much as 200 to 400 percent. But the flaw in comparing us to other businesses is that we cannot control our source of supply, whereas other businesses can. If you are in the business of making coffee cups, you can make more coffee cups if there is more demand. If something costs me $100,000, I am not bound to give it to someone for $115,000 if there are no more such objects. . . . Collectors must learn to concern themselves with what the value of the object is, not what the dealer's profit is."

Some dealers are known for charging particularly high markups;

you will have to decide whether their services and the quality of their offerings justify their prices. One experienced collector who requested anonymity noted that, in the old-masters field, Wildenstein & Co. in New York and London and Edward Speelman Ltd. in London "are high-priced but tend to have great pictures," whereas Cramer Gallery in The Hague generally has "lower profit margins because it seldom has its own money tied up in pictures; most are on consignment." David Nash of Sotheby Parke Bernet, New York, noted that the amount of a dealer's overhead may also influence the amount of his markup. "If someone has a big shop on Madison Avenue with constantly changing shows, it costs him a lot to keep it going and he is likely to charge more." A private dealer working out of his apartment, though, may be willing to take a lower markup.

Dealers assemble their wares in various ways: They may buy some works at auction (an important source of material for dealers in old masters) and they may buy or receive works on consignment from collectors, artists, estates, or other dealers. Lawrence Fleischman has a nationwide network of professional scouts who follow up leads about important works of art tucked away in obscure places. Sometimes, he said, an important work comes to a small, out-of-the-way dealer who recognizes its importance but realizes that he doesn't have the clientele for it or the money to buy it. The dealer, Fleischman said, may send such a work to a larger gallery, which pays him a finder's fee. Old-masters dealer Stanley Moss said that he relentlessly follows every lead that might help him find a desirable work. His journey to a garage sale once rewarded him with an important painting by Genoese painter Bernardo Strozzi, which he later sold to the De Young Museum in San Francisco. "If you told me your Aunt Molly had a Leonardo in her apartment in Jackson Heights, I'd go take a look," he said. "If I pass a little auction, I go to the auction." Among his auction finds were a rare Morazzone, which he picked up for only $600, and a Guilio Cesare Procaccini for $5,000.

Selling Through Dealers

Collectors are an important source of galleries' inventories, and part of the dealer's job is knowing who has the important works and whether they are available. If you decide to dispose of works through a dealer, you have three methods to choose from: trading, consigning or selling. If you trade, you may be able to get another work or works of equivalent market value to your own (provided you have a sufficiently good sense of the market to judge the fairness of the trade). If you consign or sell a work, you will almost always get less than its full retail value. On consignments, dealers take a percentage of the sale price; the commission can, on rare occasions, be as low as 2 percent (for unusually expensive, large or desirable consignments) but is more typically 10 to 25 percent. (Commissions charged by contemporary art galleries on artist-consigned works—as distinguished from works consigned by collectors—are much higher, usually ranging from 33 1/3 to 50 percent. More on this in Chapter 5.) It is perhaps even more important to deal with well-established, reputable professionals when consigning to a gallery than when buying from one: It may not matter to you if the gallery from which you *buy* an art work subsequently goes out of business, but (according to lawyers Franklin Feldman and Stephen Weil in their book, *Art Works: Law, Policy, Practice*) if the gallery where you left a consignment goes under, your property may, under provisions of the Uniform Commercial Code, be legally subject to the claims of the gallery's creditors. (However, according to Feldman and Weil, the code holds dealers legally responsible for loss of or damage to consigned works, unless you have made an agreement to the contrary.) A disreputable dealer may fail to pay you promptly when your work is sold or may tell you he sold your consignment for an amount lower than the actual sale price; he will then pocket the difference and net considerably more than his commission of 10 to 25 percent.

If you sell, rather than consign, a work to a dealer, you will know that you are getting exactly what you bargained for, but (given what you already know about dealers' markups) you will also know that you are getting considerably less than the work's current (or probable future) retail value; in almost all cases, the dealer will buy from you only if he thinks that he will eventually make a profitable resale. "If I purchase a painting, I buy it at a 'dealer's price' and expect to make 30 to 40 percent on my investment," said Stephen Hahn. If he thinks a work will retail at $135,000, for example, he will buy it for about $100,000, he said. Selling to a dealer also means that you will be negotiating with a seasoned professional who will ask you to name your price and then will probably try to bargain it down. "I will not make an offer to a collector," said Eugene Thaw. "He has to offer a work at a price. If I want to, I can then make a counter-offer. If the collector says, 'I don't know what to ask,' and then I say, 'I'll offer $30,000,' the collector will find an excuse to get out of my gallery and take the work to someone else to see if he can get $35,000. I will have lost it, but I will have established the value for it. If someone doesn't know what to ask, I say, 'Take it to someone else, see what they offer and let me know.'"

There is, of course, an entirely different system for buying and selling art—the auction system. It carries its own set of rules and traditions, advantages and pitfalls. The auctioneers and dealers are engaged in a growing and not always friendly competition for the art trade, and some collectors feel so strongly about the relative advantages of one system over the other that they rely on it almost exclusively. You will probably find, though, that both are worthy of attention and neither can be overlooked if your goal is to form a first-rate collection.

Chapter 3

THE ACTION AT AUCTION

Auction houses seem more casual and less intimidating than the hushed establishments of big-name dealers. This gives auctions an especially strong appeal for the new collector—an appeal that is enhanced by the air of drama at auction, which no gallery exhibition can possibly match. You may feel a surge of excitement when the moment approaches for you to bid. "You'd better not attend if you have heart trouble," observed collector Paul Singer. Auctions also give the inexperienced buyer a chance to make his decisions (and his mistakes) in relative anonymity, without an all-knowing dealer looking over his shoulder, sizing him up as a neophyte or a fool. Sotheby Parke Bernet's director of fine arts sales, David Nash, likened the difference between auction houses and galleries to the difference between a big department store and a smaller specialty shop. Some people prefer to buy things "off the rack," without a salesperson following their every move and trying to influence their choice; others enjoy the personal assistance and service that the smaller, more specialized establishments can offer. "New buyers tend to come to auction," Nash said, "because they feel they will not be pressured here to buy something they don't want." Auctions also give the new collector a sense of security about the appropriateness of the price he pays. A successful bidder appears to pay only slightly more than another potential buyer—the underbidder —is willing to part with. In an article on "Today's Auction Boom" (May 31, 1980), *New York Times* art critic John Russell observed that auction houses owe much of their increased popularity to the fact that "in the archetypal situation today, the owner doesn't know what he is selling, and the buyer doesn't know what he ought to pay." The openness of auctions, he suggested, gives buyers and sellers the sense that they are probably getting a fair deal. Similarly, the collector and industrialist Armand Hammer commented that if collectors are worried about getting a fair price, they are protected when they buy at auction.

This is not necessarily so. Nor is it true that new collectors should buy at auctions in order to make their first mistakes anonymously. Auctions are essential training grounds for new collectors, but only if the collector applies as much analytical skepticism to auction purchases as to purchases from dealers. The intelligent collector will not bid at auction without thoroughly examining the object he is considering and the policies and practices of the auction house he is attending.

Preparing to Buy at Auction

The first step in preparing to buy at auction is finding out which particular auction sales may interest you. The two biggest international auction houses—Sotheby Parke Bernet and Christie's—organize hundreds of sales a year in New York, London and many other cities around the world. Each sale usually concentrates on a particular collecting area (e.g., old-master paintings); sometimes further distinctions are made among sales in a particular area, so that one sale contains works of a higher price and quality, while another contains the more run-of-the-mill offerings. (The catalogue for the higher-quality sale may be entitled "Fine [or "Important"] Old-Master Paintings," while the catalogue for the more ordinary sale may be entitled simply "Old-Master Paintings.") The various categories by which auction houses (and also dealers) classify art may differ from a layman's understanding of these terms. Sales entitled "Nineteenth-Century European Paintings," for example, generally include only realistic works done in the early and middle nineteenth century but not the Impressionist or Post-Impressionist works of the late 1800s. "Modern Art," in the lingo of the art market, generally means nonrealistic work produced by European artists in the first half of the twentieth century. American artists from the same period are usually lumped into sales of "American Paintings and Sculpture," while American artists associated with later movements, beginning with the Abstract Expressionists (such as Pollock, Rothko, de Kooning and Motherwell), are included in sales of "Contemporary Art." Sales of "Old Masters" include not only the great names like Rembrandt and Rubens, but virtually anyone who painted between 1400 and 1800. Smaller auction houses have fewer specialized sales and broader specialties. They often hold "estate sales," which offer all of the auctionable property of the deceased, including furniture, silver and fine art. A "specialized" sale at a smaller auction house may be a sale of all paintings recently consigned to the house from various sources, regardless of the paintings' periods or countries of origin.

Once you have determined which auction houses interest you, you must find out when they will be holding their sales of the types of material that you want to buy. Auction houses publish their schedules in their own newsletters and in advertisements in newspapers and magazines; they are, of course, delighted to answer all telephoned and written inquiries about their sales. You will find that the various auction houses in a particular city try to schedule their sales of similar material within several days of each other, to make it easy for out-of-towners to attend all the sales in their field of interest. The most important sales of Impressionist and modern works at Sotheby Parke Bernet and Christie's in New York, for example, are generally scheduled during one week in November and one week in May; major collectors and dealers from around the world converge on New York at those times, making the rounds of the galleries as well as the auction houses. Other specialties have their big sales at other times of the year; you will soon learn the seasons for auction-going in your particular field or fields, and if you are not from New York, you may time your art-gallery visits to coincide with the periods of greatest auction activity. Although they are fiercely competitive, the auction houses do not schedule similar sales to conflict with each other; a scheduling conflict would divide the pool of potential bidders and hurt all the houses. The desire to avoid conflict extends to international scheduling. The houses in London schedule their big Impressionist, modern and contemporary sales, for example, at different times of year from their New York counterparts.

Once you have determined which specific sales interest you, the next step is to find out just what they will offer. Catalogues are usually available from the auction houses several weeks before each sale; they may be purchased singly or by subscription. (At the big auction houses, you may subscribe to all catalogues or only to those in the fields that interest you.) If you intend to visit the auction house before the sale, it is not absolutely necessary to buy the catalogue. (At this writing, catalogues at SPB and Christie's can cost anywhere from about $5 to $20 or more. The higher prices are for hardbound catalogues of major sales.) The catalogues are available for free inspection at the auction house, and the works themselves can be examined at a special exhibition, open free to the public, during the days before the auction. If you intend to collect a particular type of art in depth, it is a good idea to build a personal library of relevant auction catalogues that you can study carefully before the sales and refer to later when you want to evaluate the price and quality of other potential purchases. Subscribers are generally sent price lists after the sales.

The sale catalogue usually contains a detailed rundown of the auction house's general policies, practices and conditions of sale (more on this later), as well as important information about each specific object being offered. Information may be given about an object's attribution, date, dimensions (height by width), medium, edition size (where relevant) and, occasionally, its condition, provenance (history of ownership) and exhibition history; the amount of detail varies from object to object and from auction house to auction house. Important offerings tend to be described at greater length, and the larger auction houses, with their larger and (usually) more expert staffs, generally do more research than the smaller organizations. The catalogue entry for an object may have a line or two describing its subject matter, importance or physical appearance, and may also list any books or articles in which the object has been mentioned. Many catalogue entries include a photograph of the object. In general, the offerings judged by the auction-house experts to be more important are given photographs; color photographs are usually reserved for the top offerings in the catalogue.

Like their descriptions of different categories of art, auction houses' descriptions of specific art works may confuse the layman who has not yet learned the auction-market lingo. A work catalogued as "attributed to" a certain artist is likely not to be by that artist at all. The "attributed to" designation means that the auction-house specialist is less certain of its true authorship than if he had simply catalogued it under the name of the artist, without any words of qualification. (If the auction house makes any guarantees of authorship, such guarantees apply only to works catalogued as by the artist, without qualification.) If the specialist catalogues a work as "signed" or "dated," he is more certain of the signature's or date's authenticity than if he says the work "bears signature" or "bears date." (In some cases, false signatures or dates may have been added to works to enhance their value.) These and other nuances are spelled out in the glossary at the front of the catalogue, which is essential reading for any potential purchaser.

Auction catalogues usually supply one additional important piece of information about each offering: the approximate price that the auctioneer expects it to fetch. These "presale estimates," usually expressed as a range of values (e.g., $800–$1,000), are sometimes printed as part of each catalogue entry and sometimes compiled in a separate list, arranged according to lot number, at the back of the catalogue. Some lots—usually only highly important items in important sales—do not carry published presale estimates but are, instead, designated "Refer Dept." This means that you must contact the experts in the department that is running the sale (the Impressionist/modern paint-ings department, for example) to be told the expected price. "We use 'Refer Dept.' estimates for unusual and important works because we don't really know what they are worth," said Christopher Burge of Christie's. "We recently had a Picasso drawing for which the original estimate was $100,000. Everyone was raving about it, so we then told people that we thought it would bring $150,000. It made $210,000."

Auction-house specialists usually set presale estimates at the level of recent prices fetched by comparable objects. But other factors may also come into play—the wishes of the consignor (who may have bought the object at a high price and be willing to let it go only if he can make a profit), or recent market trends (which may lead the special-ist to believe that prices will be higher or lower than suggested by the last comparable sales). Burge said that he likes presale estimates to be "accurate but conservative." That way, he said, the seller gets more than he expects and the buyer is encouraged to bid because the esti-mate is enticing. A high estimate, on the other hand, may deter people from bidding. Nash of SPB said that estimates tend to be lower than actual prices in areas where the market is escalating rapidly. (He cited American paintings and nineteenth-century European paintings as two fields where this estimate-lag had recently occurred.) In areas where the market has been more consistent, he said, estimates tend to be more accurate. Estimates tend to be particularly low for those "block-buster" items that are of such quality or rarity that the auction-house expert has few recent comparable yardsticks to go by. The Turner painting *Juliet and Her Nurse,* which became the most expensive art work ever auctioned when it sold for $6.4 million on May 29, 1980, at SPB, New York, had originally been estimated by the auction house to bring "over $1 million." The estimate was based partly on the rarity of Turners on the market, but was also tempered by the fact that *Juliet,* a transitional work of 1836, was not considered to be among Turner's most important paintings. "Art-historically speaking," according to Judith Landrigan, SPB's expert for nineteenth-century European paint-ings at the time of the Turner sale, "what we think of as Turner's greatest masterpieces were yet to come." No major Turner had been auctioned for ten years, Landrigan said, and the last one, a very early work sold in 1970, had brought $750,000. By three weeks before the auction, Landrigan had witnessed enough presale excitement to raise her estimate to between $2 million and $3 million, but almost no one (least of all the seller, Flora Whitney Miller of New York) had dreamed that a middle-quality Turner could fetch $6.4 million, topping the

J. M. W. Turner, *Juliet and Her Nurse*

previous record for any art work at auction—$5.5 million paid in 1971 at Christie's, London, by the Metropolitan Museum of Art for a Velázquez masterpiece, *Juan de Pareja.*

Auction prices may also greatly exceed presale estimates when several bidders are convinced that an art work is more important than the auction specialist has realized. At a 1980 old-masters sale at Christie's, New York, a painting catalogued as "School of Francesco Guardi" and estimated at $8,000 to $12,000 sold for $115,000, and a painting catalogued as "School of François Boucher," estimated at $8,000 to $12,000, sold for $112,000. The auction-house specialist, Ian Kennedy, commented that the bidders must have believed that the works could be securely attributed to the artists themselves.

According to Robert Schonfeld, formerly SPB's liaison with the investment and financial community, auction-house experts are skilled at estimating the "floor price" that an object will bring. Speaking at a 1979 seminar on art investments sponsored by the New York Society of Security Analysts, he observed that it is often very difficult to estimate the "ceiling price," especially of unique objects, because interest in a particular lot can change as the date of the sale approaches. But regular auction-goers and disappointed consignors know that overly

Above: **School of Francesco Guardi,**
The Rialto Bridge
Left: **School of François Boucher,**
The Birth and Triumph of Venus

optimistic estimates are also frequently encountered. At a 1980 auction of old-master paintings at SPB, New York, for example, a painting expected to be one of the star lots in the sale, *The Singel, Amsterdam* by Gerrit Berckheyde, consigned by the Fine Arts Museums of San Francisco, was unsold at $47,500, about half its presale estimate of $80,000 to $100,000. Brenda Auslander, then SPB's old-masters expert, considered the painting to be "a rare, nice view, in good condition." The bidders apparently did not share her enthusiasm. According to SPB's photography expert, Anne Horton, a large percentage of unsold works at auction indicates a tendency on the part of the expert to assign estimates that are too high. Speaking at a 1980 seminar on photography collecting sponsored by the Association of International Photography Art Dealers and by Images Gallery of New York, Horton suggested that collectors take note of the "buy-in" rate at auction (the percentage of the knockdown total that represents bids on works that failed to sell) to gauge whether an expert's estimates are reliable. An unsold total that is 20 percent or more of the knockdown total (as would be the case if $20,000 or more of a $100,000 knockdown total represented bids on works that failed to sell) is usually considered high, although in very speculative fields, such as contemporary art, a relatively high buy-in rate is common. Auction houses, preferring to emphasize their successes rather than their failures, often do not publicize their buy-in rates. You may get this information, however, by contacting the auction-house staff or by reading published accounts of auctions in newspapers and art-market newsletters (see Bibliography). Unsold works are generally omitted from the price lists sent to catalogue subscribers after the sales. (More later on "buying in" and the reason why certain works fail to sell.)

Examining catalogue descriptions, photographs and presale estimates is an important first step in deciding whether to buy an object, but is not a sufficient basis for making a final decision. You can usually return an object that you have obtained on approval, sight unseen, from a dealer, but you cannot do that at an auction house. David Nash of SPB asserted that collectors should never buy something at auction from a photograph. "If you cannot attend the sale, unless you are really expert on what the problems might be, don't buy without seeing the object or having someone see if for you," he cautioned. Firsthand inspection is necessary because auction-catalogue photographs often give a very different impression from the one you would get viewing the work itself, and auction-catalogue descriptions are often sketchy and sometimes inaccurate. The auction house understandably wants to put its offerings in the best possible light, and may therefore overpraise their merits while neglecting to mention their defects. In certain collecting areas, such as prints, condition defects are often thoroughly noted in auction catalogues. In many other areas, condition defects are not even mentioned. An auction house based in Bolton and Boston, Mass.—Robert W. Skinner—is known for meticulously cataloguing the condition defects of its offerings, but such forthrightness is the exception, not the rule. Another important limitation of auction-catalogue descriptions was noted by auctioneer William Doyle, president of William Doyle Galleries in New York, at the 1980 ARTnews art-market conference: "An auction catalogue never tells you the quality of a painting. Childe Hassam painted quite a few dogs." It is important to note that even those auction houses that guarantee the authorship of certain works do not guarantee the accuracy of the rest of the description in the catalogue. (More on guarantees later.)

To assess quality and condition—as pointed out by David Nash, above—attendance (by you or your representative) at the auction house's presale exhibition is essential. In contrast to the "hands off" policy at museum exhibitions, the policy at auction-house displays is entirely hands on. "Viewing" an object at a presale exhibition can mean fondling it to assess its shape and surface texture, moving it to examine its back or underside, or (in the case of a work on paper) removing it from its frame to get a better idea of its appearance and condition. (The finest old-master prints in a sale are often exhibited unframed and off the walls, according to SPB's print specialist, Marc Rosen, "because people want to see the paper unimpeded by the coloration or the look of glass"; glass ordinarily protects the surfaces of framed works on paper.) It is best to request assistance from the auction-house personnel stationed around the exhibition area before attempting any physical examination of potential purchases. They will unlock cases, help you move objects and caution you about works that may be too fragile for a particular type of handling. Many people like to run their fingers lightly over the surface of a painting to determine whether the texture of the brushstrokes has been flattened by cleaning, relining or other handling. Some people even spit on old-master paintings and rub the spit over the surface, to get some idea of the true colors beneath the layers of grime. (Brenda Auslander, formerly of SPB, says that she knows when a painting has aroused unusual interest by the amount of spit that has accumulated on it.) But some paint surfaces may be seriously damaged by such treatment; if you don't know, you must ask.

Discreetly listening to the comments of dealers and other expert buyers as they peruse an auction house's offerings (and noticing whether your favorite works seem to have caught the eyes of others) can be an interesting and informative part of your visit to the presale exhibition. You may even try to strike up conversations with fellow viewers, to get an idea of their tastes and opinions. But beware of taking presale chatter too seriously. The "expert" you overhear may be no more knowledgeable than you, or may have selfish motives for making others think that a certain work is very desirable (if he is in some way connected with the seller, or if he himself owns a similar work). The most disparaging presale remarks about a work sometimes come from the person who winds up purchasing it. When dealer Richard Feigen was commissioned by a collector to buy an Impressionist painting that Feigen considered "an exceptional work of art," he actively tried to discourage other people. "I did not extol the painting when people asked my opinion and I tried to put people off it, if they were people to whom I did not have a fiduciary responsibility. I sent a note to the auctioneer, saying that I would only proceed at certain increments if he wanted to accept my bid. They lowered the increment [the amount by which one bid exceeds the last] when I entered the bidding. I got the painting for about 60 percent of what the client was prepared to pay. He was ecstatic."

Consultation with dealers or other outside experts can sometimes save you money at auction, but is most often used to get additional insights about a work's authenticity, quality and condition. "A collector who has any sense and buys in a public sale should consult a specialist," asserted dealer Stephen Hahn, who said that he performs such consultation free for clients and for a "nominal fee" for those who have not bought from him. David Nash of SPB noted that many collectors— particularly those who are well known for spending large sums on a particular type of art—like to have dealers bid for them at auction; they rightly fear that others in the room may push up the price if they know an important collector has entered the competition. Such a collector (or, indeed, anyone) can also leave a bid with the auction house, to be exercised anonymously on his behalf (more on this later), but he may not want to let the auction house know that he is willing to pay a price greatly exceeding the presale estimate. He may also believe that a personal representative can best serve his interests by getting a feel for the competition and, perhaps, using certain salesroom tricks (à la Feigen) to keep the price down.

Nash observed, though, that dealers are not likely to give auction assistance to strangers who are interested in small, less important items. For the beginning collector, the best available source of auction advice may be the auction house itself. Just as it is important for collectors to get to know the directors of galleries, so is it important for them to cultivate good relations with auction-house specialists. The specialists are often available for consultation at the presale exhibitions and they are always available to talk to potential buyers and sellers by appointment. You should ask them the same questions that you would ask dealers about a work's quality, condition, history and price. Sometimes the specialist may learn important new facts about a work after the sale catalogue has gone to print; you will discover these facts only by talking to him. Both Burge of Christie's and Nash of SPB say that they and other specialists give collectors candid advice about the quality and condition of their houses' offerings. "If a new collector, looking for advice, says, 'What do you think is good in the sale?' I will tell him what I would personally want to own," said Burge. "I will give totally unbiased advice about a picture that a collector is interested in, although my own taste might be quite different. I might personally like a Monet from 1872 and not like one from the 1880s, but I will advise a collector about what I think a good 1880s picture is. . . . If I loathe a picture, I will not say, 'This is the nastiest thing I've ever seen. It's a piece of rubbish.' But I will say, 'It's not all that great. I think it's overpriced, but that's the market. I cannot recommend it, because it's not a good example of the artist's work.' " Similarly, Nash observed that "most specialists will speak candidly about the quality of a work, but a lot of cases are fairly subjective." He noted, though, that because of the auction house's responsibility to consignors, "we can't be too dissuasive. We try to be as factual as possible." (It should also be noted that the auction house has a definite financial interest in promoting consignors' interests: the higher the bidding, the more the auction house earns in commissions.)

Both Burge and Nash said that auction-house specialists will reveal to potential buyers everything they know about a work's condition and will even let collectors examine works with the auction house's ultraviolet light in a dark room, to determine how much restoration has been done to a painting. Surprisingly few people ask to use the ultraviolet light, according to Nash and Burge. "I'm amazed that so many people just look at a picture and bid on it," said Nash. Sometimes the specialist will be aware of defects that do not show up under ultraviolet, and will point these out to any collector who takes the trouble to ask. Nash said that SPB will also put collectors in touch with restorers who can tell how well a dirty or damaged work can be cleaned or restored.

A talk with the specialist can also give you more guidance on price. He will reveal the basis upon which he arrived at his original presale estimate (telling you what recent prices were fetched by which comparable works) and he will say whether he has revised the estimate since the catalogue went to press (due to unexpectedly high presale interest in the work, for example). If the provenance listed for the work in the catalogue indicates that it was auctioned previously (the date and place of the sale will usually be listed in the catalogue, but the price often won't be), you can ask what the previous auction price was (or you can look this up in an art library that collects auction catalogues and price lists).

Once you have done all the groundwork and decided whether to bid, you are ready to decide how much to bid. Nash suggests that the neophyte who wants a few paintings to decorate his apartment should probably not go more than 20 to 25 percent above the high end of the presale estimate range, unless he is absolutely set on a particular picture. But he added that if someone seriously specializes in collecting a certain type of art, and a particularly good example comes up for sale, "he should pay whatever he can afford." Similarly, Burge said that a new collector will probably not overpay if his bid is within the presale estimate. Many people, he said, overpay in the beginning for something they ultimately don't like, because their taste is not yet developed. To guard against "auction fever"—the temporary madness that causes amateurs and even seasoned collectors to bid prices beyond the limits they had just set themselves (and even beyond what the same item could be expected to fetch in a dealer's gallery the next day)—Burge suggests that bidders "write their maximum in their catalogue in red and underline it six times. Once you've decided on your maximum, you've got to stick to it." One of the most amazing sights at the celebrated 1980 auction at Christie's, New York, of ten important Impressionist and modern paintings from the collection of Henry Ford II was a woman's impulse-bidding at the $5-million level. When her unseen rival for van Gogh's *Le Jardin du Poète, Arles* bid $5 million over the telephone, she firmly signaled to the auctioneer that she no longer wished to compete. Then she changed her mind, offering $5.05 million and, finally, $5.15 million before dropping out of the bidding for the last time, allowing the hammer to fall at $5.2 million—the highest price in the sale, one of the highest prices ever paid for an art work at auction, and more than twice the auctioneer's presale estimate of "around $2 million."

The final step in preparing for auction is finding out about the auction house's policies regarding credit and payment. Some auction houses require bidders to register before a sale and to establish their credit in advance. You may have to pay in full or leave a deposit immediately after the sale. "All auction houses will require that checks clear (or that a bank confirm there are sufficient funds to clear) before goods may be removed," wrote *New York Times* auction reporter Rita Reif in her article, "Buying or Just Browsing, the Action Is at the Auctions" (Nov. 9, 1979). "But purchases may be made by cash, money order, traveler's checks or with a bank letter of credit. . . . Because each house has rules about how long a buyer is given to pay, it is best to ask what is required."

Selling at Auction

Approaching an auction as a potential seller rather than as a potential buyer requires a different sort of preparation. Occasionally, if you own a desirable work that would neatly fill a gap in an upcoming sale, the auction house may actually initiate negotiations, in the hope that you may want to sell. "When I begin to put together a sale," said Burge, "I have fantasies of Tahitian Gauguins and still lifes by Cézanne. I try to keep a balance in a sale. I already have too many Sisleys and Pissarros in my next sale, and if someone offered me another one, I'd probably say no. But I need a Matisse: I'm going to go through the Matisse catalogue and call up some people who have Matisses."

While, in special cases like this, the auction house may put feelers out to potential consignors, it is more usual for consignors to initiate discussions with the auction house. Consignors to an auction typically include collectors, dealers, estates and, occasionally, museums or other institutions. In deciding which auction house to favor with your consignments, you should consider the reputations, track records and consignment terms of the various houses, as well as your personal rapport with their staffs. Burge said that the prices fetched at Christie's and SPB are likely to be "pretty much the same," and that rapport is often what influences a client to choose one house over the other. "People finally decide to go here or there because somebody was more polite on the phone," he said. Robert Eldred, Jr., of Robert C. Eldred Co., the East Dennis, Mass., auction house, suggested that making consignment decisions on the basis of personalities is not as arbitrary as it may seem. "Personality may be the key to how much money an item brings," he maintained, speaking at the 1980 *ARTnews* art-market conference. "It shows the auctioneer's ability to convince buyers and sellers that he can do the best job for them." At the same conference, Robert Skinner of Robert W. Skinner, Inc., in Massachusetts said, "I want to talk to people. If I can instill confidence in me, I've won most of the battle."

There are, however, more concrete factors to consider in choosing among the auction houses. Perhaps the most important are their levels of expertise and the quality of their track records in handling the types of objects that you are planning to sell. The expertise of specialists in different fields varies at the different auction houses; the most highly respected expert is likely to attract the best consignments, and the sale with the best consignments is likely to attract the greatest interest and fetch the highest prices. When, for example, Martha Baer became the contemporary-art specialist at Christie's, New York, in 1978, she brought with her the contacts and reputation gained from previous experience as vice-president at André Emmerich Gallery and, after that, president of Acquavella Contemporary Art (both top-flight galleries in New York). Although Christie's was a newcomer to the New York auction scene (opening its New York auction premises in 1977),

Baer was soon able to assemble sales that surpassed those of the long-entrenched rival house, SPB, in both dollar volume and (in the eyes of many observers) quality of offerings.

"You should pick an auction house based on how well it's done with similar items," said dealer-collector Ben Heller, who scoffed at the notion that personalities should be the deciding factor. A rough idea about which auction houses specialize in which types of art can be obtained by comparing their annual sale figures in different categories. (You can ask the houses for this information, or read about it in the various art-market publications listed in the Bibliography.) If an auction house has a greater sale total for nineteenth-century European paintings than its competitors, or if such paintings account for an unusually large proportion of the house's total sales, the firm is probably considered a leading seller of nineteenth-century European paintings. Similarly, an auction house that deals primarily in lower-priced items may sometimes be the best place for lesser consignments. Robert Skinner pointed out that smaller auction houses tend to get more money for lesser merchandise. "As a seller in the middle of Massachusetts," he said, "we can make a lot more excitement [for lower-priced goods] and bring in more buyers than can be done in New York, where there are tremendous goods and all but the great things are run-of-the-mill and happen every day." John Marion, president of SPB, New York, predicted that "with the spread of wealth and interest to different areas of the country, the role of the small auction house and dealer will increase in the future."

Recognizing the importance of the lower-priced market, both SPB and Christie's have developed their own strategies for attracting such consignments. SPB holds regular "Arcade Auctions" at its York Avenue facilities (opened in 1980 to relieve the space crunch at the Madison Avenue headquarters), where objects valued from $100 to $5,000 are sold within four weeks of consignment. Christie's East, a satellite of the main New York auction house, holds frequent sales of lower-priced goods in many of the same categories (e.g., American paintings, tribal art and antiquities) that are auctioned at the main branch. Christie's East also auctions certain other lower-priced categories not handled at the main branch, such as photographs, costumes, and dolls and toys.

Discussions with other collectors and dealers will help give you an idea of the relative strengths and weaknesses of different auction houses in different categories, and discussions with the specialists themselves at the various auction houses (and requests for information about their backgrounds and experience) should give you some idea of their relative expertise. Questions about the works already consigned to an upcoming auction should help you determine whether the sale as a whole is likely to attract high bidding interest that may help boost the price of your own consignment. Nash suggested that potential consignors should ask about the expected number of works in the sale; the expected number of color photos in the catalogue; the expected total value of the offerings; how your consignment is expected to rank in quality and price relative to the other offerings; the extent of the catalogue's distribution; whether a group of works from a good private (or museum) collection will form the nucleus of the sale (attracting greater bidding interest).

In general, the level of expertise at the large international auction houses is greater than at the smaller regional ones. Nash noted that knowledgeable buyers can sometimes pick up bargains at the smaller firms because their auction-house specialists may not recognize the true quality and worth of some items that come their way. For the seller, such undervaluation is clearly undesirable. But officials of the smaller auction houses argue that their firms offer important advantages to certain consignors, aside from the greater visibility for lower-priced goods. "A smaller house gives more personal service," said William Doyle. "There is no Mr. Christie, no Mr. Parke and no Mr. Bernet, but there is a Mr. Doyle at William Doyle Galleries." One of the services provided (particularly to estates) by Doyle and other smaller auction firms is the rapid, complete disposal of all the property in a household. "We buy out the whole apartment," Doyle said, "and sell to second-hand dealers whatever is not auctionable."

Auction houses can differ considerably in the fees they charge consignors, and this too may enter into your decision about which house to choose (although it should weigh less heavily than your assessment of the firm's expertise, track record and integrity). Following the lead of Christie's, many auction houses in the United States now charge a commission to buyers as well as sellers; the "buyer's premium" is a fixed percentage of the purchase price (usually 10 percent) and cannot be negotiated; the seller's commission (also usually 10 percent, but as high as 15 percent for goods valued at $3,000 or less at Christie's, or at $2,000 or less at SPB) *is* negotiable, and some people "play one house against the other to get the commission down; they go back and forth several times," according to Burge. (It should be noted that all auction prices cited here are hammer prices and *do not* include the buyer's premium. It should also be noted that the auction-house fees, policies and practices discussed in this chapter are those in effect at this writing, but may have changed in some respects by the time you read this. To check on current policies, it is important to read the statements in auction-house catalogues and ask staff members about anything that needs clarification.)

Burge said that, despite the heavy competition among auction houses for consignors, he is "against commission-cutting" for sellers. "I like to suggest that people pay *more* commission if the house does well. If we say we will charge the consignor 5 percent on a $5-million collection, I like to suggest that he pay 7 percent if we get $5.5 million." Nash said that SPB will "negotiate about the seller's commission if a consignment is sufficiently valuable or if the consignor does frequent business with the auction house. "If you have a nice Guercino drawing worth $10,000 to $15,000, we might accept a 6 percent commission," Nash said. "The commission might also be reduced for a big collection." At the art-investment seminar sponsored by the New York Society of Security Analysts, SPB's head of appraisals and estates, C. Hugh Hildesley, said that negotiation is common for consignments worth more than $50,000. Dealer Eugene Thaw said that a good negotiator with a top-quality consignment can get the seller's commission reduced to zero (in which case the auction house collects money only from the buyer). Nash said that seller's commissions were charged even for such highly important single-owner auctions as the 1977 Mentmore sale, the 1978 Robert von Hirsch sale and the 1979 Paul Rosenberg sale (all held in England). "A 2.5 percent commission is the lowest I've ever done," said Nash. However, in a later interview with the *Wall Street Journal* (July 7, 1981), John Marion, president of SPB, New York, acknowledged that the seller's commission may have been eliminated "once or twice."

Other auction-house fees can also be negotiated. SPB generally charges consignors for catalogue photos, insurance and transportation of works to the auction house, but sometimes, for highly desirable consignments, the auction house pays it all, said Nash. Some other auction houses (including Christie's) make no charge for photos or short-distance shipping. SPB (but not Christie's and many other firms) charges sellers for special advertising of their consignments and for visits to inspect prospective consignments at the sellers' homes. (The inspection fee is refunded if the works are consigned within a year to SPB.)

If you bring your potential consignment to the auction house (it is best to make an appointment for this) or if you send the auction house a clear black-and-white photograph, a specialist will give you a free oral assessment of what it is and what it is worth. You should supply as much information about the object as you can: its provenance, exhibition history, and any supporting documentation. It is not necessarily a good idea to consign your wares to the house that gives you the most optimistic appraisal. A high appraisal may reflect the specialist's sincere enthusiasm for the object, or it may just reflect his desire to round up some merchandise for sale, even if it means giving some consignors false hope.

A truer gauge of the specialist's feelings about an object may be his suggestion about the level of the "reserve"—the price below which the object will not be sold. Consignors are allowed to set a reserve price to protect themselves against an object's going for too low a price. Certain circumstances may sometimes cause auction prices to be unnaturally low—for example, a snowstorm that keeps bidders away or a secret agreement among a group of dealers not to compete against each other for a particular offering. (Such a group of dealers—known as a "ring"—may then hold their own private auction to determine which of them gets the work. Auction-house officials say that the effectiveness of rings has been greatly diminished in recent years by the broadening of the auction-going public to include collectors and dealers from around the world, all in active competition with each other.) Although an auction-house specialist may sometimes flatter a consignor's expectations by putting a high presale estimate on an object, he will be less willing to agree to a reserve that he feels is excessive: The auction house loses all or most of its commission on works that do not sell because the reserve is not met. In addition, a sale with a high number of unsold works gives the auction house an aura of failure that may hurt its chances for future consignments. To discourage owners from insisting on unrealistic reserves, some auction houses charge consignors a "buy-in fee" on works that do not sell. (In auction lingo, a work that is not sold because its reserve is not reached is said to be "bought in.") At SPB, for example, the buy-in fee is 5 percent of the reserve price. (This fee is sometimes waived if the auction-house specialist and the consignor agree on the appropriate reserve.) Christie's, at this writing, makes no such charge.

The level of the reserve is a secret between the auction house and the consignor; the bidding public is never told what the reserve is for any object. At SPB and Christie's, the reserve for a given object is usually below the low end of the presale estimate range published in the catalogue, and is never above the high end. Nash said that reserves at SPB are usually equal to about two-thirds of the median estimate.

Many lots have no reserve at all, he added, because the seller is willing to take whatever he can get. Unreserved items are found mostly among the lower-priced offerings, but even the high-priced Impressionist and modern works in the 1980 sale of the estate of Edgar William and Bernice Chrysler Garbisch had "almost no reserves," according to Nash. "The estate didn't want them back."

At Christie's, according to Burge, reserves are "ideally 75 percent of the low estimate" but are usually (due to the wishes of consignors) somewhat higher—about 90 percent of the low estimate. Some lower-priced lots have no reserves, but the consignors usually expect the auctioneer to use his discretion in not allowing the objects to go for prices that are ridiculously low, Burge said; such objects usually can be bought for no less than half their low estimates. Other objects, Burge said, are auctioned "to go": any bid will buy them. Potential buyers are not told by Christie's or SPB when an object is being offered without reserve; all items are marked in the catalogue as subject to a reserve. Reserves are much less common at the smaller auction houses, and their catalogues sometimes do differentiate between those objects that are sold with reserves and those that are not. "Maybe 1 percent of our items are reserved," said Skinner, and the fact that there is a reserve (but not the price at which it is set) "is indicated in the catalogue, next to the estimate. Some people won't bid on items with reserves." Eldred said that he sometimes offers a lower seller's commission to people who agree to sell without reserves. Richard A. Bourne Co. of Hyannis, Mass., does not (at this writing) allow reserves on any of its offerings.

For particularly desirable consignments, the larger auction firms sometimes devise more complicated arrangements to protect the seller from risk. A collector who consigns several works (or an entire collection) to an auction can sometimes negotiate a "global reserve" for his consignments—a reserve figure that applies to the total price for all his consignments, rather than to the price for each individual lot. If the first items in such a collection go for more than expected, the auctioneer can let some of the later items go for less than expected, provided that the total for all items reaches the global reserve price. For example, if there is a global reserve of $100,000 on two items and the first is sold for $60,000, the second can be sold for $40,000. If bids on the second item do not reach $40,000, it will be bought in for the consignor.

Some auction houses also protect certain sellers from risk by buying their property outright and later auctioning it for the auction firm's own account. This has the same advantages and disadvantages as selling works to dealers. It provides the seller with immediate cash but, given the fact that the auction house obviously hopes to make a profitable resale, the amount paid to the seller may be less than the property's full fair market value. Some people (including some auction-house officials) consider it a conflict of interest for an auction house to sell some goods for its own account as well as for outside consignors. Among those that do not buy property from sellers are Christie's, Adam A. Weschler & Son in Washington, D.C., and Samuel T. Freeman & Co. in Philadelphia. SPB occasionally (but rarely) buys property from sellers, only after standard arrangements have been rejected by the client. SPB-owned property is identified in the catalogues as "Property of Sotheby Parke Bernet Inc." or "Property from [name of estate or previous owner] sold by order of the present owner Sotheby Parke Bernet Inc." Other auction firms that purchase property from sellers include William Doyle Galleries in New York and Du Mouchelle Art Galleries in Detroit.

A final decision related to selling at auction is whether or not to do so anonymously. Most consignors opt for privacy, but it may sometimes be financially advantageous to allow your name to be used (particularly if you are well known or have acquired a reputation as a distinguished collector); bidders sometimes will pay more for a work with a desirable or interesting provenance.

How Auctions Work

Almost all auctions are open free to the public; all you have to do to attend is to arrive at the right time. You can usually walk in any time during the sale without causing any disruption or attracting any notice; if the lot you are interested in is one of the last to come up, you need not arrive early. In the case of a very popular or important sale, however, it is best to come early to assure yourself of a seat. Tickets (which are distributed free) are required for admission to important evening auctions of Impressionist, modern and contemporary works at SPB and Christie's. The demand for tickets is great; it is best to request them early and to describe yourself as someone who intends to bid. Depending on how the auction house assesses your importance, your ticket may admit you to the main salesroom or to one of the auxiliary rooms that are opened to accommodate the overflow crowds at the major auctions. (There are spotters ready to take your bids in any of these rooms, and you can watch the main action via closed-circuit television.) Certain charity auctions or estate sales on the premises of the deceased require the purchase of an auction catalogue as the price of admission.

Objects are auctioned according to their order in the catalogue; the auctioneer or his assistant holds up or points out the particular lot being offered. Some lots appearing in the catalogue may have been withdrawn from sale; the auctioneer will usually identify any withdrawn lots at the beginning of the auction, and again at the points in the sale where those lots were originally scheduled to come up. A work may be withdrawn at any time up to the start of the sale, for a variety of reasons. The owner may have changed his mind about selling or may have decided to sell the object privately; doubts may have been raised about the object's authenticity or the consignor's title to it.

Bidding usually begins at a level considerably below the presale estimate. Nash said that SPB's auctioneers generally start the bidding at one-third of the low estimate, proceeding at increments of 5 to 10 percent of the first bid. (In other words, if the presale estimate is $3,000 to $5,000, bidding will begin at $1,000 and will probably advance $100 at a time.) At Christie's, according to Burge, bidding usually begins at one-third to one-half of the low estimate, with 10 percent increments. Doyle said that his auction house starts the bidding at the low estimate. "If nobody bids, we go down," he said.

To make a bid, all you need to do is raise your hand (or your numbered paddle, if the auction house gives you one). This will almost certainly attract the attention of the auctioneer or one of his "spotters" stationed around the room. Once you have gotten his attention, you can continue bidding with more subtle gestures—a nod of the head, a flick of a pen, or even a wink. Some people who do not want to be conspicuous in making even the first bid notify the auctioneer in advance of their intention to compete for a particular work and arrange a subtle bidding signal that only the auctioneer will recognize. (One such signal might be to pull the corner of a handkerchief out of your pocket to enter the bidding, and to stuff it back in again when you no longer wish to bid.) There is a danger, though, in excessive subtlety: Prearranged signals may backfire when one or the other party forgets the arrangement in the excitement of the auction. And a barely perceptible bidding style may cause the auctioneer or his spotters to miss your bid entirely or even to think you are bidding when you are not. The classic story is that of Norton Simon bidding for Rembrandt's *Titus* in 1965 at Christie's, London. The painting had been knocked down to another buyer when, according to the front-page account in the *New York Times* (March 20, 1965), Simon "rose ashen-faced to demand that the bidding be resumed because the auctioneer had missed a secret signal." Simon got his way and got the painting for $2.23 million. The signal, which was read aloud to the astonished auction-goers, was: "When Mr. Simon is sitting down, he is bidding. If he bids openly, he

Above: **Rembrandt van Rijn,**
Portrait of the Artist's Son, Titus
Right: **Paul Cézanne,**
Paysan en blouse bleu

is also bidding. When he stands up, he has stopped bidding. If he sits down again, he is not bidding unless he raises his finger. Having raised his finger, he is bidding until he stands up again."

Even the most simple (but subtle) bidding signals can cause trouble. At the 1980 Henry Ford II sale at Christie's, New York, dealer Heinz Berggruen of Paris strode from the auction room believing he had just been the successful bidder for Cézanne's *Paysan en Blouse Bleue,* at $3.9 million. As he left, while the sale was still in progress, he met his friend and colleague Eugene Thaw, the New York dealer, who said that *he* had just been the successful bidder. The two rushed back to the auction room and discovered that auctioneer David Bathurst, Christie's president, had missed Berggruen's subtle signals completely and had knocked the painting down to Thaw, who was sitting behind Berggruen. On a less dramatic level, a dealer of American art who signaled his bids by a subtle wink was disconcerted to find that a spotter was still calling out bids for him after he had stopped winking. "He's bidding *for* me!" the dealer exclaimed to his associate in astonishment. Finally he made it plain to the spotter that he was not bidding and the painting was knocked down, at a price that was several bids too high, to another buyer (who, unknown to the winker, was a rival dealer).

To avoid any misunderstandings, it is best to signal unambiguously that you are dropping out of the bidding: firmly shake your head from side to side, as if to say, "No!" One misunderstanding that is *not* likely to occur (although it is feared by many new auction-goers) is the auctioneer's entering you into the bidding because you have scratched your head, craned your neck or waved to a friend. If you are convinced that the auctioneer *has* made such a mistake, and he seems to be looking at you for another bid, shake your head negatively. If something is mistakenly knocked down to you, immediately tell the auctioneer or his staff that you were not bidding; the lot will almost certainly be reoffered.

It is also possible, as previously mentioned, to bid without either you or your representative appearing in the auction room. Many auction firms allow potential buyers to leave bids with the house, to be executed in competition with other bids. Such "order bids," as they are called, may be placed in writing (often on a special form provided in the catalogue) or, in some cases, by phone (to be followed by written confirmation). Depending on the policy of the individual auction house, a bank reference, a deposit, or both may be required of order bidders (particularly those not already known to the house). "Bids of varying complexity may be submitted to the Bids Department representatives," according to SPB's January–February 1980 newsletter. "Sometimes a client will submit an alternative bid (either lot X *or* lot Y). A client may request that if he is not successful on a particular lot, then an increased dollar amount may be applied to another lot. Finally, a client may select several lots and request that a maximum *total* amount be spent. Representatives of the Bids Department are pleased to accommodate any such special requests, within reason." The auction firms all say that they buy works for order bidders at the lowest possible price, subject to other bids and to the consignor's reserve; in many cases, order bidders have purchased works for prices considerably below their top limits. The New York offices of the international auction houses, SPB, Christie's and Phillips, will arrange to place bids for Americans at any of their other auction locations around the world.

For absentee bidders who do not want to give the auction house advance notice of how much they may spend and who also do not want to have anyone else bid for them, there is another possibility—bidding by telephone. Occasionally (especially for highly important works, for which the bidding is expected greatly to exceed the published presale estimate), auction-house staff members will convey bids made by clients over telephones located in the auction room. Anne Horton, SPB's photography specialist, warned, though, that "telephone bids generate excitement in the room and the prices, as a result, are generally higher."

Those who regularly attend auctions may develop various bidding strategies to try to outwit the competition. None of these strategies will prove very effective against another determined bidder. But auctioneers say that some bidding tricks do work under certain circumstances, and knowledge of them may help you to obtain a lower price or, at least, make you aware that an auction rival may be trying to influence you by his own bidding techniques. David Nash said one trick that "has worked on occasion" is entering the fray after everyone else has finished bidding. "It is very discouraging for someone who has just won a bidding duel to see a bid come from a new place," Nash observed. One dealer in an old-masters sale in London, Nash recalled, ostensibly dropped out of the bidding when only one person remained against him. At that point, an auction-house clerk entered the bidding for an anonymous client, who happened to be the same dealer who had just appeared to drop out. "He wanted to give the impression that he was out of it and someone new was bidding," Nash said. "Whether he got the painting any cheaper because of this, I don't know." Also potentially discouraging to other bidders, Nash said, is calling out a bid that represents a large jump over previous bids. He recalled that a collector who wanted to buy a Pissarro that was estimated to fetch $150,000 to $200,000 "intimidated everyone" by bidding $200,000 after someone else's bid of only $50,000. The obvious danger of jump bidding, as Christopher Burge observed, is that the purchase may be made at a higher level than would have been reached in the ordinary course of bidding. Burge listed the following additional strategies that he has seen bidders use: varying the pace of the bidding; bidding boldly, which may rattle another person who is squeezing out his bids; bidding just on the hammer, which can discourage the person who thought he was just about to buy the piece.

There are times when a bidder's strategy is not to achieve the lowest price for himself, but to push up the price that somebody else will pay. Dealers, in particular, like to see high auction prices for works comparable to those they have in stock; auction prices that seem to indicate a jump in the market may help dealers to justify increases in their own prices. Sometimes a dealer may be bidding on behalf of a client who wants to buy a work; other times he may be bidding because he thinks a work will make a good addition to his gallery's stock. But occasionally, he may be bidding to try to create a new, higher level of prices in his field, or to try to prevent prices from dropping too low. In such a case, his goal will not be to buy the work (although he must be prepared to do so if no other bids are forthcoming) and he will probably drop out of the bidding when he feels an appropriate price level has been reached. (You will, of course, have no way of knowing a dealer's motives for bidding on a particular work. You will have to be guided by your own sense of appropriate market values.)

In his Nov. 9, 1975, letter to the *New York Times,* contemporary-art dealer Leo Castelli gave some insight into how dealers use auctions to promote their interests and those of their artists: "I myself have from time to time bid at auction on the works of artists whom I represent, have bid to prices which I thought those works were worth, and have paid the prices which I have bid as the best evidence of my conviction that the prices were justified." He further described his attitude towards auctions in an interview with *Times* reporter Grace Glueck published on Jan. 20, 1976. "Most dealers hate the auction houses—I don't. In my case, auctions have established prices for me over a long period of time. How could I ask the prices I do for, say, Johns, if the work hadn't gone over $100,000, then over $200,000, at auction? . . . I've boosted prices for my artists at auction in extremes—when I see that a really good painting is going too low, for example. Generally, the reserve you put on a painting takes care of that situation, but I don't want to see a work go for an indecent price." When asked about some dealers' practice of bidding up price levels artificially, Castelli said, "To rig auction prices you'd have to come up with a fantastic amount of money. You can't maintain such prices unless there's a real market." At the aforementioned 1980 dealer-sponsored seminar on collecting photographs, Jim Hughes, editor of *Camera Arts,* said, "I have gone to auctions where one dealer and his associates will bid each other up and set a market price for their photographs. This is a common practice and happens at least a few times at almost every auction."

The fact that you may be bidding against someone who is trying to raise the level of the market, rather than someone who genuinely wants to buy a work, is one reason why you cannot assume that auction prices always truly represent fair market value. Another reason is that, even if there are no other bidders interested in your potential purchase, you may possibly be bidding against the owner's reserve; the reserve may reflect a realistic market level or it may merely represent the owner's (or auction house's) wishful thinking. In his memoir *The Glorious Obsession,* Paris auctioneer Maurice Rheims recounted his sale of a Benin (southern Nigerian) bronze for what was then the unprecedented price of 300,000 francs. The owner, a colonel, had set his reserve at that amount based on the percentage increase of colonels' salaries over the years since he bought the bronze for 3,000 francs in 1931; he refused to listen to Rheims' pleas to lower the reserve. Protecting the reserve against a lone bidder, Rheims managed to push the price up to 300,000 francs, setting a world record. But after the sale, the colonel informed Rheims that he had made a mistake in his arithmetic; he really should have set his reserve at only 175,250 francs. The unsuspecting buyer turned out to be a doctor who was not a collector and had never been to an auction; he had, by chance, seen a photograph of the bronze in a periodical and decided he liked it enough to buy it.

If you are the only bidder for a work and your bid is beneath the level of the reserve, the auctioneer himself will protect the consignor's interests by putting in a bid on the consignor's behalf. If you do not choose to rebid and no one else enters the bidding, the work will be bought in for the consignor at that price. Once the bidding has gotten under way, auctioneers at SPB and Christie's do not put in several consecutive bids for the consignor after all other bidding has stopped, according to Nash and Burge. Burge noted, though, that "when the bidding starts on an item, usually no one enters the bidding right away, so the auctioneer will probably enter two or three bids himself." Trying to guess whether the auctioneer is recognizing a real bid or merely protecting the owner's reserve is a skill that no auction-goer has completely mastered. You can try to follow the auctioneer's gaze to the place where the bid is supposedly coming from, but the bidder's signal may be too subtle for you to detect, or the auctioneer may be implementing a genuine order bid that he has on his books. You may also suspect that an item is about to be bought in if the bidding stops at a level considerably below the presale estimate; such an item may be sold, however, if it has a very low reserve or none at all.

Reserves are, understandably, a subject of great controversy in the art world. Some bidders resent the charade by which auctioneers pretend to recognize real bids when they are, in fact, merely protecting a consignor's reserve. "The preliminary bidding before the reserve is reached is meaningless," asserted Gilbert Edelson, secretary and treasurer of the Art Dealers Association of America, at the 1979 seminar on art law sponsored by the Practising Law Institute. "It's a game for people to put their hands up and feel good." In 1974, ADAA took a leading role in a move to get the New York City Department of Consumer Affairs to require auction-house disclosure of the amount of the reserve price for each lot. (After reviewing the arguments on both sides, the department decided not to impose this requirement.) The dealers argued that auction houses should start the bidding at the reserve price, in order to eliminate "useless and misleading bids below that price." SPB argued that the reserve, once disclosed, "is bound to be viewed as a price beyond which the buyer should not and will not go, even though, in fact, it may be nothing more than a minimum protective figure placed well below the appraised value." At a Practising Law Institute art-law seminar held in 1978, C. Hugh Hildesley of SPB said that disclosing the amount of the reserve "would remove the speculative excitement of competitive bidding. . . . It would tilt the whole process to the buyer's advantage."

There are other reasons (aside from the possibility of excessive reserves or price-puffing by self-interested dealers) why you cannot have complete confidence that auction prices represent appropriate market levels: You may be bidding against someone who has no more knowledge of market values than you do, or the bidding may have been inflated by "auction fever." Under the competitive pressure of auction, many bidders are loath to stop at their own previously established limits; just one more bid, they reason, may bring success. One unplanned bid leads to another, and soon the hapless collector finds himself not only over his limit but over his head. For some, the compulsion to bid is an expression of love of art; for others, it is a display of nerve and financial clout. Prices fetched under such irrational circumstances are considerably above normal market levels and they are often (but not always) only partly related to the aesthetic merit of the sought-after object—a Dürer watercolor landscape that was undeniably rare (the last in private hands of thirty-two such works), but not generally considered to be of the highest aesthetic importance, set a record for any watercolor ever auctioned when it sold for $1.18 million to a consortium of German museums intent on recapturing their nation's cultural patrimony. On a less dramatic scale, an alabaster head of John Barrymore by American sculptor Paul Manship fetched $25,000 from a Barrymore fan who was willing to pay more than ten times what the auctioneers had estimated it would bring.

As the above examples illustrate, auction fever is most likely to strike at the heavily promoted, single-owner "blockbuster" sales that attract strong interest from around the country or around the world. The Dürer price was one manifestation of "Hirschteria"—the wild bidding that greeted the collection of the late Robert von Hirsch (a Frankfurt-born industrialist who fled Nazi Germany in 1933) at the legendary 1978 sale at Sotheby's, London. The Barrymore head was one of the offerings at the much-touted 1979 sale of the collection of the late Benjamin Sonnenberg, the New York City public relations man, at SPB, New York. "It would be hard to exaggerate the power of a name—the pedigree which gives extra character to objects by personalizing them—so that by printing the owner's name on the catalogue one is offering not only each lot in itself but a portion of his sensibility," wrote auctioneer Rheims in his memoirs. The power of a name, he added, is particularly strong when its owner is deceased.

> Where lots at auction are concerned, death is the equivalent of an official decoration. It is reassuring. A living man who suddenly parts with his collection is inevitably under suspicion: are the things fakes? Or is he perhaps just speculating? With a dead man's goods, no such question arises; they *smell* right. They are the portion of the quarry which is thrown to the hounds at the end of the hunt. . . . If the deceased happens to have been well known, prices often move well beyond the fringe of rationality. In 1950 Mme. Emile Gaboriaud, widow of the journalist, gave me the task of dispersing the collection of old pictures created by her husband. The press caught fire. At the time, Gaboriaud's name symbolised a combination of power and taste, so much so that a portrait of the Flemish school which he had acquired fifteen years earlier for 135,000 francs and which was now valued at 500,000 francs made 1,600,000 francs.

Auction fever tends to rise to its greatest heights with objects that are rare, have interesting histories or have been hidden away for many years. "The mystique of buying something that has not been seen in recent years is very strong for private collectors and museums," observed John Walsh, Jr., of the Boston Museum of Fine Arts. This mystique was particularly compelling in the sale of Frederic Edwin Church's *The Icebergs,* which set an auction record for any work by an American artist when it sold for $2.5 million on Oct. 25, 1979, at SPB, New York. In its presale publicity, the auction firm emphasized that the huge (64 by 112 inches) painting had been "lost for more than 100 years," until it was discovered at a home for delinquent boys near Manchester, England, which had decided to sell it (without having any idea of its value) to raise needed cash. Many observers (including some at SPB) thought, however, that the bidding enthusiasm for the painting was wildly out of proportion to its aesthetic merit, whatever its history. *Time* magazine's art critic, Robert Hughes, referred to the painting (in a Dec. 31, 1979, article on the art market) as "a lummocking spread of icebergs by Frederic Church, a salon machine whose pedestrian invocations of the sublime are not worth one square foot of a good Turner." David Nash of SPB said several months after the sale that he "frankly thought *Icebergs* was worth about $100,000. It's not a very good painting. It's not up there with Cézanne, Monet and Turner." When asked at a press preview of the Garbisch sale whether the high prices expected

Frederic Edwin Church, *The Icebergs*

for the top lots reflected the auction house's opinion that these were works of the highest quality, Nash obliquely replied that prices at auction are "a question of supply and demand. The demand may not necessarily be informed demand."

The possible aberrations of auction prices should not deter you from buying at auction. But they should serve as a warning against the common misconception that you cannot seriously overpay at auction because someone else is willing to pay almost as much. Despite the occasional anomalies, auction prices—publicly arrived at and readily available for study and analysis—often are reliable indicators of the true level of the market. They are, in fact, the main gauge used by officials of the Internal Revenue Service in determining art's fair market value for tax purposes. (More on this in Chapter 9.)

After the Auction

Once you have bid successfully for an object, you may be asked to sign a bid confirmation form, particularly if you were not required to register with the house before the auction and you are not already well known there. Under many circumstances, you will have to pay considerably more than the amount you actually bid; you must always take this into account in deciding upon your top bidding limit. As previously mentioned, many auction houses now charge a buyer's premium—usually 10 percent of the hammer price—which is used by the auction house to help defray its expenses and to boost its profits. On top of the hammer price plus buyer's premium, the successful bidder may have to pay state and local sales taxes, depending on whether he lives in a state where the auction house has offices. Those who live in states where the auction house does have offices must pay sales taxes according to the rate of their home state (not the rate in the locality where the auction took place). Those who live in states where the auction house does not have offices may (if the home state has an agreement with the state in which the auction took place) have to pay a "compensating use tax" equal to the tax of the home state. Auction houses usually require payment within several days to a week after the sale, and goods not paid for and removed within the specified time are stored at the buyer's risk and expense. Depending on the policy of the particular auction house, consignors are usually paid within a week to thirty-five days of the sale.

A work that fails to sell at auction does not necessarily go straight back to the consignor. Depending on the owner's wishes, the auction house may try to negotiate a sale privately after the auction. The highest bidder is sometimes contacted, and other offers are also entertained. If you are interested in buying a work that you think may not have sold, it sometimes pays to check with the auction-house specialist after the sale. You may occasionally manage to pick up a bargain, since the seller may have decided that his expectations were unrealistic and he may also be worried by the prospect of trying to sell privately a work that has already been publicly "burned" (tainted by the stigma of being unsold). According to Nash, after-auction prices at SPB are usually below the level of the last public bid. (The last public bid is one bid below the price at which the work is bought in by the auctioneer for the consignor.) Burge said that at Christie's, after-auction prices usually equal the last public bid. Sometimes, though, an auction house can succeed in negotiating a higher price than was achieved during the sale. The aforementioned painting consigned by the Fine Arts Museums of San Francisco to a 1980 old-masters sale at SPB—Berckheyde's *The Singel, Amsterdam*—was bought in at $47,500 and sold later for its undisclosed reserve price (which was still, however, considerably below its presale estimate of $80,000 to $100,000).

Occasionally the person who is "burned" at auction is not the consignor but the successful bidder. Some auction houses, like William Doyle Galleries, flatly refuse to guarantee the authenticity of anything they sell. "Every lot is sold 'as is' and without recourse," according to the conditions of sale in Doyle's catalogue. "I have an old-fashioned philosophy: Buyer beware," Doyle said at the 1980 *ARTnews* art-market conference. "If you don't know what you're buying, you shouldn't be buying it here," he asserted. Other firms do offer some protection, but their guarantees are strictly limited in terms of what they cover and the length of time that they are in effect. Auction houses generally stand behind their merchandise to a smaller extent than top-flight dealers, who take a greater personal interest in their clients and screen their offerings more carefully than is possible in the high-volume auction business. The risks of buying at auction are compounded by the fact that some sellers try to unload their fakes or damaged works at auction, hoping that the defects will not be noticed by auction-house specialists or bidders.

Among the most generous (though by no means far-reaching) auction-house guarantees are those offered by Christie's in New York. In its catalogues, Christie's "warrants for a period of six years from the date of sale that any article in this catalogue unqualifiedly stated to be the work of a named author or authorship is authentic and not counterfeit. The term 'author' or 'authorship' refers to the creator of the articles or to the period, culture, source or origin, as the case may be, with which the creation of such article is identified in the description of the article in this catalogue." The warranty applies only to the accuracy of the heading, in bold type, at the beginning of the catalogue entry for each lot (i.e., the name of the artist or other identification of the object, such as "EGYPTIAN LIMESTONE RELIEF FRAGMENT, 19th Dynasty." The warranty does not apply to any heading defined in the catalogue's glossary as a "qualified statement as to authorship" (such as "Attributed to JEAN BAPTISTE CAMILLE COROT") nor does it apply to any of the descriptive material beneath the heading (such as dimensions, medium, date of execution, provenance, exhibition history, etc.).

The policy at SPB, New York, is similar to that at Christie's, except that SPB's guarantee is effective for five, rather than six, years and does not cover a large number of works that would be covered under the terms of Christie's warranty. Unlike Christie's, SPB does not guarantee "the identity of the creator of paintings, drawings and sculpture executed before 1870 unless these works are determined to be counterfeits [i.e., deliberate forgeries rather than misattributed works], as this is a matter of current scholarly opinion which can change." Also not covered at SPB is "the identification of the periods or dates of execution of property which may be proven inaccurate by means of scientific processes not generally accepted for use until after publication of the catalogue." At both houses, buyers of inauthentic works that fall under the terms of the guarantee can receive complete refunds. Interestingly, the refund policy at the London branch of Christie's is much less far-reaching than it is in New York. In London, buyers at Christie's are eligible for refunds only if they notify the auction house within twenty-one days of the sale that they can prove an object to be a deliberate forgery (not merely a misattributed work). At Sotheby's, London, buyers have five years to return deliberate forgeries. The smaller auction houses in the United States either have a no-refund policy (e.g., Samuel T. Freeman & Co., Philadelphia; Robert W. Skinner, Bolton and Boston, Mass.) or a policy that is measured in days rather than years (i.e., Phillips, New York, ten days; Adam A. Weschler & Son, Washington, D.C., fourteen days; Butterfield & Butterfield, San Francisco, twenty-one days; Du Mouchelle Art Galleries, Detroit, twenty-one days).

Despite their efforts to limit their liability, many auction houses do go to much greater lengths than are legally necessary to protect their customers from misrepresentation and fraud. Nash said that if a controversy arises before a sale at SPB about the authenticity of a particular object, "we will not sell it unless the seller allows us to disclose the difference of opinion. If there is a disagreement after the sale, we generally submit it to a third party and abide by that decision." He added that if a specialist was found to have given incorrect advice to a buyer, "we'd cancel the sale. . . . If the buyer finds that a painting was relined and repainted and the specialist said it was not, the buyer would have a legitimate complaint." Although representations by specialists and descriptions in auction catalogues are not covered by the terms of auction-house guarantees, you should promptly notify the house of any discrepancies that significantly affect the value of your purchase. At the very least, this will put the firm on notice that it will have to exercise more care in the future if it is to deserve public confidence. At best, you may win yourself a refund.

Dealers vs. Auctions: The Pros and Cons

When asked whether they prefer to buy or sell at galleries or auction houses, many collectors will answer, "It all depends." Each system has its own advantages and shortcomings in terms of types of service and quality of goods, and each has its own pricing peculiarities which may, under different circumstances, favor the buyer or the seller. In general, dealers offer the more personal and confidential service, but relations with dealers depend more upon trust and good faith than transactions at auction, where business is conducted openly and prices are publicly arrived at. Sellers who have no idea what their possessions are worth often prefer to sell at auction, for good reason: objects offered to a wide public in open competition will usually find a proper (although not necessarily the highest) market level. Selling an object to or through a dealer means setting a price in advance—a daunting prospect to someone who has no idea of what price he should set. Dealer-collector Ben Heller noted that auctions are attractive to sellers (such as administrators of estates) who "don't want the responsibility" for deciding what objects are worth, and to those "who want to move a mass of merchandise quickly" (such as collectors who want to dispose of a large part of their holdings). Similarly, Gilbert Edelson of the Art Dealers Association observed that a public sale offers "unquestioned safety" for a fiduciary (i.e., someone entrusted with disposing of an estate). It is especially useful, he said, when there is a large estate with small items to be cleared out quickly.

Sellers may also choose disposal at auction when the market in a particular field is so volatile or so untested that no one, not even an expert, really knows what the right price would be. "When something is running hot," said Heller, "the dealers are embarrassed to ask their clients to pay the prices that the dealers can get by selling the items at auction"; in such fields, many high-quality works are sent to auction by dealers and collectors. Collector Paul Singer observed that the tendency to sell Chinese art at auction has increased enormously, because such art has risen sharply in value. "Neither the collector nor the dealer today knows the value of anything," Singer said. "Today's auctions are full of top material from collectors and dealers. Dealers have bought objects at auction, put them back up for sale six months later and gotten three or four times what they paid for them." If a work is extremely rare and nothing comparable has recently appeared on the market, an auction sale may be the only way to determine its value. The $6.4-million Turner, *Juliet and Her Nurse,* "would not have sold for that price at a dealer's," according to collector Norton Simon. "There hasn't been a Turner sold for a long time, and a dealer wouldn't know that someone would pay that much."

In addition to helping problematical objects find their own level, auctions give a seller the assurance that a work will be sold on a particular day (unless it is bought in for failure to meet its reserve) and that he will "know exactly what price it has been sold for," according to Nash of SPB. "There is no room for hanky-panky. A dealer may tell you he sold your painting for $100,000, when he in fact got $125,000. And when you consign something to a dealer, you never know when it is going to be sold." In addition, Nash noted that "a dealer has only a limited number of prospects for a picture. It is unlikely that someone from South America is going to walk in and say he wants that picture. An auction catalogue gets circulated widely." Selling directly to a dealer, rather than selling through him by consignment, eliminates the uncertainties about the time and amount of payment, but it does, as noted, mean you may get much less than full market value for your property. When the need for cash is urgent, a sale to a dealer is often faster than an auction sale (although many auction houses are also willing to buy works or to give owners an advance on potential sales).

Dealers generally show greater personal concern for their clients than is possible in the fast-moving, high-volume auction business and, as previously discussed, dealers offer many services that auction houses provide only to a much smaller degree, if at all (such as opportunities to take a work home on approval, pay for it over a period of time, and receive the benefits of a dealer's many years of scholarship and connoisseurship). In general, the level of specialized expertise at top-flight galleries is higher than that at auction houses; auction specialists are often relatively young and inexperienced, and they must deal quickly with a large volume of extremely varied goods. Dealers have the freedom to be choosy about the type and quality of merchandise they handle. They *must* be choosy if they are to develop reputations as important, high-quality sources for particular types of art. When asked what criteria are applied to the selection of works for auction, Nash candidly replied, "Not many. . . . At the top end, we have equal quality with dealers, if not better. At the bottom end, you would have to go to York Avenue to see some of the junk we sell." (Nash was referring to certain "schlock" galleries on York Avenue, not, obviously, to SPB's own facilities there.) Heller observed that "auctions often get the leftovers that couldn't be disposed of any other way," and other dealers, like Lawrence Fleischman, said that they unload their "deadest merchandise" at auction. In certain fields, like classical antiquities and contemporary art, dealers are generally felt to dominate the quality end of the market. In almost all fields, the inventory of dealers is more consistently of high quality than that of auction houses, since dealers can be more selective in deciding what to sell. Along with the dross, though, auction houses do obtain many top-quality consignments, thanks to their low seller's commissions and their attractiveness to estate administrators and other sellers of large collections.

In addition to offering more personal services and more consistent quality, dealers offer buyers and sellers greater assurance of confidentiality in art-related transactions. Auction houses do allow clients to buy and sell anonymously, but the art world is a small and gossipy place, which almost guarantees that the names of "anonymous" buyers and sellers of important objects at public sales will eventually become known and, in some instances, even be published in the newspapers.

The day after Turner's *Juliet and Her Nurse* was bought at SPB by an "anonymous" collector, the *New York Times* reported that the mysterious multimillionaire had been identified by someone who had attended the sale as Amalia Le Croze Fortabat, widow of Alfredo Fortabat, an Argentine cement producer. The *Times* article also named her as the "anonymous" purchaser of a $2.9-million Gauguin and a $1.9-million van Gogh at the Henry Ford II sale two weeks earlier at Christie's. When an "anonymous" European private collector consigned an important collection of Benin art to Sotheby's, London, in 1980, the name of Adolph Schwarz of Amsterdam was soon picked up by the press. Conducted quietly and without publicity, transactions at private galleries are far less likely to attract unwelcome notice. For this reason, collector Edward Carter said that when he wants to dispose of a work, he most frequently trades with a dealer for another painting. According to dealer Stephen Hahn, "many important collectors don't want people to know what they have bought and don't want to compete with someone else to buy things. For this, they are willing to pay a little more."

It is generally thought that purchases at galleries do cost more than purchases at auction houses. Conventional wisdom has it that auction prices fall somewhere between wholesale (what a dealer would pay for a work) and retail (what he would sell it for). But, as already suggested, there are many circumstances under which auction prices may greatly exceed what the same or comparable objects would fetch at a gallery. Observers say that in certain fields, such as modern masters and American paintings, auction levels often exceed dealers' prices. In other fields, such as old masters and prints, auctions are still a basic source of supply for many dealers; the auction prices in those fields are, in general, lower than what the dealers feel they can charge. With a growing number of private collectors competing against dealers for auction-house offerings, the opportunities for picking up "bargains" are rapidly diminishing; dealers are finding that objects which they might have bought for their inventories often get bid up to levels beyond what they feel they can pay (in light of their need to resell the objects at still higher prices).

For sellers, the question of whether a particular item will fetch a higher price at a gallery or at auction is particularly important. Unfortunately, the question has no easy answers. Dealer Klaus Perls (who would, of course, prefer that everyone sell through dealers) says flatly that auctions are the best method for getting the highest price. Auctions, he observed, start at a low price and work their way up, with no limit on how high the bidding can go; at private galleries, any adjustment from the initial asking price is downward. No dealer, he said, "would dare charge the prices" fetched by many works at auction. "If you see objects at auction which realized prices in excess of their top presale estimates, you know that they sold for more than a private gallery would ask," he said. "The top estimate usually equals the top retail price." While not ready to concede the entire field to the auction houses, Gilbert Edelson of the Art Dealers Association noted that certain objects probably do sell better at auction than with dealers—old masters that cannot be securely attributed, and works in large, important collections. "I'm not sure that dealers could have gotten the prices that Sotheby's got in the Von Hirsch sale," he observed at the 1979 art-law conference sponsored by the Practising Law Institute. Edelson noted, though, that dealers' close contacts with museums and important collectors, "some of whom do not buy publicly," may enable them to negotiate a better price by placing a work privately. Museums often find it difficult to buy at auction, because their staffs and trustees need a long time to consider potential purchases and raise the required funds. "In the last month," said Edelson, "a very important work was sold by a dealer to an institution only after three or four months of patient negotiation and agreement on terms of payment." He observed that dealers' patience and willingness to allow payment over a period of time may ultimately result in "a more favorable price" to the seller than could be obtained at auction.

Similarly, dealer Richard Feigen observed that "some collectors don't like to operate in public or by a time schedule." Dealers, he said, are best suited to place works with such buyers. "Paul Mellon," according to Feigen, "doesn't buy at auction." When asked about this, Mellon chuckled and said he was glad that some people had that impression: He tries to buy at auction anonymously. He revealed, though, that probably about half of his paintings collection came from public sales. Even the most privacy-conscious collectors are not likely to pass up important buying opportunities at auction.

Like Edelson, Feigen conceded that certain types of works may sell better at auction than privately. Good candidates for auction, he said, are offbeat works for which it is difficult to find potential buyers. The wide dissemination of auction catalogues and presale publicity, according to Feigen, increases the likelihood that some interested collectors can be found. When a client of Feigen's wanted to sell a Monet that was so large (almost 80 inches high) as to discourage most buyers, Feigen had it consigned to the spring 1980 Impressionist-modern sale at Christie's, New York, where it was estimated to bring $550,000 to

$650,000; it sold for $650,000. Feigen observed that one danger of consigning to auction is that some works fail to sell (because bidding does not reach the level of the reserve) and get burned—a danger that is particularly great for works (like the Monet) that are easily remembered because of their size or some other unusual characteristic. Burned art works are often difficult to sell, either publicly or privately, for a period of two years or more. But auction-house officials maintain that if consignors follow their advice in setting reasonable reserves, the danger of burning is slight. Sellers who fear that bad weather or some unforeseen calamity may keep important bidders away can rest assured, according to Hildesley of SPB, that potential buyers will make a special effort to show up, in the hopes that the unusual circumstances may yield them some unusual opportunities. Speaking at the seminar sponsored by the New York Society of Security Analysts, he observed that "the bargain-hunting mentality offsets the problem of inclement weather very, very handily on every occasion."

Auction-house officials do concede, though, that certain works probably sell better at galleries than at their own firms. Nash said that prices for Impressionist paintings are generally 20 percent lower at auction than at galleries and he added that a "tough, difficult work," for which there is a limited audience, would probably get a better price at a gallery specializing in that type of work than at auction: "If you have a van Gogh, everyone knows what it is, and there are twenty-five people who can buy it. If you have a Klimt, maybe five people know what it is, and you might do better at a gallery." A work for which there is "one obvious candidate—a particular person who should buy it" should also probably be sold through a dealer, Nash said. Also best sold privately, he said, is a work that is "so rare that you could ask almost anything for it." The buyer of such a work at auction, Nash observed, would have to pay only slightly more than an underbidder was willing to pay, even if his own top limit was considerably higher. If a dealer had asked more money for the same work, the buyer might have been willing to pay it. (However, as previously noted in relation to Turner's *Juliet,* a dealer might not know how much he could ask for a rare work, particularly if there have been few or no recent comparable sales.) Similarly, Burge noted that "more $5-million pictures have been sold privately than at auction. . . . People who buy and sell at that level like to be secretive about what they are doing." Hildesley of SPB observed that an object might be better sold through a dealer if it is in a "very rarefied field and it needs a very specialized expertise to identify it. We have said to some clients, 'We believe this is so specialized that there may be only two potential buyers for it in the world.' " Such clients, he said, are steered toward appropriate dealers.

Even certain types of art that are not particularly unfamiliar do not, for some reason, seem to perform well at auction; the only way to get a feel for these trends is to analyze auction results and to consult with dealers, collectors and other experts. Feigen observed, for example, that "since 1969, Braque has been singularly unsuccessful at auction." One field that is generally considered to be weak at auction is contemporary art, except for works by the most established, popular masters. "Contemporary art is the most speculative end of the market," according to Hildesley. "An auction is not necessarily the best mode of approach for selling it." Similarly, Burge noted that for contemporary works by artists who are not of top reputation, auction houses get less than retail. Dealers offer important advantages to both buyers and sellers of contemporary art, because they give potential purchasers the time and attention needed to study works that may be unfamiliar and initially hard to grasp. The mass-merchandising approach and frenetic atmosphere of the auction house does not lend itself to the careful education and undistracted viewing that are often needed before one can "see" contemporary art. In addition, when a collector of contemporary art visits a dealer, he can usually choose from many works by an artist who interests him; at an auction house, there may be only one work by that artist, and it may or may not be a particularly good example. Snapping up the types of work that tend to be underpriced at auction can be a useful strategy for collectors who are long on connoisseurship but short on cash. If you are one of the vast majority of art lovers with limitless desires but limited resources, all the art-market publicity about record prices may discourage you from even trying to get closer to objects that you have admired from afar. But while the publicity always emphasizes high prices, the vast majority of art transactions—those that are too common to interest the media—occur at levels within most people's reach. The trick is to find the art at those levels that is interesting as well as affordable.

Chapter 4

NOT FOR
MILLIONAIRES ONLY

It is one of life's sad ironies that many people who have developed highly refined tastes have not developed their bank accounts to the same degree. Some become museum curators or advisors to more financially fortunate collectors, satisfying their acquisitive urges by spending other people's money. Others become scholars and critics, determined to possess art mentally, if not physically. Some give up without a fight and make the dishonorable retreat into the world of reproductions, settling for imitation art when the same outlay could have bought modestly priced originals. Committed and persevering art lovers manage to find affordable originals by choosing appropriate fields and then making their purchases at the right place and the right time. If you covet only the top works by the most fashionable artists shown at the fanciest galleries, you are doomed to a life of frustration, unless you are very rich. But if you are flexible, persistent, knowledgeable and occasionally lucky, you can build a fine collection on a modest budget.

The Right Place at the Right Time

While impecunious collectors can sometimes enlist the sympathy and help of the most prestigious dealers, it is obvious that elegant establishments, with their high overhead, big-name artists and monied clientele, are not the most promising sources for low-cost art. New dealers, by contrast, are almost always receptive to new collectors who may grow along with them, and such dealers also may price their works more moderately to attract new clients. There is always the risk, however, that a gallery with no track record may be undistinguished or even disreputable. As always, you must be a judge of both art and character. Between the two extremes of venerable institution and fledgling venture are the vast majority of galleries—those that are well established but still down-to-earth enough to offer many works at attractive prices. Once again, your art-world contacts and readings in art-related periodicals should give you important leads.

In the auction world, it is easy to find out where the low-priced goods are, simply by consulting the presale estimates in the catalogues. In general (as previously mentioned), the smaller auction houses consistently offer low-priced goods. Both Christie's and SPB also compete for that end of the market—at Christie's East, SPB's "Arcade Auctions" and at other sales throughout the year that are not labeled "important" or "fine" on the catalogue cover.

Collectors seeking low-priced art sometimes circumvent the established system, buying directly from other collectors or (in the case of contemporary art) from alternative spaces, co-op galleries or individual artists (more on the options available to contemporary collectors in Chapter 5). But if you do this, you are completely on your own in judging quality, condition and authenticity. Before going this route, you should be confident of your ability to recognize when a "bargain" is really a swindle.

In art as in other markets, being a smart shopper means knowing not only where to buy but also when to buy. When a particular field is in vogue, prices may be unduly inflated. When the market for a particular type of art declines owing to a change in fashion or a general economic slump, good buys often turn up. Analyzing the ups and downs of the auction market, or subscribing to the art-market periodicals that provide such analysis (see Bibliography) can help you develop a sense of timing. There is, however, an important drawback to buying in a down market: owners of top-quality works are not eager to sell when prices are deflated. A booming market tends to bring out more desirable offerings.

Finding Affordable Fields

The first step in finding a field in which you can realistically hope to collect is to lower your sights. Almost everyone would prefer to collect major masterpieces by big-name artists, but that hope is no more easily realized than the wish to become an instant millionaire. There are several ways of working your way down to the level that you can afford: by *medium,* by *artist* or by *field.* If works in a relatively expensive medium—oil on canvas, for example—are beyond your reach, you might look into the market for works on paper, which are usually priced much more modestly. There is a hierarchy of price among different types of works on paper, as well. Multiples (such as lithographs or etchings) are almost always less expensive than one-of-a-kind works (such as drawings or watercolors) by the same artist. An admirer of Daumier, unable to afford a first-rate painting at $500,000, might easily purchase a print clipped from *Le Charivari* (a French periodical for which Daumier worked) for under $100. Charles Moffett, European paintings curator at the Metropolitan Museum of Art, collects French nineteenth-century drawings because "it is still possible to buy fine drawings by lesser-known masters for $750 to $4,000." All other things being equal, small works are usually less costly than large ones, and damaged works (even if beautifully restored) are less expensive than those in perfect condition. In the print market, an image that lacks a signature (when other examples of the same image are signed) or one that was printed without the artist's supervision, some time after the original edition was made, may cost only a fraction of the price of similar images without such deficiencies. "People are paying 100 percent more for the signature," said Nicholas Stogdon, print specialist at Christie's, after an unsigned Picasso print from the Vollard Suite, *Faune Devoilant une Femme,* sold at a 1979 auction for $5,000, considerably below its presale estimate of $7,000 to $10,000. The deficiencies that lower the prices of prints or damaged paintings may make those works poor choices for those who buy art as an investment or for purists who find such faults glaring, but for the less affluent and less picky collector, imperfections can bring important works within reach.

Those who are inflexible about medium, size or condition may be able to buy top examples of an artist's work if they are willing to be flexible about who the artist is. While the work of a famous master may be out of reach, works by his less well-known contemporaries, who perhaps worked in the same style as the master, can often be had for reasonable prices. In the old-master field, paintings attributed to the "school of" or "follower of" a great painter are often plentiful and inexpensive. Occasionally, they turn out to be better bargains than they originally seemed, if a scholar later firmly attributes the painting to a particular artist. An admirer of van Gogh might never obtain that artist's work, but might easily afford a painting by Adolphe Monticelli, the French colorist of whom van Gogh once wrote, "Altogether I am obliged to lay the colors on thick in Monticelli's way. Sometimes I think I really am a continuation of that man." A Toulouse-Lautrec enthusiast might find affordable alternatives among the works by the artist's friend, Charles Maurin, a printmaker who played an important role in reviving color etching in the 1890s and who was well admired by the important artists and dealers of his time. Every era had artists who were very popular (and expensive) in their own time but who, sometimes deservedly but sometimes not, later fell into obscurity. Careful research (and discussions with dealers, who are always looking for less-known artists to balance out their higher-priced inventories) will lead you to likely prospects. The contemporary field (as will be further discussed in the next chapter) offers perhaps the greatest selection of high-quality works by little-known artists who may become tomorrow's big names.

Another approach to the quest for affordable art is to look for alternative fields—whole areas of collecting that are inexpensive because they are relatively new or have been overlooked by most collectors. Art historian John Rewald, who advises some of the world's richest collectors in one of the most expensive fields (Impressionist and Post-Impressionist paintings), collects African art, a field in which "you can still get things for a few hundred dollars that are aesthetically satisfying." African art and the other moderately priced fields mentioned on pages 7–8 offer good opportunities for new collectors. But the criteria that distinguish high-quality works in those fields often differ markedly from the criteria applying to mainstream Western art. Before you can collect in such fields, you will need to open your mind and eyes to new ideas and perceptions. Admirers of American folk art, for example, must learn to put aside conventional expectations about perspective and proportion in order to appreciate the special vitality, boldness and charm of works that were created (in the words of Nancy Druckman, SPB's American folk art specialist) "for ordinary people by ordinary people." Even within an alternative field, there may be some subcategories that are less widely appreciated and less expensive than others. In the field of American Indian art, for example, contemporary Pueblo pottery is much less expensive than wood carvings produced in the late nineteenth and early twentieth century by the Northwest Coast tribes. In the field of primitive art, according to Douglas Newton, chairman of the primitive-art department of the Metropolitan Museum of Art, two of the most reasonably priced areas are Australian aboriginal art and South American Amazonian pottery. Unpopular fields are always sources of good buys for those collectors who manage to find charm in works that others regard as unappealing. The landscapes of American Barbizon and Tonalist painters (such as George Inness, Alexander Wyant and J. Francis Murphy) strike many as dark and dreary. Because of this, they are underpriced in relation to the more popular Hudson River and American Impressionist schools.

Another "alternative" field that attracts some collectors is reproductions—copies of high-priced art that, themselves, may cost several
hundred dollars or more. Popularized by, among others, the Metropolitan Museum of Art (which has reproduced hundreds of objects from
its collections and exhibitions) and the late Nelson Rockefeller (who,
shortly before his death, launched a reproduction venture that marketed high-priced copies of works from his own collection), the acquisition of meticulously crafted reproductions is seen by some as a way to
enjoy the finest in art for a fraction of what that art would cost if
original. But while it is a time-honored practice to buy posters and
other low-priced reproductions to serve as reminders of great works of
art, it seems senseless to spend hundreds of dollars for art substitutes.
As reporter Grace Glueck wrote in the *New York Times* (Jan. 11, 1979),
the amount of money charged for Rockefeller clones could buy "original objects by the same makers, or at least produced in the same
periods, as the reproductions struck off by Mr. Rockefeller." Among
the examples cited by Glueck: a $7,500 Rockefeller reproduction of
Rodin's *The Age of Bronze* vs. early casts of a seated woman and a
woman's head, both by Rodin, at $8,000 and less than $4,000, respectively; a Rockefeller copy of Picasso's *Girl with Mandolin* for $850 vs.
signed original Picasso prints from the 1960s and 1970s for $650 to
$1,500; a Rockefeller copy of an American running-horse weathervane
from the late nineteenth century for $975 vs. authentic nineteenth-
century American running-horse weathervanes for $500 to $800. Admittedly, the originals cited by Glueck were not as fine as Rockefeller's
originals, but they convey much more of the artists' essence than could
ever be conveyed by high-priced copies.

One of the drawbacks of reproductions as an alternative field is
shared by many other alternative fields: they are not necessarily good
investments. Reproductions often have little or no resale value. Prices
for works in new or less traditional fields of collecting are often unstable and are much more susceptible to the influences of fashion and
economic conditions than works in well-established fields (more on this
in Chapter 10). Collecting with limited funds is much harder work than
collecting where money is no object. It is far easier to find fine objects
in a high price range than a low one. The unmonied collector must
compensate for his lack of financial clout through extra research (to
learn which fields and artists are important but neglected), connoisseurship (to be able to distinguish fine objects from the vast array of
mediocre ones in the low price ranges) and, especially, patience (to be
able to wait until worthwhile but affordable objects come onto the
market).

Art-world contacts are, as always, important, but are less accessible to collectors who can interest dealers and other experts only through a knowledge of and devotion to art, rather than through a large supply of cash. At a 1981 seminar on art collecting sponsored by the Metropolitan Museum of Art, Chinese art dealer Robert Ellsworth reiterated that dealers are often sympathetic to collectors who are poor in funds but rich in sensitivity. "We love people who love objects," he said. "If they have the eye to see and enjoy, you help them. That's what any dealer should do for any young people." Dealers, who may themselves have started out with limited resources, are often the best sources of leads about collecting well on a tight budget. But to get their help, you have to interest them in your case. That takes knowledge, sincerity and, especially, a passion for fine things that others who are similarly afflicted find very hard to resist.

Chapter 5

FEED A HUNGRY
ARTIST TODAY

Contemporary art offers some of the best opportunities for collectors of limited means, but this field has its own peculiar ground rules and traditions because it involves one element that all other fields lack —a living artist, producing new work that may challenge your (and maybe even his own) preconceptions about what constitutes great art. Collecting contemporary art means becoming a part of the cultural colloquy of one's own time. No other field offers more opportunities for making brilliant discoveries and foolish blunders, and no field makes greater demands on a collector's time, imagination and sensitivity. "In the twentieth century," said dealer Sidney Janis, "the artistic concept has changed so radically from generation to generation that it is difficult for someone watching what has happened to keep abreast of it, and if he does keep abreast, to be able to distinguish the good from the indifferent. An experienced eye has the ability to come closer to having a significant reaction and to judging aesthetic value through that experience." Even among experienced observers, though, opinions on the latest artists, movements and styles are constantly debated and revised, and, because the final returns are not in yet, collectors of contemporary art must rely on their own vision and judgment to a much greater degree than collectors in safer, more thoroughly sifted fields. They must also work hard just to keep up with the latest developments in the fluid, far-flung contemporary art scene—visiting museums, galleries, artists' studios and "alternative spaces" (exhibition areas, often publicly funded, that frequently display new, unfamiliar art), talking to dealers, collectors and artists who are in contact with promising new talent, and reading the books, museum catalogues, art magazines and newspaper columns that try to put the latest developments in perspective.

The Peculiarities of
the Contemporary Art Market

For those who feel an affinity for today's art (and for some the response is immediate and intuitive), the advantages of choosing this field of collecting are unparalleled. In many other fields, where museums and collectors have long scoured the market, you will have to settle for the second-rate or pay top dollar for the few high-quality examples that occasionally come up for sale. The contemporary art market, by contrast, offers collectors an abundant supply, continually swelled by new work. If you are attracted to the work of a lesser-known artist, you will probably have no difficulty finding an available example of one of his best efforts. If you are attracted to one of the bigger names, you may sometimes find it difficult to acquire good examples of past work, but if you make an effort to be one of the first to see a gallery show of the artist's recent work (preferably at the show's installation or opening), you will probably be rewarded with a chance to buy. Admittedly, the works of a few "superstars" may be beyond the reach of new collectors. Dealer Leo Castelli said there are long waiting lists for new work by Jasper Johns and Frank Stella, and added that such works are sold only to his most favored clients. "They are not available to the general public, except by pure accident," he said. For the most part, though, the supply problems in contemporary art are those of overabundance rather than scarcity. The "art boom" in this country seems to have spawned more contemporary artists and galleries than anyone can keep track of, and all compete for the interest of adventurous collectors. "It is helpful to spend a great deal of time looking," says collector Richard Brown Baker. "In the 1950s, there were fewer contemporary art galleries, and they were more reachable. Now, there are so many that it is very difficult to cover the gallery scene thoroughly."

In addition to offering unusual supply advantages, collecting contemporary art also offers important price advantages to collectors with sharp eyes and strong legs. If you discover an important artist early enough, before his work is generally appreciated, you can usually pick up a fine example of his work for only a few hundred to a few thousand dollars. "I'm a miserly New Englander. I try to find inexpensive paintings," says the Rhode Island–born Baker, who bought works by such artists as Jackson Pollock, Hans Hofmann, Jean Dubuffet and Roy Lichtenstein long before their reputations blossomed. In his article in *Art International* on the formation of his collection, Baker said that he "decided to ignore the artists (for price reasons) whose reputations had been achieved in the prewar years. However much I might admire Braque, Picasso, Miró, Soutine, etc., I could not afford their work. I even eliminated the older generation of Americans from consideration: better to buy a major oil by Franz Kline, for instance, whose work was cheap because nobody then bought it, than a watercolour by the aged John Marin whose prices I thought beyond my reach." Similarly, collector Ralph Colin passed up works by Cézanne when he began collecting in the 1930s, because "they then sold for $20,000 to $25,000, and that was beyond our range." Instead, Colin and his wife bought a Soutine for $200 from a show at the Valentine Dudensing Gallery in New York. Soutine, whose work was not widely appreciated until after his death in 1943, "was considered wild and way-out" when the Colins made their first purchase, he recalled. "We were not interested in investment, and we didn't have the faintest idea that things would go up the way they did." When Colin bought Juan Gris' *Violon et Guitare* for $3,500 in the 1940s, "word went up and down Madison Avenue that Colin had gone crazy," he recounted. "None of Gris' works had sold for more than $2,000 at the time." Colin said he has since turned down an offer of $800,000 for his "overpriced" Gris.

What Baker and Colin accomplished—the discovery of great artists before their works achieved great prices—is the dream of almost every collector, whether his main motive is to make a good investment or simply to see his adventurous, offbeat choices confirmed at last. Colin insists that he and his wife "weren't as smart as we appeared to be. We weren't picking Picasso and Matisse in 1900. We were picking artists who were not known here but who we knew had some reputation in Europe for quality. They had thirty years of oeuvre behind them; you could see it in museums and books." Baker mostly credits his success to his own eyes, aided by the guidance of certain perceptive dealers. Two of today's top New York dealers, Castelli and Xavier Fourcade, say that collectors can get valuable leads about the possible stars of tomorrow if (in Fourcade's words) they "listen to what informed people, such as artists and some museum people, say. There is a certain milieu and things get known." Castelli observed that collectors must "become part of the environment" of the contemporary art scene if they want to be among the first to recognize important new artists. "I tell collectors that a certain consensus develops about artists, and they should become part of the group of people who are aware of that consensus." Castelli added that he himself is happy to give collectors the names of lesser-known artists whom he believes have promising futures (including artists not represented by his gallery), and he advises collectors on what they should buy, "if they have the same feeling." Part of becoming

Juan Gris, *Violon et guitare*

aware of the developing consensus is, of course, reading the reviews of recent exhibitions in newspapers and art magazines. The influence of critics on art and the art market, however, is much weaker today than it was in the 1960s when "dealers, curators and collectors were guided by the ratings doled out so carefully by leading critics," according to the article by poet and art critic Carter Ratcliff in the Nov. 27, 1978, issue of *New York* magazine. "A few of these writers came to be seen, with only slight exaggeration, as starmakers. For the investor, they were the art-world equivalents of Moody's or Standard & Poor's. The nod from Clement Greenberg could provide a young color-field painter with a blue-chip rating. . . . So the early seventies were crawling with young art writers announcing their ambition to be the Clement

Greenberg of the new decade. But no latter-day Greenbergs or [Lawrence] Alloways have appeared. One reason is that the three-way situation of the sixties (pop, Minimal, and color-field) has developed into a pattern of sub- and sub-sub-styles so complex no critic can follow more than a fraction of it. Earthworks, conceptual art, performance, video, realist revivals, pattern painting, narrative literary-visual hybrids —all this and more makes for a contemporary art world more like a labyrinth than a neat set of launching pads for stars. . . . Exhibits are reviewed in the art magazines, if and when they happen, but no single critic has decisively affected a career begun in this decade."

Better than relying heavily on the advice of critics, dealers and collectors is developing a mind of your own, since there is no other field where "expert" opinion diverges so much or shifts so dramatically. Matisse's colorful paper cut-outs, which are now widely admired and exhibited, were generally regarded as "the playthings of a senile old man" when he produced them in the 1940s and early 1950s, recalled Paris dealer Heinz Berggruen in an interview with the New York–based newspaper *Art/World* (November/December 1978). Matisse consigned the cut-outs to Berggruen, who showed them in 1953, "because I believed in them. . . . They were priced at $300 to $500 and we sold them all." Baker observed that because there is always a "legitimate difference of opinion as to which work by an artist is the better work," dealers generally price works by living artists according to size rather than quality. A sharp-eyed collector may be able to buy a superior work for the same or even less money than he would spend for a lesser work.

The merits of even the most established of today's superstars are still hotly debated: Jasper Johns is "certified as a genius at the highest art-world levels," observed Carter Ratcliff, yet Hilton Kramer (then the senior art critic of the *New York Times*) described the 1977 Johns retrospective at the Whitney Museum in New York as "something of a bore. . . . Johns has never mastered the big picture, and it is the big picture that he has attempted again and again and again since the 60's when he was not occupied with his endless production of variations on the same old prints. . . . One's final impression is of an artist victimized by his own success. An artist of smaller reputation might have been content to work on a scale appropriate to his talents."

Another drawback to relying too heavily on the advice of experts in the fast-changing contemporary field is that an expert who is marvelously attuned to the merits of the art of a particular style or time may be completely insensitive to the methods or objectives of a new, different group of artists. An old-time collector or dealer who quickly caught on to what the Cubists and Fauves were doing early in this century may be totally nonplussed by later movements like Abstract Expressionism, Pop and Minimalism. Ralph Colin says that he does not collect today's art because "I cannot tell the difference in quality between one work in a show and the other nine. I am used to being able to say, 'I like this better than the others,' and I can't say that with the contemporary things. People say to me that it's a different generation, that I'm an old fogey." Similarly, dealers who have made big reputations by picking the stars of one generation are often the wrong people to consult for auguries about new artists. In his *Art/World* interview, Berggruen observed that "one has only to look at [Daniel-Henry] Kahnweiler to see how a great dealer can make a mistake. He began with Braque and Picasso but disastrously decided to take on younger artists like Lascaux and Roux, who are decidedly second-rate. His eye was not attuned to the art of the next generation." New York dealers who helped make the big reputations of the 1960s frequently lament the absence of up-and-coming artists of comparable stature; meanwhile, new young dealers have no trouble discovering exciting new talent, and they attract their own followings among adventurous new collectors. "The new sort of collector," according to writer Annette Kuhn, "tends to know what goes on in tucked-away alternative art spaces and in small art publications, and likes to keep up with the latest political and personal concerns among young artists." Writing in the September/October 1977 issue of *Art in America,* Kuhn observed that "many of these collectors find a certain pleasure in the reverse chic of going to the often grubby spaces where new art can be found. They take their collecting very seriously, persistently looking for interesting, lesser-known artists, often buying directly from artists they like. . . . Of course, collectors had better be eclectic these days, since so many art currents flow without creating a mighty mainstream. Current art-world diversity (or confusion, depending on how you view it) may actually encourage the purchase of new and difficult art, for in the absence of a stampede in one direction, collectors can feel comfortable buying in various unlabeled and undigested modes."

Some of these modes are not only unlabeled and undigested but also almost uncollectable. Trying to get away from the concept of art-as-commodity, many artists have turned to performance, large installations and earthworks (large-scale manipulations of the earth's surface) as new means of expression. These new art forms pose new challenges for the collector. A collector can sometimes buy a document that attests to the fact that a certain performance took place at a certain time, acquire plans or drawings for large-scale works, or (if he has a great deal of space at his disposal) install a large-scale work on his own property or even commission one to be specially designed for him. Count Giuseppe Panza, an Italian collector who has assembled one of the world's largest and most important collections of recent American art, uses his villa's stables "to accommodate the large works and environments, among his latest acquisitions," according to Milton Gendel, writing in the December 1979 issue of *ARTnews*. "Numerous artists have been invited to the villa to create works for its halls and salons. Two former horse stalls became a mysterious penumbral space focused on two tall slits of light—an environment by Maria Nordman. Another stall, with its 18th-century vault, granite supporting column and flagstone pavement, has a wainscoting of metal panels by Donald Judd. Bruce Nauman's resonating and suffocating parallel walls, a colossal concrete half-egg by Jene Highstein, his penetrating eye-level beam, boom or pipe, a luminous disk by Robert Irwin and pavement sculptures by Richard Nonas are among the Italian stable pieces. In the aggregate they add up to a variety of found objects interrelated as much by the character of their owner and the villa as by their own affinities."

The bewildering diversity of the contemporary art scene, while adding to the field's excitement, greatly complicates the collector's task of distinguishing mere facility from greatness. "It is difficult now to distinguish the really good work from the imitative," Castelli observed. "What I look for is people with great new vision, someone who has something to say that no one has said before him." Similarly, in his essay on the formation of his collection, Baker wrote: "I now hold that it's a small problem to differentiate between a bad and a good work of art. The untutored eye should usually, after comparing the two, make the right choice. The real problem is to recognize the exceptionally good, with its oddness of originality, from amidst the ordinarily good, which is to say, the workmanlike and competent, because the ordinarily good can be analyzed as good, while it is not easy to spot an elusive super-excellence in what is possibly unorthodox."

The task of making distinctions is further complicated if a collector's main motive is to buy inexpensively and sell at a large profit, rather than to acquire work to which he intuitively responds. While contemporary art can offer unequaled opportunities for making a "quick killing" (if an artist emerges rapidly from obscurity to renown), such windfalls are rare. According to Gilbert Edelson of the Art Dealers Association, 95 percent of works sold in the primary market (the market for first-time sales of contemporary works, as distinguished from resales) never appreciate in value. In his memoirs, *Merchants of Art,*

Above: **Michael Heizer,** *Double Negative*
Below: **Donald Judd,** *Galvanized Iron Wall*

Germain Seligman wrote that "much of the speculative buying today in the contemporary field can be described as blind buying. Choices often are made not because of any particular enjoyment of the paintings themselves or for their quality, but for purely mercenary ends. The simple of mind, knowing the golden opportunities which their fathers missed—the Cézannes, the Van Goghs, the Seurats which went begging for purchasers during the lifetimes of the artists—imagine that they are assured of future profits when they invest in any painting by a young artist around whom enough publicity has been woven. In their haste to take advantage of a good thing, the speculators—dealers and collectors alike—urge the artist to produce beyond his capacity. The artist, unless he has great force of character, may allow himself to be drawn into a hot-house atmosphere, under an obligation to work at double time. Genius cannot be created by force of will, an artist's tempo of production cannot be accelerated beyond its normal pace, nor can his creative direction be set by another.

"The clamor that accompanies every exhibition of the work of some much advertised young newcomer (the younger, the better, as he will have longer to live and more time to produce) creates a climate difficult to escape unless strict objectivity is guarded. Real and lasting recognition has seldom come to an artist in a single showing of a few canvases; his talent can only be truly evaluated upon aesthetic progress. This needs time. And it is not the quality of his publicity which must stand the test of time, but the quality of his creative ability."

With today's emphasis on superstars and hot investment opportunities, the distorting influence of hype on the contemporary art market is greater now than it was in Seligman's time. Andy Warhol and Salvador Dali are two of the art world's greatest media stars, and many critics feel that their art-market stature owes more to their talent for publicity than to their artistic achievement (though Dali's earlier work, at least, still entitles him to be ranked as a major artist). "It is probably idle to complain that the work itself is shallow and boring, and that it is the phenomenon of Mr. Warhol's media career, rather than its intrinsic quality, that endows the art with whatever interest it commands," wrote Hilton Kramer in his *New York Times* review (Nov. 23, 1979) of Warhol's portraits show at the Whitney Museum. "Mr. Warhol long ago outdistanced such criticism, and turned it to his own advantage. (Surely he would not be having his second major show at the Whitney if he were not a media hero. To paraphrase a famous quip about the Sitwells, his art belongs less to the history of painting than to the history of publicity.)" In his *New York* magazine article, Carter Ratcliff observed that "Andy Warhol's 'paintings' are hand-colored silk screens on canvas and, as such, are outrageously overpriced at $50,000 or so each." Hype-inflated prices can be difficult to sustain, and Castelli, Warhol's dealer, conceded that there had recently been some weakening in the market for his paintings. "He's done a tremendous amount of work. There are so many paintings available that there is a bit of a glut on the market," Castelli said. He added that the attractively mounted Whitney show had not caused any upsurge in the market for Warhols.

During the late 1960s and early 1970s, the market for contemporary prints was particularly susceptible to inflation-by-hype. The rise in prices was accompanied by a great surge in print production, and "some dreadful prints came out with the names of some very important artists attached to them," according to dealer Sylvan Cole, Jr. The market began to soften in the mid-1970s, when collectors began to take a cooler look at value. Richard Solomon, president of Pace Editions (the print-publishing arm of Pace Gallery in New York), now says that "the print explosion is over." He maintains that the works sold today by major galleries, while still high-priced, are of consistently higher quality than was true in the market's go-go years. "I don't sell the frivolous stuff that I used to, like the hard-edge prints that were sold to decorators. Now, I must charge at least $1,000 to $1,500 for a print, and I won't sell work for that amount unless it is serious."

Cole, however, maintains that unreasonably inflated prices persist: "Contemporary prints created by the so-called stars have achieved a very high cost factor, often without discernment," he said. "A lot of contemporary prints today are created very much as a way of providing additional income for the artist. For people like Motherwell, Warhol, Rauschenberg, Johns, Lichtenstein and Dine, prints are a logical adjunct of the artist's effort. There is more demand for their art than they can possibly fill by unique works. . . . Many artists who produce or authorize production of a lot of images are under pressure from publishers, who couldn't care less about the integrity of the image." In his *New York Times* article on print collecting, critic John Russell observed that "the first thing that a print collector has to do . . . is to learn to distinguish between prints to which the artist has entrusted his deepest feelings and prints that result from a more or less honorable form of replication."

Prices for contemporary art may be distorted not only by the manipulation of demand (through excessive hype), but also by the manipulation of supply. In her *New York Times* article about the pricing of art works (Jan. 20, 1976), Grace Glueck reported that New York lawyer Lee Eastman, managing the affairs of Josef Albers, declared a moratorium on all Albers sales for a year in the early 1970s so that, in Eastman's words, they became "like black tulips. Everybody wanted one." Works that would have sold for no more than $5,000 to $6,000 before the moratorium sold afterwards for $40,000 to $50,000. Sometimes the contemporary art market can be disrupted by a sudden flood of works. If a large number of works remain unsold in an artist's studio or in an estate, according to dealer Xavier Fourcade, and if huge prices are asked for what is slowly placed on the market, it is not certain that those prices will be sustained when, for one reason or another, a sudden flood of works becomes available.

The Arrangements Between Artist and Dealer

Like collector-dealer relationships, artist-dealer relationships are usually much less structured and formal than traditional business arrangements; although some artists negotiate detailed written contracts with their dealers, most rely on oral assurances or simple letters of intent to define the terms of their gallery connections. For the most part, artists consign works to their galleries for sale, but instead of paying a commission of 10 to 25 percent (the typical commission for consignments by collectors), they usually pay 33 1/3 to 50 percent. In other words, if you buy a contemporary painting for $10,000, the artist will probably get only $5,000 to $6,666. (The price is usually set by agreement between the artist and gallery.) Dealers charge much higher commissions for artists' consignments than for collectors' consignments because of the greater degree of commitment, service and risk inherent in representing an artist. Whereas consignment by a collector is usually a one-shot affair, representation of an artist is potentially a long-term marriage. A dealer who brings an artist into his stable makes an implied (or, sometimes, contractual) commitment to mount regular shows of his work (typically once every two years) and to promote the artist's reputation in every possible way—through publicity (such as press releases and advertisements), discussions with collectors, critics and museum officials, and assistance to those who may wish to write about or mount museum shows of the artist's work. (Some museum shows are actually initiated by dealers rather than by the museum's staff. The dealer may do a great deal of work in helping to assemble works for the show and in arranging for the publication of the catalogue; some of the funds for the catalogue and other aspects of the show may come from the dealer rather than the museum.) In some cases, the costs of exhibiting and promoting an artist's work may result in a financial loss to the dealer, who has no way of knowing when or if the collecting public will catch on. At the 1976 art-market conference sponsored by *The ARTnewsletter,* Ivan Karp of O. K. Harris Gallery commented that "between 80 and 90 percent of my shows don't sell. A few others do well, and they support the rest of the gallery. When we sell a print, we do a little dance in the back room." Business apparently picked up a bit after Karp made these remarks. In an article appearing on Aug. 18, 1978, the *Wall Street Journal* reported that "about 70% to 80% of all works exhibited at O. K. Harris never sell." In some cases, dealers try to reduce their financial risks by charging little-known artists for certain expenses (i.e., photography, framing, shipping, insurance, publicity). A commercially operated gallery where artists pay *all* the expenses is regarded as a "vanity gallery"; at this type of gallery, an artist essentially buys himself a show—a situation that confers little or no prestige and usually few or no sales. (Such galleries should be distinguished from artist-run-and-financed "co-op galleries," to be discussed later.)

There are a number of variations on the standard artist-gallery arrangement: sometimes an artist may sell works outright to a dealer; sometimes he and his dealer may agree upon a set dollar amount that the artist will receive upon the sale of a work, with the excess going to the dealer (the "net price" method of compensation). Castelli said that he has used the latter arrangement for some important older works by Rauschenberg and Johns; the artists decide how much they want to receive for the works, and, if a discount is given to an important purchaser, the gallery's share of the sale price may be as low as 10 percent, according to Castelli. Important artists may sometimes negotiate lower gallery commissions than those available to other artists. Castelli said his commission is usually 40 percent, but it may be 50 percent for an artist who is very prolific or only 25 percent for one who produces very slowly, or for an important work that the artist is reluctant to part with. Lawrence Fleischman said his commission is 50 percent for young artists, 40 percent for established artists.

Established artists sometimes arrange for galleries to pay them regular stipends, assuring them a steady flow of income, regardless of sales. Stipends are usually advances against sales or are applied towards purchases of the artist's work by the gallery. If the stipends are deemed advances, and sales within a certain period of time do not cover the amount of the advances, the artist may be required to reimburse the gallery in cash or in art. Some galleries may take a larger sales commission in exchange for paying a regular stipend.

Other aspects of oral or written artist-gallery agreements may cover territorial exclusivity (the gallery's right to be the artist's sole representative in a city, country or the world), the duration of the agreement, and procedures for accounting and payment to the artist. Irregularities in accounting and payment are among the most frequent causes of artists' complaints against their dealers. Because of galleries' occasionally haphazard record-keeping or their failure to provide artists with detailed, documented information about sales and inventories, artists sometimes have no sure way of knowing what has been sold, for how much or to whom. Artists who do not find out about certain sales until long after they occur complain, with justification, that their share in the sale proceeds is being used to help solve their dealers' cash-flow problems.

To protect artists who consign works to dealers, the legislatures of certain states (including California, Connecticut, Massachusetts, Michigan, New Mexico, New York, Texas, and Wisconsin) have enacted laws spelling out dealers' legal responsibilities. Specific provisions differ from state to state, but most of these laws provide that a dealer must treat sale proceeds as funds held in trust for the artist-consignor, who has first claim on such funds. Works consigned by the artist are, under the terms of most of these laws, also held in trust by the dealer for the artist's benefit and are not subject to claims by the dealer's creditors. Some states also make the dealer liable for loss or damage to artist-consigned works, and two (Connecticut and Wisconsin) require dealers to enter into written contracts with their artists, specifying such things as the minimum sale price and the schedule of payment to the artist after a work is sold.

It is common for artists to switch galleries when their complaints go unanswered or when they believe that another gallery, with a better reputation, can do a better job for them. To find out which gallery represents a particular artist, you can ask the curatorial staffs of museums showing contemporary art, or consult reference sources such as *Who's Who in American Art; Locus,* a guide to artists represented by a large number of New York galleries; or *Locus Select,* a guide to artists represented by selected top-name galleries around the country (see Bibliography). You may also check the entry under the artist's name in the *Art Index* (the art world's version of the *Readers' Guide to Periodical Literature),* which lists articles published about the artist during a given year, including reviews of gallery shows.

Dealing Directly with Artists

Part of the thrill of collecting contemporary art is the chance to talk about the works you buy with the people who actually created them.

You can meet artists in their galleries (at openings or sometimes on regular exhibition days) or by appointment at their studios, where you can often get a fascinating inside look at how art is created. "Sometimes visiting an artist's studio is marvelous; sometimes it's very disappointing," said dealer Fourcade. "You don't necessarily have to know how things are done, but if the artist is willing to show you, it can be very interesting." At the 1979 panel discussion at the New Museum on collecting contemporary art, collector Barbara Schwartz commented that knowing the artists whose work she bought was "a very treasured experience. . . . A collector can support an artist by going to the studio and giving feedback. You can also tell other collectors, curators or art dealers about an artist." Schwartz observed that she and her husband, Eugene, had developed close friendships with many artists, including some whose work they did not collect. An artist who is struggling for recognition is likely to be particularly receptive to the advances of interested collectors. Ben Heller, who bought Rothkos from Rothko, Pollocks from Pollock and Motherwells from Motherwell at a time when their art was largely ignored by collectors, observed that "I was as much a freak as the artists were. When they heard that there was a live one, they wanted to meet him." His first visit with Pollock, he said, was arranged simply by calling the artist on the phone.

The simplest way to arrange a studio visit is to contact the artist through his dealer, if he has one. Explain that you want to make the visit to see as much of the artist's work as possible and to learn more about his methods and his ideas about his art. The dealer will then tell you whether such a visit is possible and, if so, he will set up the appointment. Dealers and artists are understandably much more favorably disposed toward making such arrangements for people who are (or who are expected to become) serious collectors of the artist's work.

Some collectors do not like to make such arrangements through dealers because they have another motive for visiting the artist's studio —to make their purchases directly from the artist, without the dealer's knowledge or participation. Some artists' addresses and phone numbers are easily found in the phone book (provided that you can find out where the artist lives from *Who's Who in American Art* or some other source). Others can be gotten only through knowledgeable art-world contacts. Many collectors try to circumvent dealers, according to Fourcade. Whether it works, he said, depends on the relationship between the artist and dealer. Collectors reason that if they cut out the middleman, they can save a great deal of money in commissions. The artist may charge more than he would ordinarily receive as his share from a gallery sale, but this could still be significantly less than the collector would have to pay for a gallery-negotiated purchase. Collectors may also try to contact a popular artist directly in order to circumvent a dealer's long waiting list for the artist's work. "People who come to an artist's studio have a wide choice of works that they shouldn't have," said Castelli. "Other people should come before them. Sometimes people get a good painting who should not be getting it." For obvious reasons, most galleries insist that artists inform them of any studio sales and pay the gallery a commission for such sales. (In some cases, the dealer may accept a lower commission on studio sales than he would charge for sales from the gallery.) Fourcade says that when collectors try to make purchases from his artists' studios, the artists contact the gallery and the gallery sends the bill. In his biography of Joseph Hirshhorn, Barry Hyams reported how the collector "took the shortcut" to an artist represented by New York dealer Pierre Matisse, inviting the artist to lunch and then visiting her studio. "But his artifice didn't work," according to Hyams: the artist, Loren MacIver, referred Hirshhorn to Matisse. If an artist decides not to cooperate with his gallery, however, there is little the gallery can do to police studio sales. Artist Larry Rivers said he is "kind of a sneaky number" in his own way. "I don't tell my gallery everything, but they seem to tolerate it. Under my former contract, if I sold something out of my studio, I was supposed to give Marlborough 20 percent. [His regular commission for sales from the gallery was 33 1/3 percent.] I didn't always do that."

While studio visits can sometimes benefit equally the artist and the collector, they have also been used by collectors to exploit certain artists who are financially vulnerable. Known as an inveterate bargain hunter, Joseph Hirshhorn (according to Hyams' book) visited the studio of Milton Avery, "who was then [in the early 1940s] on hard times. Hirshhorn peered about the studio. He pulled out a wad of hundred-dollar bills, peeled off 120 of them, pressed them into Avery's palm, and swept the studio clean of forty paintings. In the center of his studio, Avery stood stunned by the windfall, staring from the bare walls to the $12,000 in his hand. Regaining his voice, he exclaimed in dismay, 'I've been robbed!' "

Some artists may avoid studio sales because they feel that their galleries can protect their financial interests better than they can themselves. Others just don't like to have their work interrupted. "A young artist is pleased when anyone comes up," said Castelli, "but famous artists don't want to be bothered. They are only willing to see important collectors who are very involved with them." Similarly, Sidney Janis observed that some artists will not make sales from their studios because "they feel this infringes on their creative life." Some collectors take it upon themselves to tell artists how to paint—an approach that may be viewed by some artists as constructive criticism but by others as an obnoxious intrusion into their private domain.

Collectors who fear making such an intrusion sometimes prefer not to meet artists personally. "I make it a point not to visit studios because I don't want to be in the position of being dishonest or brutally frank," said Ralph Colin. Richard Brown Baker said that he tends to tell artists what he thinks is wrong with their work and added that he is frequently contacted by aspiring artists who want him to come to their studios. "I visit studios very little," he said, "although it is marvelous to visit the studio of an artist whose work you admire." In his essay on his collection, Baker observed that most artists are "suspicious . . . of the motives of collectors. Collectors are judged to be greedy and mindless, ignorant and slaves to fashion. Some, whose names are synonymous with great wealth, are disliked for arrogance and meanness; they're always trying to get something for nothing at the expense of the artist. . . . I know I am myself rather afraid of the human factor and prefer to know and become friends with artists after, not before, I have seen and admired their art. I don't want to be bribed into a purchase by personal charm rather than artistic merit." Similarly, at the New Museum panel discussion, collector Sondra Gilman said, "If I were to become friendly with an artist, I would find it emotionally impossible to separate myself from the art; it would be difficult to judge. . . . I can't deal with walking into an artist's studio and walking out without buying."

Finding New Talent

There is a large group of artists with whom you *must* deal directly if you are interested in their work—the new or undiscovered talents who lack any gallery affiliation. The major contemporary art galleries can give exposure only to a small percentage of the thousands of working artists, and most of the artists represented by those galleries are the ones who have already established major reputations. Such galleries are not usually the places to discover new talent. "Our calendars tend to be filled by the artists we are already representing," said André Emmerich at the 1979 panel discussion on the interior designer and the New York art market, sponsored by the Art Dealers Association and the American Society of Interior Designers. Many top dealers or their assistants do look at the slides submitted by hundreds of aspiring artists; if they think the work is good, they may suggest galleries or other spaces where the artists may be able to get exposure, or they may even occasionally take on a fledgling artist themselves. "If I produce something new," said Fourcade, "people are prepared to look at it.

They will not necessarily buy it, but they will at least look at it. I deal in a certain number of artists who are recognized as extremely important and, because of my reputation, a lot of people trust us." As previously suggested, the younger, less well-established dealers are more likely to appreciate and show larger amounts of new work by emerging artists. In his *New York* magazine article, Carter Ratcliff said that the following New York galleries are "mostly for new artists": Patricia Hamilton, Droll/Kolbert, Robert Miller, Brooke Alexander, David McKee, Susan Caldwell, Sculpture Now, Holly Solomon, Willard, Max Protetch, Pam Adler, O. K. Harris. But some adventurous collectors may occasionally wish to strike out on their own, seeking artists who lack any gallery's patronage and who are at the stage in their careers where they most need the financial and emotional support that an interested buyer can supply. Some established dealers maintain that such an approach is not just adventurous, it is foolhardy. They point out that most of today's little-known artists will always remain little known. If an artist is genuinely talented, they maintain, he will eventually be embraced by the gallery system. "A lot of people feel they would rather buy two or three dozen unknown artists than one recognized artist," observed Sidney Janis. "I think that's an error. Why go for a long shot?" But some of the best-known collectors of contemporary art think it is important to range more widely. Roy Neuberger, much of whose collection is now housed at the Neuberger Museum in the State University of New York, College at Purchase, told the audience at a 1980 seminar on investing in art, sponsored by the New York City Bar Association: "I feel there are hundreds or perhaps thousands of living artists who do not make the grade in a commercial way and whose quality can be just as good as some of those contemporary artists who get tremendous prices." Similarly, Herbert Vogel commented at the New Museum panel that "I know a lot of artists who don't have galleries and who are very good," and Ben Heller noted that he had "bought a fair number of works by contemporary artists who were not represented by galleries."

How can a collector find the most promising unaffiliated artists? As is usual in the art world, word-of-mouth plays an important role. Castelli said that collectors who search for new talent "most of the time make horrible mistakes," but can minimize the risks by getting leads from "dealers or artists who know the scene. You can't do it on your own." Ivan Karp, who sees about 150 unaffiliated artists a week, keeps a list of about 50 who he thinks show unusual promise. Collectors, he said, can have this list (with studio addresses) on request. Artists are often the first to discover and appreciate important new work by other artists; they are particularly good sources for leads on emerging talent. Barbara Schwartz said that collectors seeking such leads should "listen to curators and especially to artists you respect." Dorothy Vogel said that she and her husband go to alternative spaces to find new talent. Such spaces, which include the Clocktower and Artists Space in Manhattan and the Washington (D.C.) Project for the Arts, are usually willing to help arrange sales of works from their shows and may even maintain slide files, available for viewing by collectors, of works by artists lacking gallery representation. Occasionally, a group of unaffiliated artists may band together to form their own artist-run gallery. These co-op galleries, as they are called, are generally more sales-oriented than alternative spaces, give more one-person shows, and have a regular stable of artists.

Standards of quality vary, of course. Some co-ops are widely respected; others are regarded as little more than vanity operations. You can discover which alternative spaces and co-op galleries have the best art-world reputations through word-of-mouth, reviews in respected publications, and track records in attracting government grants. (A list of co-ops, alternative spaces and other organizations funded under the "Artists' Spaces" program of the National Endowment for the Arts, a federal agency, can be obtained from Visual Arts Program, National Endowment for the Arts, Washington, D.C. 20506.)

The National Endowment and many state arts agencies award fellowships to artists, and lists of their grantees may also lead you to promising prospects. If you explain that you are a collector interested in supporting new artists, the agencies' staffs may be willing to help you find those grantees whose works are most likely to appeal to your taste. The New York State–funded Creative Artists Public Service Program, for example, maintains a slide file of works by its grantees and other selected applicants, and encourages perusals and inquiries by collectors. Slide files are also kept by the National Endowment for the Arts, the U.S. General Services Administration (which commissions art for federal buildings) and many museums and artists' organizations. A listing of slide files around the country is provided in the *Directory of Artists Slide Registries* compiled by Suzy Ticho, and published by the American Council for the Arts, 570 Seventh Ave., New York, N.Y. 10018.

Juried exhibitions, where selections are made by judges of distinguished reputation, may also provide useful leads. Some museums, including the Baltimore Museum of Art, the Detroit Institute of Arts and the Corcoran Gallery in Washington, hold regular exhibitions of works by area artists; all artists from the state or region are invited to submit works for possible selection by respected jurors. Art fairs and exhibitions that have few or no criteria for selection (such as the well-known outdoor shows in New York's Greenwich Village) are, obviously, less likely prospects for collectors seeking high-quality work by emerging artists. Also uneven in quality are many of the shows mounted by large local artists' organizations (such as the Boston Visual Artists Union and the New Organization for the Visual Arts in Cleveland) and the "open studios" events (which allow the public to visit participating artists' studios during specified days) organized by artists in various cities (including "Artweek" in Boston and "10 Downtown" in New York).

High-quality art may, at times, be found in the most unlikely places, just as mediocre work may, at times, be found in the most prestigious galleries. The trouble with exploring the alternatives to the gallery system is that it requires strong legs, discerning taste and much patience. It is far easier to choose intelligently among artists and art works that have already been preselected by experienced professionals. It is certainly not advisable to rummage around art fairs and grant lists if your goal is to buy art that will prove to be a good financial investment; the chances of today's commercially untested art becoming tomorrow's hot commodity are minuscule. But if your goal is to buy art that appeals to your taste and can be had at a reasonable price, the search for new talent can add an element of adventure and excitement to collecting, while providing some badly needed support for unrecognized artists.

Artists' Rights and the Collector

While contact with living artists adds to the excitement of collecting, it can also add some complications. Owning a work of contemporary art is a little like being a foster parent: the real father is still alive and can attempt to assert certain rights and make certain demands. The civil rights movement of the 1960s had its art-world analogue in the "artists' rights movement"; some artists began to demand changes in the system which allowed collectors, dealers and museum personnel to profit from the labors of artists, while most artists, except for a few stars, were unable to make a living from their own art. The rebellion took a variety of forms: the search for alternatives to the commercial gallery system, demands for reforms in the practices of galleries and museums, and attempts to increase the collector's accountability to the artist. The collector-artist relationship has been the most resistant to change. Most collectors feel strongly that once they buy an art work, they have the absolute right to do with it what they wish, without being subject to any conditions imposed by a previous owner or creator. While such artists'-rights concepts as resale royalties and moral rights (to be discussed below) are still live issues (and have, in California, even been embodied in legislation), they have, as yet, had little practical effect on the conduct of the art market.

The one area where there has been significant change is copyright. A 1976 revision of the federal copyright law increased the copyright protection of artists in several ways. Previously available for a maximum of fifty-six years, copyright protection is now available to artists and their heirs for the lifetime of the creator plus fifty years. (For works created before Jan. 1, 1978, the maximum term is seventy-five years.) Before the 1976 revision, if a work was "published" (i.e., distributed or offered to the public by sale, transfer, rental, lease or lending) without notice of copyright, the artist lost all possibility of copyright protection and the buyer of the work was presumed to have complete property rights in it, including reproduction rights (i.e., the right to arrange for and profit from the reproduction of the image on posters, wallpaper, bedsheets, etc.). Under the new law, collectors cannot assume they have these rights if they buy a recent work that lacks copyright notice. An artist who omits copyright notice from a published work can retain copyright protection if he registers the work with the U.S. Copyright Office within five years of its date of publication and makes an effort to add the copyright notice to the work. (Copyright notice is the word "copyright," the abbreviation "copr.," or the symbol ©, accompanied by the name of the creator and the year of publication.) When you own a recently created work, you do *not* necessarily own the copyright in it; if it is important to you that you own the copyright, you should request a written agreement from the artist transferring the copyright. You do not have to own the copyright of a work to be able to display it publicly, but you do have to own the copyright (or the work has to have entered the public domain because of the artist's failure to meet the requirements of the copyright law) to arrange to make reproductions. A New York–based organization called the Visual Artists and Galleries Association was formed in 1977 to monitor and take action against violations of artists' reproduction rights, and a number of prominent artists, concerned about unauthorized reproduction, have become members of VAGA. Other groups, including SPADEM in France, perform a similar service abroad. Still, despite the growing awareness of the benefits of copyright protection (and despite the fact that copyright notice can be attached to the back or base of a work, so as not to deface the work itself), most artists still

Robert Indiana, *Love*

do not use copyright and their work eventually winds up in the public domain. The financial folly of this, from the artist's point of view, is most frequently illustrated by the example of the widespread commercial exploitation of Robert Indiana's design of the letters "LOVE". Having failed to copyright the work, Indiana received nothing from the numerous commercial spin-offs.

Far more controversial than copyright, which has a long-standing legal tradition here, is the concept of resale royalties (the French "droit de suite"), which sharply conflicts with American notions of property rights. Some artists feel that when a collector resells a work at a profit, the artist (who is responsible for the art work's value but who may have sold it cheaply at a time when he was struggling for recognition) should share in the windfall. Most collectors, predictably, disagree. They feel that once they have bought a work for a price mutually agreed upon with the artist or his representative, they have absolute title to that property and their financial obligation to the artist ceases. Most contemporary-art purchases, they note, do not appreciate in value, and they feel that the collector who risks his money on little-known artists deserves to reap any financial benefits that may occasionally come his way. Dealers generally feel that requirements for payment of resale royalties are difficult or impossible to enforce, and that attempts to impose them would hurt sales of contemporary art. The difficulties of administration and enforcement have been illustrated in California, where a 1976 law requires the seller to give the artist 5 percent of the resale price on paintings, drawings and sculpture that are sold at a profit, provided that the seller resides in California or the sale occurs there. (Works resold for less than $1,000 are not subject to the law.) The law has been largely honored in the breach, with enforcement left up to artists. They can protect their rights only if they keep track of sales and sue offenders for unpaid royalties. The law has survived a court challenge to its constitutionality, and proponents hope it will serve as a model for future federal legislation. So far, attempts to enact similar bills in other states and federally have failed. Certain European countries (e.g., France, Germany, Italy) do have laws providing for payment of resale royalties under certain circumstances.

In the absence of legislation, artists can try to get purchasers of their works to sign contracts requiring the payment of resale royalties. But few artists are willing to jeopardize sales by pushing collectors for unusual concessions, and few collectors are willing to make such concessions. A widely disseminated (but little used) contract drafted in 1971 by New York attorney Robert Projansky requires the collector to pay the artist *15 percent* of the *profit* from a resale (as distinguished from the royalty under the California law, equal to 5 *percent* of the *entire resale price*).

Some artists feel that while collectors may not be willing to sign royalty agreements, they can reasonably be expected to agree to other non-economic stipulations that are important to the artist and yet are not likely to impose a significant burden on the collector. Artists sometimes seek assurances that if they want to borrow a major work from a collector for display in an important gallery or museum exhibition, the collector will cooperate. Also receiving increased attention from artists are "moral rights" (the French "droit moral"), including the artist's right to protect the physical integrity of his work. The moral rights of artists are protected by law in France, Germany and Italy. In this country, California has, again, led the way. A 1979 state law prohibits any person other than the artist "from intentionally committing, or authorizing another to commit . . . any physical defacement, mutilation, alteration or destruction of a work of fine art." (As with California's resale-royalties law, enforcement is left up to the artist, who is unlikely to know whether a violation has in fact occurred.) In the absence of such legislation or of a contract between the artist and collector containing similar provisions, the collector's property rights over his purchase extend to changing its physical character to suit his whims—a power that can lead to distortion of the artist's work and, perhaps, injury to his reputation. The California act also prohibits defacement, mutilation, etc. by framers, conservators and restorers, and holds them to an even higher standard of responsibility than that for collectors: collectors are prohibited only from *intentionally* destructive acts, but the professionals are liable for damage or destruction that results from "any act constituting gross negligence," whether intentional or not. Concerned that the work of unskilled (or sometimes even skilled) restorers can seriously distort their work, some artists may ask collectors to consult them before any restoration is performed on their work and to give them "first opportunity to restore it, if practicable" (the language of the Projansky contract).

As previously suggested, few contemporary-art transactions are likely to be complicated by stipulations involving artists' rights, unless these stipulations are a matter of law, as in California. If you are confronted by artists'-rights demands, you have two choices: either look elsewhere and buy only works by the many artists who do not make such demands, or accept the restrictions as a small price to pay for the excitement of becoming involved with an artist whom you admire. If you see your role as a supporter of contemporary artists rather than an accumulator of contemporary art, you may even want to do the outrageous: voluntarily offer to give the artist certain rights and privileges that he would not himself have dared to demand.

Chapter 6

BECOMING
A CONNOISSEUR

Beginning collectors, even of contemporary art, usually rely very strongly on the knowledge and advice of sellers. Dealers and auction-house specialists are the most accessible of all experts and, if they are well established and have a reputation for integrity, their descriptions of their wares can usually be assumed to be reasonably accurate. But as you begin to spend more time and money on your collection, you will probably want to become less dependent on the word of those who are trying to sell you their goods. One way of doing this is to develop relationships with other experts. They will give you a more disinterested and often more scholarly perspective on the works that interest you and they may help you develop your own taste. Even the most experienced collectors often consult scholars or conservators. Norton Simon, whose wide-ranging collection includes old masters, Impressionist and modern art, as well as antiquities from India, sometimes consults with several different experts for a single purchase. Armand Hammer, whose collection contains old masters, Impressionists and moderns, regularly consults with John Walker, former director of the National Gallery of Art, with Kenneth Donahue, former director of the Los Angeles County Museum of Art (where Hammer is a trustee and to which he has bequeathed his paintings) and with Konrad Oberhuber, drawings curator at the Fogg Art Museum at Harvard University.

The key to benefiting from expert advice is to know whom to consult and how to gain access to them. For beginning collectors, the first logical step is to develop relationships with local museum curators. "Art collecting is a rare hobby," noted Eugene Thaw, "and museum people are usually enthusiastic about anyone in the community who is interested in taking up collecting." There is, in part, an ulterior motive behind this enthusiasm. Museum officials hope that local collectors will eventually become local patrons, donating or bequeathing to the museum some of the works that the museum helped them acquire. Collectors stand the best chance of getting curators' best advice if they evince an interest in helping the museum and a seriousness of purpose in forming the collection. One way to make your helpful intentions clear is to become a donor to the museum or to the department specializing in the type of art that interests you. Curators are not apt to take an interest in building a collection to enhance a collector's personal prestige or financial position, nor are they likely to help a collector who hasn't exerted much effort to help himself through self-education. The best curator-collector relationships are dialogues whereby each learns from and helps the other. "It's a two-way street," said Norton Simon. "Rick Brown [Richard Brown, the late director of the Kimbell Art Museum in Fort Worth and former director of the Los Angeles County Museum of Art] and I often called each other about a picture. I have also advised others in museums. They may have heard that there was something I didn't like or was bothered about a few years ago when I was considering a certain picture and they want to know my opinion about it."

The types of help that museums can provide include giving you access to works in storage (so that you can sharpen your eye and compare potential purchases to museum-quality objects), letting you know about the market availability of desirable works (which the museum does not want to or is not able to purchase for itself), assessing the quality, authenticity and condition of works you are considering for purchase, and introducing you to dealers and other experts (who may treat you with greater consideration because of your museum connection). Most museums will allow any serious collector to see works in storage, even if the collector has not cultivated any special personal relationships. Many print collectors know about and take advantage of the opportunity to visit museum print rooms, but similar opportunities also exist to see other parts of museum storage collections. Each museum department usually maintains a card catalogue, which you can examine to learn about the museum's holdings in a given area. The entry for a particular work may include a photograph, exhibition history and a list of reference sources that mention the work, as well as the standard description of the work's size, medium, date, etc. You can then ask to see those works that most interest you.

John Walsh, Jr., of the Boston Museum of Fine Arts stresses the importance of seeing as many works as possible in one's field of interest —including all relevant works in museums. A prime tool of the collector, he noted, is a "large mental repertory of images that can be recalled. . . . One of our obligations," he added, "is to try to work with people with a serious developing interest. We answer their questions and go with them to galleries to see things. We do advise people on price, in a gingerly way, trying not to prejudice the art dealer's getting a fair crack at a profit. [Museum officials differ on this; some will not give monetary appraisals.] But we have to be careful not to be taken for a ride. We will not aid some scheme to speculate."

Some museums have made it easy for collectors to establish relationships with curators, by setting up formal programs for regular consultation between the museum's staff and the public. (The Boston Museum, for example, has "Thursday consultation days," when members of the public can meet with paintings curators to get advice and expert opinions.) You may also meet curators by attending lectures and other museum events. (Not all lecturers are curators, however; many are members of the museum's education staff.) Or you may simply call or write to the curator in your field of interest (whose name you can learn by calling the museum or examining its annual report or other publications), explaining your reason for wishing to see him and requesting an appointment. The subject of your first discussion should probably not be too closely tied to the marketplace. A curator who has never previously met you may be reluctant to advise you on whether or not to buy a work that you have obtained from a dealer on approval. He is more likely to be interested in discussing with you the general collecting opportunities in his field (such as what types of things are available and where they can best be obtained), issues related to connoisseurship (such as how to assess quality and authenticity), and questions that you may have about works already in your collection. (Questions about the authenticity of a particular work, however, are always delicate—a curator does not want to get drawn into a lawsuit between you and a dealer who may have sold you a questionable work.) As previously mentioned, the curator's interest in helping you will be heightened if you indicate a desire to develop a cooperative relationship with his department, including possible donations of high-quality works to the museum.

The main advantages of museum advice are that it is free of charge and untainted by commercial motives. But it may be seriously limited in its availability or quality. Since a curator's first responsibility is to his institution, he is not likely to be able to devote much time and effort to your personal collection. If your "local museum" happens to be the Metropolitan Museum of Art, your chances of gaining access to top curatorial help are greatly diminished, since the demand for that help is particularly great. European-paintings department chairman John

Pope-Hennessy, for example, says flatly that he does not work with private collectors who are not important museum patrons. A similar attitude was expressed by William Rubin, director of painting and sculpture at the Museum of Modern Art in New York. At the other extreme, if your local museum is a minor one with a shoestring budget and a weak collection, it is unlikely to have attracted a staff of sufficient caliber to provide you with high-quality advice. Dealer Richard Feigen says flatly that very few local museum directors or curators are sophisticated enough to advise on forming a first-rate collection.

As your own sophistication grows, you may want to turn to other experts—not the reigning authorities in your locality, but the top names in your region, the nation or even the world. You may learn who these people are from the contacts you have already established (who may also provide you with needed introductions), or independently, from your own reading and research. For a guide to the key people in about twenty different fields, consult the *ARTnews* article, "The Experts' Guide to the Experts" (November 1978). The New York–based Art Dealers Association of America maintains a card index of top authorities in various fields, and ADAA's administrative vice-president, Ralph Colin, said that serious collectors can get the names of these experts from ADAA's office. For a fee, collectors who lack contacts can get an assessment of a work's authenticity and correct attribution from the New York–based International Foundation for Art Research, a nonprofit group that enjoys the services of many experts, including an advisory council composed of about thirty of the world's most distinguished art scholars and museum curators. At this writing, IFAR's fee is $200 for a preliminary examination from photographs (which is usually sufficient to resolve questions of authenticity); $500 to $1,000 for a full examination (including laboratory tests and more extensive research). IFAR does not give monetary appraisals. (See the Appendix for the addresses of ADAA and IFAR.)

If you want to establish a regular relationship with an expert who will give you advice about quality, authenticity, condition, provenance and price (as well as tips on newly available works that you may wish to acquire), you may decide to hire a personal art advisor. Some distinguished art historians are available for such consultation. Most museum officials, however, will not hire themselves out as personal advisors. They must give first priority to the collecting interests of their museums. The financial arrangements between collectors and advisors vary: some advisors work on commission (charging a percentage—usually about 10 percent—of the price of works purchased on their advice); others work for a flat fee. Impressionist/Post-Impressionist expert John Rewald said he gets $1,000 to $2,000 for advice on an important picture and added that "when you are an advisor to a very big collector, it is done on retainer. Otherwise, it might look like you could recommend an expensive picture because there would be more money in it for you. Being on retainer means I am not involved in the deal. But not many collectors pay a retainer. They must be rich and collect a great deal to make it pay." One of the most prominent collectors receiving his advice, the late John Hay Whitney, began by paying Rewald a 5 percent commission on purchases. But he switched to a retainer arrangement, Rewald said, when Rewald found that he did not feel comfortable charging a commission for a particularly expensive painting.

Whereas Rewald advises no one exclusively and engages in many other art-related pursuits, some art historians work full-time for one collector. In such cases, according to Paul Mellon, who has hired such experts, an accepted rate of compensation is slightly more than the art historian could expect to earn on the curatorial staff of a museum. The most distinguished experts usually do not take on such full-time assignments, preferring not to confine themselves to serving the interests of one collector.

Reliance on advisors is not without its dangers and disadvantages. The first problem is finding someone who is competent and honest. There are many inexperienced, well-meaning people masquerading as "art consultants," who have few qualifications other than an art-history degree and a claim to understanding the mysteries of "good taste." Other advisors are not so well intentioned. Dealer Stanley Moss noted that some art historians secretly receive kickbacks from dealers whose works they recommend to collectors (who also pay them a fee for their services)—a situation that is not apt to yield the best, most disinterested advice. In his memoirs, Maurice Rheims described the temptations he faced when he began to serve as advisor to the famed Armenian-born collector Calouste Gulbenkian. Sent by Gulbenkian to investigate an "El Greco," Rheims was offered 2.5 million francs by the seller if he would persuade Gulbenkian to buy the painting for 10 million francs. Believing the painting to be by El Greco's son, Rheims refused to cooperate and later found out that Gulbenkian had also consulted another expert who had reached the same negative conclusion. Having gained Gulbenkian's trust, Rheims was rewarded with other assignments. "Buying an advisor is as difficult as buying a work of art," observed Ben Heller. "You should ask about the advisor's track record and about how his advice has worked out. . . . Most collectors I've seen, particularly with regard to expensive things, drop their business smarts when it comes to the art world. If someone wants to buy something in business, he does his research or he knows how to listen. In the art world, he looks for advisors all over the place. . . . You can get too many gurus and become very confused."

Most art-world observers agree that the best collectors find out as much as they can from as many reliable sources as possible, but ultimately rely on their own judgment. "I'll ask for opinions, but I won't take advice. Or rather, I'll listen to opinions and analyze not just the advice, but the motive of the giver, and then I'll make up my mind— in business, art, everything," said Baron Hans Heinrich Thyssen-Bornemisza, one of the world's foremost old-masters collectors, in an interview with reporter Alan Levy for a November 1979 profile in *ARTnews.* Similarly, curator John Walsh, Jr., observed that "collectors ought to feel it is their own primary obligation to evaluate things and satisfy themselves as to what things are. They should regard the help they can get as an adjunct to what they themselves can find out. They have got to build reference libraries of their own and collect photographs of art works, and they must learn what art historical monographs can tell and what they can't, what's reliable and what isn't, what value opinions have and don't have."

Most museum professionals, dealers and collectors share collector Edward Carter's belief that a group of art works is more coherent and interesting when selected by one set of eyes. "I selected my pictures by myself in the end," he said proudly. "I know a lot of naïve collectors who engage people they trust or can hire to do their collecting for them. That's not the fun of collecting." Similarly, collector Ralph Colin observed that "if you get to the position of a Paul Mellon or a Norton Simon, where you spend millions on art in various fields, you need advisors. But the greatest fun is not having one."

Self-reliance ultimately means becoming your own expert. It requires serious scholarship and a careful examination of potential acquisitions. If you are an unknown and not particularly wealthy collector, the need to develop your own scholarly expertise is especially strong, according to Chinese-art collector Paul Singer. "There is a great difference between a rich man and a poor man collecting," he said. "A poor man has to know more than anybody else—more than dealers, other collectors and even museum people. A rich man can buy successfully from dealers without knowledge, because no dealer will attempt to cheat a rich customer. The casual buyer and the poor buyer do not have that guarantee." Singer added that a collector who lacks clout has to be certain of authenticity himself, without relying on anyone else's judgment. Sometimes, he noted, a collector's superior knowledge may enable him to pick up bargains. "Many things I own," he said, "are objects that the dealer suspected might not be genuine; he had no idea what they were and sold them cheaply because they had been called forgeries by others. I was convinced I knew better, and I was later proven to be absolutely correct. Some objects which began coming out of southern China around 1937 were so different and unfamiliar that even the greatest scholars shook their heads."

The expert collector will not only analyze potential acquisitions in terms of quality and price (as discussed in Chapter 1) but will also investigate questions that less sophisticated buyers might entertain only briefly or not even consider:

- Is it really what it is represented to be?
- What kind of condition is it in?
- Where did it come from?

Any art professional would advise serious collectors to explore these questions. But what they might not tell you is how best to go about this exploration to maximize your chances of arriving at the right answers. Here's how:

Is It Really What It Is Represented to Be?

"The primary thing that collectors are asking about today is authenticity," according to dealer Klaus Perls. "They are running scared about forgeries and misattributions. They are terribly suspicious, and I encourage people to be suspicious. In this gallery, they would usually tend to be less suspicious [because of Perls' reputation], so if they are suspicious here, I can imagine what it must be like elsewhere."

Collectors' suspicions should not be confined just to the question of whether a work is an outright fake—created and sold with the intent to deceive. While this is the most dramatic and disturbing form of misrepresentation, there are many others—some deliberate, some innocent—that potential buyers should be wary of. "Real fakes are a tiny minority of what we see," according to John Walsh, Jr., of the Boston Museum of Fine Arts. "Mostly we see genuine old paintings that have some relation to the work of the master but were not painted by that master."

Misattributions can occur in many different ways. A work from an old master's studio (sometimes an exact copy of a work by the master) may be wrongly attributed to the master himself; a copy made by an artist with no intent to deceive (such as those done by students trying to learn from the masters) may somehow find its way onto the market as an original; a work by a minor artist may be wrongly attributed to an artist of greater repute. This type of misattribution may be an innocent error, particularly if the actual creator of the work was a follower of the better-known artist, or it may be a deliberate fraud on the part of the seller, who may go so far as to remove the original signature and replace it with a more salable one.

Sometimes the masters themselves have deliberately contributed to the confusion. In her catalogue essay for "Fakes and Forgeries," an exhibition mounted in 1973 at the Minneapolis Institute of Arts, the museum's researcher Kathryn Johnson noted that while the Flemish painter Rubens "made no attempt to deceive the buyer," he did write the following about a duplicate painting, produced in his workshop, "As this reproduction is not yet quite completed, I am going to retouch it throughout myself. So it can pass for an original if necessary." About other copies he wrote, "I have retouched them to such effect that they can hardly be distinguished from the originals. . . . They are perfect miracles at the price." Johnson also noted that certain artists—including the ancient Greek painter Apelles and sculptor Phidias, the French Rococo painter Boucher and the French landscape painter Corot—signed the works created by their favorite or most talented students. Corot's generosity, Johnson wrote, also extended to "followers, admirers, and especially, destitute young artists upon whom he took pity." His works, which were very popular, were also widely faked after his death, giving rise to the art-world adage that "Corot painted 1,000 pictures, of which 1,500 are in the United States."

In media that involve the creation of multiples—prints, photographs, sculptural casts—questions may arise concerning the extent of the artist's involvement in the final product. Although the artist may have created the original image for the print, the negative for the photograph or the model for the sculpture, the extent to which he is responsible for the actual piece that you buy may vary (more on this later). Editions of prints, photographs or sculpture may even be produced without the artist's knowledge—in some cases, posthumously. The confusion is further compounded by the fact that there is no art-world agreement as to how much of the artist's involvement is required before something can be deemed an "original" work of art. Definitions may vary from artist to artist and from work to work. Add to this the problems of reproductions (copies that are not produced directly from the artist's original lithographic plate, negative, model, etc.) and edition size (sometimes difficult to determine), and you can begin to appreciate the difficulties in knowing just what you are really getting when you purchase a print, photograph or sculpture.

A collector should try to find out the truth about a work's authorship and the degree of the artist's involvement (and how this involvement compares with the artist's usual working habits) if he is to avoid being conned or overcharged. By buying from established, reputable sources, you can minimize the risk of authenticity problems which, according to dealer Eugene Thaw, "usually arise if you buy from unusual sources or off the mainstream." As noted, dealers who are financially secure and have reputations for integrity stand more to lose by cheating you (in terms of the effect on their reputations if they are found out) than they stand to gain. But there are so many gray areas in the characterization of art works—so many opportunities for innocent mistakes or shadings of the truth—that collectors should take upon themselves at least some of the responsibility for investigating the facts.

Fakes and Forgeries: There are two obvious ways to guard against buying fakes in any collecting area. One is to know what the fakes generally look like, and the other is to know what the authentic works should look like. Part of a collector's education is to study photographs or actual examples of known fakes and learn both how the forger attempts to deceive us and how he gives himself away. One of the most effective but most painful ways of learning this lesson is to buy a work or works which you later discover to be inauthentic. A less costly way is to learn from the mistakes of others—by examining the fakes tucked away in museum storerooms and by studying the literature on fakes. At the 1980 art-market conference sponsored by *ARTnews,* Samuel Sachs II, director of the Minneapolis Institute of Arts, gave some instructive examples of the forger's art, drawn from his museum's "Fakes and Forgeries" show. (The illustrated catalogue from the show, which includes an extensive bibliography, is still available from the museum.) The examples fall into several categories—authentically old objects that were later reworked to enhance their value; exact copies of authentic works; modern inventions done in the style of older works. Among the examples:

• An authentic Corinthian terra-cotta vase and cover, Greek, ca. seventh century B.C., with a painted decoration of animals and stylized flowers that was added in modern times to enhance its value. "The original decor was blanched off or the vase was, more likely, unadorned," said Sachs. According to the Minneapolis show's catalogue, "the careless interior detailing and a close observation of the paint used proved the painted decor to be a recent modification." The vase was in the collection of the Cleveland Museum of Art.

• An authentic Egyptian basalt head of a man, ca. 350 B.C., on which the facial features had been obliterated but were recarved some time between 1956 (when it was offered at a Cairo gallery) and 1966 (when it was offered at a European gallery). "The head that grew a face," as it was described by the chairman of the Brooklyn Museum's Egyptian and Classical art department, Bernard Bothmer, was acquired as a forgery for study purposes by the Brooklyn Museum.

• A highly deceptive copy of a still life by the seventeenth-century Spanish artist Francisco de Zurbarán, painted in the nineteenth century on authentically old canvas. X-ray examination showed that the false Zurbarán was painted over a picture of a Spanish saint. It was originally thought that the fake, in the collection of the St. Louis Art Museum, might have been a second version of the painting done by Zurbarán himself. But scientific analysis revealed that the paint was not of the right period and (according to the Minneapolis catalogue) "the material found in the cracks of the painting was not the accumulation of centuries of dirt and aged varnish, but rather graphite of the type found in black paint, thinned." Although the painting fooled the experts for years, the Minneapolis catalogue now asserts that the original, which is in the Norton Simon Museum, Pasadena, Calif., "is basically a religious painting and, as such, is filled with a curious Spanish mysticism. The forgery is little more than a still life."

• A copy of Fragonard's *Portrait of a Young Lady,* the original of which had been consigned for sale to a dealer by its owner. When the dealer failed to sell it, the owner asked for it back. But, according to Sachs, she discovered after she received it that "she didn't like it as well as she had remembered." She also noticed that it had acquired a strange odor—the smell of recently applied paint. Further investigation revealed that the dealer had substituted a copy for the owner's original and had sold the original (which the owner subsequently recovered) to another dealer. The copy, according to Sachs, "has a visible coarseness that the original does not possess."

• A copy of Dürer's engraving *St. Jerome in His Study* that is "mind-bogglingly accurately done and would confuse all but the most expert of print connoisseurs," according to Sachs. To distinguish between the copy and the original, one must focus on the little toenail of the lion's left paw: it is shaded in the copy, but white in the original.

• A portrait of a man painted in the nineteenth century in the style of German artist Barthel Bruyn that is actually a pastiche of elements

Left: **Jean Honoré Fragonard,** *Portrait of a Young Lady*
Right: **Copy After Fragonard**

lifted from several other paintings: the face was derived from a portrait by Memling, the hand from another Memling, and the hat from an authentic Bruyn. The pastiche, from the collection of the Doerner-Institut, Munich, was done on panel (consistent with the period) but with modern pigments. "The pastiche is one of the cleverest of frauds," according to the Minneapolis catalogue, "because it takes select parts of genuine pictures and combines them in an inventive manner. It thus avoids the risk of detection that a line-for-line copy does, as there is no 'original' with which it can be compared. Only after laborious searching do the parts which the pasticheur used turn up."

• The Tiara of Siataphernes, bought in 1896 by the Louvre in Paris and, according to Sachs, considered then to be "one of the greatest objects of Scythian gold ever discovered." Purportedly made in the third century B.C., the elaborate tiara was defended by the Louvre against all doubters until the real creator, a Russian silversmith, identified himself and claimed that he had produced it as an exercise, with no fraudulent intent. "Today," Sachs maintains, ' people would not be deceived. The tiara freezes in time what people in the nineteenth century thought Scythian culture looked like. A fake is unchanged by time. The only thing that changes is our vision of it."

The last example above illustrates one of the cardinal rules of fake detection. Most fakes hold up for, at most, a generation, because they embody the tastes and prejudices of the times in which they were produced. If you can free your eyes of modern prejudices and preconceptions, you can go a long way towards unmasking modern forgeries of older works. "A modern forgery looks and feels wrong in some way that is not easily defined," according to John Walsh, Jr. "In the first instance, there may be something about the human content that's fishy, that looks vaguely dated, like a Vermeer with a 1930s look. Fakes tend to be a kind of interpretation, a playing to things that appeal to·the audience of that moment. A fake produced by an earlier generation appears as dated as the written opinion from that period about an artist."

A case in point is the work of the renowned Dutch forger Han van Meegeren, who, with painstaking care, produced works purportedly by the great seventeenth-century Dutch artist Vermeer. Vermeer's known oeuvre is very small and little is known about his life. Van Meegeren carefully studied Vermeer's technique, used old pigments and canvas (from which all previous paint was carefully removed), developed a process to harden the pigments to a degree consistent with the paintings' purported age, and produced the requisite cracks in the painted surface by rolling and baking the finished canvas. He passed off his handiwork during World War II—a time when it was difficult for art experts to cross national borders to study authenticated Vermeers, many of which were hidden away for safekeeping. Van Meegeren was finally found out after the war, when it was discovered that he had sold a "Vermeer" to Nazi official Hermann Goering. Charged with collaborating with the Germans, he confessed to his forgeries and spent the few remaining months of his life in prison.

The Minneapolis exhibition included several van Meegerens (one "Vermeer" and two paintings in the style of Vermeer's contemporary, Gerard Ter Borch). The show's organizers observed that van Meegeren was "unable in the final analysis to shed his own twentieth-century origins, and his subjects have faces and expressions curiously of our times and not of the 1600s. His 'Vermeers' are too coarse and lack the necessary lady-like qualities; his 'Ter Borchs' [are] too timid and not filled with a prepossessing self-confidence."

This short list of actual ploys used by forgers gives some indication of what you may be up against and what you should look out for. But while it is easy, with hindsight, to deprecate those who were taken in by the works that we now can see are obviously fraudulent, it is not so easy to be the first to unmask a skillful forgery. As Sachs and many others have observed, "The best forgeries are those that haven't been discovered yet."

More important than learning the styles and techniques of the con artists is, of course, learning the styles and techniques of the true artists. An expert knows almost instinctively whether a work looks "right"—whether the treatment of the subject matter and the handling of materials are consistent with the work's purported authorship. "If a painter is a genius and no sense of his greatness is communicated by a certain picture, I wouldn't buy it under any circumstances," said New York old-masters dealer Stanley Moss. Dealer Stephen Hahn, well known for his ability to detect fakes in his field, attributes his success to having "a fine memory for details. . . . An expert should know the artist's style, his taste, the way he composed, the way he used colors. The most important thing is to know his facture—the 'handwriting' of the artist [i.e., the way he applies the paint, his brushstrokes]. Some artists' facture can differ from one day to another."

Collectors should also take an interest in the artist's more literal "handwriting"—his characteristic way of signing a work. As part of his study of seventeenth-century Dutch painters, collector Edward Carter has made a point of learning what their signatures ought to look like and he says that he now can tell whether the signatures are original or were added later. Some artists almost never signed their work, and knowing this is also a necessary part of a collector's education. French eighteenth-century paintings, for example, are rarely signed. The twentieth-century Russian-born artist Soutine signed only about 10 percent of his work, but practically all Soutines have mysteriously acquired signatures, according to dealer Klaus Perls. "If you find an unsigned Soutine, you can be almost sure it's real." On the other hand, according to a dealer who requested anonymity, paintings by another twentieth-century master, Léger, *should* be signed, not only on the front but especially on the back.

To gain an intimate knowledge of a particular artist's oeuvre, a collector should not only see as many works as possible but also read about them. A much-used tool of authenticity research is the catalogue raisonné—the detailed, illustrated listing (usually prepared by an art historian, museum professional or dealer) of all known works by a particular artist. A series of small but useful catalogues in Italian has been issued by the Milan publishers Rizzoli Editore under the names "Biblioteca d'Arte Rizzoli" and "Classici dell' Arte Rizzoli." Books in the former series are titled *Tutta la Pittura di* [*artist's name*]; books in the latter series are titled *L'Opera Completa di* [*artist's name*]. The "Classici" series is also available in French translation as the "Les Classiques de l'Art" series, published by Flammarion, Paris. The French books are titled *Tout l'Oeuvre Peint de* [*artist's name*]. Many artists, of course, have not been the subject of such systematic research and not all catalogues raisonnés are equally reliable. But the catalogue raisonné, when it exists, is a logical starting point for someone interested in determining whether a particular work is considered to be an authentic part of an artist's oeuvre. The absence of the work from the catalogue, or discrepancies between the work being considered for purchase and the published descriptions and illustrations, should at least signal a need for caution and further investigation.

"You have to use these books with sophistication," says dealer Richard Feigen. "A painting can be a copy of a work reproduced in the catalogue raisonné, but not the same work. You have to try to match the provenance in the catalogue with that of the work being offered." He noted that works purportedly by certain artists—such as Braque and Gauguin, for example—are almost certainly inauthentic if they cannot be found in the very complete catalogues raisonnés for those artists. But authenticating Modigliani is "a more difficult matter, because there is not a complete book on him." Dealer Klaus Perls (a leading expert on Modigliani) noted that although collectors often feel reassured to see their prospective purchases reproduced in a book, such documentation is no proof of a work's authenticity. "Some books are published to reproduce forged things," he observed. More often, though, the mistakes are innocent. An expert, working in good faith, may publish as authentic a work that subsequent research reveals to be misattributed. One well-known, widely used catalogue raisonné by a highly regarded art historian is said to have a number of fakes in it because the mental faculties of its elderly author had greatly deteriorated by the time the book was written.

Like catalogues raisonnés, records of a work's provenance and exhibition history are useful, but not foolproof, tools in authenticity research. "Provenance is a very important consideration to me," said collector Edward Carter. "I don't always fail to buy a painting just because it doesn't have a recorded provenance. . . . But if it has had a strong ownership record throughout most of its life, you know it has stood the test of experts. It gives you more confidence in the authenticity of the painting." It is an art-world adage, however, that all fakes have impressive provenances. It is a relatively easy matter to invent a fine-sounding history for an art work and to forge the necessary documentation. One watercolor purportedly by Paul Signac that came to the attention of the International Foundation for Art Research, for example, sported two splendid labels on its back, one indicating that it had been sold by a well-known New York gallery and the other indicating that it had been exhibited at an American museum. Both labels, IFAR discovered, were fraudulent.

It is depressingly clear that while there are various ways to explore the question of authenticity—through stylistic analysis, book research and examination of the work's purported provenance and exhibition history—none of these tests is foolproof. The expert con artist can fool not only unsuspecting buyers but even suspicious ones. In light of this, you may sometimes want to call in an expert of your own—an art historian with an exhaustive knowledge of the field in which you are interested, or a conservator who can, in some instances, examine art scientifically to determine its true age and possible authorship. Even dealers and auction-house specialists, who are more knowledgeable in their fields than many collectors, frequently consult outside experts to get a second opinion on works they are unsure about. When old-masters dealer Stanley Moss, for example, was given the chance to sell a portrait from a famous Italian collection (that of the late Count Alessandro Contini-Bonacossi) that Moss thought was by Piero della Francesca, he first sought the opinion of British art historian Kenneth Clark (who had published a book on Piero that had not included the Contini-Bonacossi painting). The Italian authorities, who impose severe restrictions on exports of art works, would never have let a Piero out of the country, according to Moss. "The fact that it was a Piero was denied by all the experts and the Italians let it go through as not a Piero." But when Kenneth Clark saw the newly cleaned painting, he exclaimed, "That's a Piero. Congratulations!" and Moss sold it to the Louvre in Paris for $2 million in 1978.

Scientific Analysis: Whereas art historians can confirm a work's authenticity from stylistic evidence, conservators take a more scientific approach. They examine the materials comprising the art work to see whether their age is consistent with the purported age of the object, and they may also try to determine whether the technique used in applying the materials is consistent with the usual working methods of the purported creator. Such analysis is particularly useful in resolving doubts about old-master paintings and antiquities. "A painting should not be on machine-woven canvas if it was supposed to have been done in the 16th century, it should not be on oak panel if it is supposed to be Italian and it should not be on cypress if it is supposed to be Dutch," observed C. Hugh Hildesley of Sotheby Parke Bernet, New York, at the 1979 seminar on art law sponsored by the Practising Law Institute. With a detailed knowledge of the history of pigments, the skilled conservator will be able to determine whether the pigments used in an "old master" are consistent with its purported age or are, instead, of relatively recent manufacture. He will also be able to tell whether the crackle pattern (the network of fine cracks in the paint surface) is consistent with the pattern that would be expected on such a painting. Some forgers produce artificial crackle patterns by rolling and baking their handiwork (in the manner of Han van Meegeren) and some less sophisticated practitioners paint a "crackle pattern" right onto the surface of a work.

Conservators also may use X-rays or ultraviolet light to reveal changed signatures or new painting on old canvas. Lawrence Majewski, cochairman of the Conservation Center of New York University's Institute of Fine Arts and a special consultant to the Metropolitan Museum of Art, once examined under ultraviolet a painting, purportedly a David, that was about to be purchased by a museum; he found that the original signature had been scraped off and "David" had been painted in its place. He also performed an X-ray examination of an "old" Spanish still life that a museum was considering for purchase and found that the original painting on the authentically old canvas was a portrait; the still life had been painted over it in more recent times. (Examination of the still life under a microscope revealed that there was no crackle pattern in the paint.) A process called autoradiography, whereby paintings treated by neutron radiation become slightly radioactive, can reveal whether the techniques used in a particular painting are consistent with the techniques used in works that are known to be by a particular artist, provided that a substantial body of that artist's work has already been subjected to autoradiography and the patterns analyzed. John Walsh, Jr., of the Boston Museum of Fine Arts noted that such analysis of Rembrandt's paintings has helped to create "a very sharp shrinkage" in the number of works generally accepted as his. "The warm sympathetic humanity that has long been taken to give form to much of Rembrandt's art is something we're now inclined to take less seriously than we take the need for a certain technical consistency in what he painted," Walsh observed. "The sentimental stuff, painted broadly and thickly, that seemed to have the blessing of Rembrandt's great spirit upon it now looks more like the work of Rembrandt's admirers in the nineteenth century, when spirit was paramount."

In the case of antiquities, certain tests can be performed on certain types of materials to determine their true age. Bronzes can be tested to see if their composition is consistent with that of bronzes known to be from a particular period. (The presence of zinc in a Chinese bronze, for example, indicates that it is a late piece.) The patina on a bronze can be tested chemically to see whether it is truly the result of long-term corrosion or whether it has been recently applied. Clay objects such as ceramics and terra-cottas can be dated according to the light they give off when subjected to a heating process called thermoluminescence. Works in marble can be viewed under ultraviolet light, and the way they fluoresce is sometimes helpful in determining whether they are authentic. (For example, Cycladic sculpture—ancient Greek art from the Cyclades islands in the Aegean Sea, including small marble figurines that look strikingly modern—should appear yellow-brown under ultraviolet; a blue-violet color indicates recent manufacture or substantial recent reworking.) The wear and encrustations on stone objects can be examined to determine if they are authentically old. Gold, however, is risky territory: there is no scientific test for age and "you have to be very careful," according to collector Norbert Schimmel. A strong believer in connoisseurship, Schimmel maintains that "all the machinery" that has been devised to test antiquities does not replace the expert's eye.

Antiquities and Primitive Art: According to Schimmel, the key to distinguishing a fake from an authentic piece is remembering that the ancient artisans made most objects to be used, not just to be admired. "You must see if the objects are functional," Schimmel said. A handle, for example, should be designed to be grasped comfortably. Similarly, collector Paul Singer noted that early Chinese culture did not produce "art for art's sake." Everything, he said, was made to be used—even tomb material, which was made for use by the dead in the afterlife. Singer and Schimmel also both noted that a purportedly ancient object should not be considered fake merely because it does not resemble other known objects of the period. In fact, according to Singer, if something looks outrageously different from familiar objects, it is much more likely to be genuine than fake. A forger tries to copy genuine pieces to produce something salable. He will rarely produce something that is very unusual. Singer noted, for example, that many people initially regarded with extreme suspicion any Chinese bronzes that did not have a green patina; such patination was considered a necessary consequence of centuries-long burial. Singer began collecting unpatinated bronzes early, and subsequent excavation of tombs in southern China unearthed many more such objects. (The lack of patination, he said, was due to the fact that objects in the southern tombs were surrounded by clay that was not permeable by water.) Similarly, Schimmel recently acquired a small stone bird with a lizard seal carved underneath, the likes of which he and others he consulted had never seen before. (The European collector who had given it to him in exchange for another piece thought it was from Anatolia.) Schimmel said he would continue to try to find out more about the piece, but he was not put off by its uniqueness. "It has to be genuine," he said, fondling it contemplatively. "It's a beautiful piece."

Dealer André Emmerich (who sells ancient and Pre-Columbian as well as contemporary art) applies what he calls "the true believer's test" to antiquities and primitive art that he examines for authenticity. "I look at a work and ask, 'Was it made by someone who was a true believer in the culture that the object represents?' The forger does not believe that he is creating something of great spiritual meaning. If an object is a human or animal representation, you ask, 'Does the subject portrayed look stupid?' If it does, it's highly suspicious; powerful spirits do not look stupid. There is a certain degree of tension and conviction that is carried by things made by true believers. This is a very subjective yardstick, but it is something to use before deciding whether a piece is even worth examining further."

Similarly, the most valuable and sought-after African art, according to collector-dealer Ben Heller, is that which was "produced by a tribal group for its own use, driven by its own strong cultural needs and generally before contact with the outside world." But there are many gradations between such pieces and outright fakes, he noted. Some objects were made not for tribal use but to be given to missionaries or other foreigners who wanted originals but actually got "replacement pieces"—copies made by tribal craftsmen to satisfy foreign demand. Such pieces may have sharp, clean edges, distinguishing them from pieces extensively handled and used by the tribe. Although used objects are considered the most valuable, "even objects with minimal use can be extraordinarily beautiful if they are from a great artist's hand," according to Heller. Further down on the scale of value, he said, are objects made considerably after the first contacts with foreigners (often in repetition of earlier styles). On the bottom rung is "airport art"— modern pieces for the tourist trade. Part of a collector's education is to study the differences among objects in these different categories.

The Fallibility of Experts: Experienced collectors and dealers agree that while consultation with scholarly or scientific experts is often desirable and sometimes essential, it is no substitute for developing one's own connoisseurship. Even experts make mistakes, and the intelligent collector should carefully weigh expert advice and then come to his own conclusions. As the body of knowledge about art and artists expands, the opinions of scholars regarding authenticity often undergo revision; different experts may have opposing views of the correct attribution of a given work. "There is a myth of scholarly authority and scientific evidence that lets amateurs kid themselves about what can be determined reliably and what can't," said John Walsh, Jr. "The amount of securely documented older art is surprisingly small. The amount of material whose attribution rests on opinion is high, and opinions are constantly being revised, occasionally with shocking results," such as the recent reattributions of works formerly thought to be by Rembrandt. "A great painting without a name attached to it will probably find a very good artist some day. A mediocre painting will probably not remain in the accepted work of a great artist." Even the world's greatest museums make mistaken attributions. In a front-page article on Jan. 19, 1973, the *New York Times* reported that the Metropolitan Museum of Art (where Walsh was then on the staff of the European-paintings department) had downgraded the attributions of some three hundred old masters in its collection, including works that had formerly been attributed to Rembrandt, Vermeer, Velázquez, Rubens, Goya, Dürer, van der Weyden, El Greco, Giorgione and Raphael. "What you read on a label in a museum hardly ever represents the latest state of scholarship," the *Times* quoted eminent art historian H. W. Janson as saying. "There is an inevitable time lag, in part not to offend donors, in part not to disillusion the public."

Sometimes "expert" opinion should be regarded with as much suspicion as the work itself; the key to profiting from advice is to know which advice is most likely to be reliable. Notably unreliable, in the view of today's experts, are certificates of authenticity provided decades ago by art historians to accompany dealers' offerings. "Certificates, most of the time, accompany sick pictures," according to art historian John Rewald. "A healthy person doesn't go to the doctor. A sick person goes to the doctor and gets a prescription." In addition, dealer Klaus Perls noted that "nothing is easier to forge than a certificate"; if someone has already gone to the trouble of forging a painting, it is a relatively simple matter to forge a document to go along with it.

When responsible experts differ about a work's attribution, the collector has to rely on his own instincts. Two respected art historians —the late Alfred Frankenstein, critic and former curator of American art at the Fine Arts Museums of San Francisco, and another museum curator who requested anonymity—were asked to examine two paintings purportedly by the American still-life painter William Harnett before they were to be offered by the auction firm of Phillips in the 1980 bankruptcy sale of the collection of Massachusetts art dealer Steven Straw (who had been accused by several dealers and investors of selling them interests in paintings that Straw did not actually own). Because of doubts that had been raised about the Harnetts' authenticity, the auction firm commissioned a report from the International Foundation for Art Research which, in turn, consulted the two art historians. Frankenstein, who had written a book on Harnett, pronounced the works genuine and backed up his opinion with a certificate of authenticity. The anonymous curator turned thumbs down, suggesting that the works might have been done by one of Harnett's German followers. Both paintings failed to find buyers at the auction.

Sometimes differences of opinion can result in unusual buying opportunities for the expert with the sharpest eye. One of the most celebrated recent cases was a purchase by London dealer David Carritt at Sotheby's much-publicized 1977 Mentmore auction in England of a painting attributed by the auction house to Carle van Loo. Carritt knew that the painting was, in fact, a documented Fragonard masterpiece, the whereabouts of which had been unknown since the eighteenth century. He bought the work, *Psyché,* for about $15,000 and sold it a year later to the National Gallery in London for a much larger (undisclosed) sum, thought to be about $1 million.

Even scientific opinion about an art work is not infallible. In a *New York Times* article ("Is Science Ahead of the Forger?" Aug. 19, 1979), reporter Bryan Rostron wrote that several leading art scientists, when asked if they could provide a new object with a false age that would deceive their colleagues, replied that they definitely could. It is possible, they said, to fool thermoluminescence and to apply a "perfect patina" to a bronze that scientists could not tell was recently produced. The experts from the scientific and stylistic camps sometimes come up with conflicting conclusions on authenticity. In the Summer 1978 issue of *ARTnews,* Sylvia Hochfield reported on the seemingly "insoluble controversy" surrounding the Egyptian art collection of the late M. A. Mansoor, a Cairo antiquities dealer. Most Egyptologists, according to Hochfield, are convinced that the collection, some of which was recently offered for sale at high prices, "consists almost entirely of forgeries." But the approximately fifteen scientists, "many of them extremely eminent," who have analyzed parts of the collection over the last thirty years "overwhelmingly believe the objects are genuine antiquities," she reported.

Jean Honoré Fragonard, *Psyché*

Multiple Originals: When it comes to "multiple originals"—prints, photographs, sculptural casts—a whole new set of questions arises about what one is really getting. Quality and price can vary greatly depending on the circumstances under which a particular work was produced, and a collector should attempt to learn the facts to make sure that he gets what he pays for. Entire books can be written on connoisseurship in each of these fields (see Bibliography); this general discussion outlines some of the main issues. In all three media, there is a question of the degree to which the artist was involved in the creation of the final product. The printmaker may have created the design for the print but may or may not have personally drawn it on the matrix (the block, plate, stone or stencil from which the design is printed). He may closely supervise the printing, or he may leave everything up to his publisher. The photographer may have taken the picture but he may have left the printing to others, whom he may or may not supervise closely. The sculptor may make a maquette (the preliminary model for the final work) but he may or may not be closely involved in translating his idea into bronze or another final form. The extreme case of noninvolvement is the edition made without the artist's knowledge or even after his death. If the matrix from which a print is made is not defaced or destroyed after the edition is pulled, subsequent editions (called "restrikes") may be made, with or without the artist's knowledge. Similar reissues can exist in photography and sculpture.

This is not to say that you should scorn all works produced with limited artist-involvement or even posthumously. The final test is the quality of the piece and how it ranks in relation to other works by the artist and his contemporaries. Some artists just don't care to get involved in the "manufacturing" end of their craft and entrust such details to printers, foundry workers and assistants whom they consider reliable. If you like their work, you must necessarily accept the way it was made. "Jasper Johns will do a silkscreen and work directly in the screen because that is the process by which he can both directly and completely express himself," noted Marian Goodman, director of Multiples Gallery in New York, speaking at a 1980 prints seminar at Artexpo, New York, an art fair. "But when Josef Albers did a silkscreen, he wasn't going to paint on the silkscreen, because his work was never about that. It was about a kind of mechanical perfection and the interaction of color. The process that an artist uses is a valid one if the way in which he uses the process is an extension of his attitude about his unique work." Similarly, Cornell Capa, executive director of the International Center of Photography in New York, noted that Henri Cartier-Bresson does not make his own prints, but is nevertheless considered one of the century's most important photographers. "A photographer doesn't need to make his own prints to establish his importance," Capa observed at the 1980 *ARTnews* art-market conference. On the other hand, Washington photography dealer Harry Lunn, Jr., noted at the same conference that "if you come across an Ansel Adams that was not printed by Adams, forget it"; his work in the darkroom is part of what makes an Adams an Adams.

Ideas about how closely an artist should be involved in the production of graphics have changed considerably since the Print Council of America issued its guidelines in 1967 on "What Is an Original Print?" (In fact, many people feel that the guidelines were already outdated when issued.) A prime requirement, according to the council's guidelines, is that "the artist alone has created the master image in or upon the plate, stone, wood block or other material, for the purpose of creating a print." The guidelines were meant to apply only to prints made after 1930; many earlier printmakers engaged specialists to transfer their designs to blocks, plates, etc. Dürer, for example, did not cut all his own wood blocks. Today, certain modern printmaking techniques—transfer lithography, offset lithography and silkscreen, for example—are often carried out by printers following the artists' designs and instructions, not by the artists themselves. The Print Council took a dim view of photomechanical processes, calling works produced by such means "reproductions," rather than originals. But some of the most prestigious galleries today carry photomechanically produced prints by some of the biggest contemporary names: Rauschenberg, Lichtenstein and Warhol, for example. "This is heresy, but if Toulouse-Lautrec were alive today, he would not make his posters the way he made them [as lithographs]. They would be made photomechanically," asserted Sylvan Cole, Jr., director of Associated American Artists, the New York print gallery.

Photomechanical "prints" can be traps for the unwary, however—when they are passed off as originals but are actually mere copies of works originally produced by other means (e.g., lithography). Such reproductions can often be unmasked under the magnifying glass, where you can see the small halftone dots that are like those seen in newspaper photos. But some print reproductions are less obvious and more difficult to detect, except by close comparison with the original. Some artists (the late Ben Shahn, for example) have been known to sign reproductions of their prints. Norman Rockwell, the American illustrator best known for his *Saturday Evening Post* covers, approved and signed lithographic and photomechanical reproductions of his paintings and drawings which were then (and still are) marketed as prints and sold in limited editions. (Rockwell never personally made any of the prints, but they nevertheless have enjoyed a strong market among his fans.)

Reproductions of sculptural works have often been made from the originals and sold for high prices to the unwary. In 1974, the College Art Association (an organization of art historians and other art professionals) issued a "Statement on Standards for Sculptural Reproductions" which, among other things, branded as "counterfeit" any bronze copy made from a finished bronze—the copy is called a "surmoulage" —except those made under the artist's direct supervision. (A surmoulage is usually slightly smaller than the original and lacks some of its definition, making detection possible on close comparison.) Also counterfeit, in CAA's view, are "all unauthorized enlargements and all transfers into new materials, unless specifically condoned by the artist." The Art Dealers Association of America promptly endorsed CAA's statement, asserting that "the unauthorized reproduction of artists' sculptural work has become a plague to the serious art world." But as long as a work is in the public domain (i.e., not subject to copyright restrictions), the owner has the legal right to make copies—which may eventually find their way onto the market as originals.

In the field of photography, skillful reproductions can also be made and passed off as originals. But photography dealers say that, so far, fakes and reproductions have not been a significant problem in their field, perhaps because, despite a dramatic rise in recent years, photography prices (and the potential profits from fraud) are still relatively low compared to prices in other areas. It is possible to photograph a photograph in such a way that the copy would look deceptively like the original, but differences in contrasts and nuances could, in most cases, be detected on close comparison.

While fraudulent copies of originals are clearly undesirable purchases, the situation is more ambiguous in the case of prints, sculpture or photographs made posthumously from the artist's own plates, models or negatives. There is, for example, a healthy market for Rembrandt restrikes, which cost only a fraction of what the originals fetch. They were made from Rembrandt's original plates which, because they were worn from use, were reworked by later printers. In addition, many collectors and museums knowingly buy posthumously cast sculpture. Certain sculptural works—by Degas, Daumier and Boccioni, for example—are mainly known through posthumous castings because the artists themselves did not make casts from their models. Some modern sculptors' widows—the wife of the late Alexander Archipenko, for example—have supervised the production and sale of significant numbers of posthumous castings. Posthumous editions of photographs have also been sold with the authorization of the photographers' estates.

The size of an edition is also a factor to consider in buying prints, sculpture or photographs. The general rule is that greater rarity brings a higher price. But like almost all art-world rules, this one has many notable exceptions: One of the highest-priced twentieth-century photographs on the market is Ansel Adams' *Moonrise, Hernandez, New Mexico* (1941). There are said to be more than eight hundred prints of this image, making it one of the least rare of all photographs. The quality of the prints varies greatly. Some are luminous, some relatively dark. But the image is so popular that, for a while, it set a new auction record for a twentieth-century photograph at almost every sale. (Finally, in May 1980, collectors' ardor for Adams began to cool, and

Ansel Adams, *Moonrise, Hernandez, New Mexico, 1941*

prices began to fall to what the experts termed "more realistic" levels.)
Marc Rosen, print specialist at Sotheby Parke Bernet, New York, noted
that "rarity cuts two ways. If something is very rare, some people may
be passionately interested in it, but rarity also reduces the breadth of
the potential market. Prices for Toulouse-Lautrec posters are high, not
because of rarity, but because of familiarity, which has encouraged
greater appreciation. Repeated seeing can make things more desirable.
Paradoxically, you often see higher prices for the things that are most
common. People think that the size of an edition determines the price
of prints. But what's most important is how good the thing is in the first
place. Prints at their best are in that medium for aesthetic rather than
convenient reasons. If a lithograph is made to look like a crayon drawing, why should it be a lithograph?"

Determining the true size of an edition is sometimes no easy matter.
It is simple enough to read the numbers penciled onto the border of
the print: "1/20" ostensibly means that a print was the first impression
in an edition of twenty; "20/20" denotes the last. But some editions
may never have been completed (so that there are actually fewer copies

than the stated size of the edition), some editions may be unlimited (with no numbers on the prints), and some works may be issued in several different editions (usually on different types of paper). Chagall, for example, sometimes did one edition numbered with arabic numerals and another of the same image with roman numerals. It does not necessarily matter whether a work was the first or last produced in an edition; the sequence is important only if there is a falling off in quality from the first to the last. The first few impressions of drypoints, for example, are the most sought after because they are fresher, richer and show signs of "burr"—the raised area of metal along the edge of the line that was cut into the plate by the artist with a hard needle. The burr holds some ink and produces a soft, velvety effect on the first few impressions, but it is quickly worn down during the printing process. The numbering sequence on most contemporary prints, however, matters very little. In fact, the numbering is often done haphazardly and bears no relation to the order in which the prints were actually pulled. In photography, "vintage photographs"—those printed very soon after the negative was made—are often the most valuable since they are considered "a truer rendition of the artist's intention," according to collector Samuel Wagstaff. But Richard Pare, director of photographic acquisitions for the large corporate collection of Seagrams Distillers Co., noted that some artists learned to print better as they got older and may value a later printing more highly than the first ones. (Both Wagstaff and Pare spoke at the 1980 seminar on photography collecting sponsored jointly by the Association of International Photography Art Dealers and Images Gallery.)

The collector who is aware of all these subtleties and how they may affect value will try to pin down the seller to an exact, detailed description of what is being offered. Only then can the collector determine that he is being charged the right price for the right object. The collector should then try to verify some of the purported facts independently— through book research or through comparison of the print, photograph or sculpture with other works from the same edition that can be found in museums and galleries. The following are some of the key questions to consider in evaluating a print, photograph or sculptural cast:

• Where was it made (i.e., at what sculpture foundry or print workshop)?

• When did the artist first create the work? When was this particular print pulled (or photograph printed, or sculpture cast)? How does the quality of this piece compare with those produced later (or earlier)?

- By what process was this made (for prints—etching, lithography, photo offset, etc.; for photographs—platinum print, silver print, etc.; for sculpture—lost-wax casting, surmoulage, etc.)? What kinds of materials (e.g., type of paper) were used?

- To what extent was the artist involved in the printing (or the casting)? How closely did he participate or supervise? Is this his usual method of operation?

- What is the size of the edition (or how many other copies are there)?

- Is there more than one edition and, if so, how large are the others and how do they compare in quality and price? Were any additional works (i.e., "artist's proofs") made outside of the regular editions, and if so, how many are there?

- Is is possible that other copies may be made in the future? (Lithographic plates are often defaced, after an edition is pulled, to prevent this; photographic negatives are sometimes destroyed.)

- If the piece is not signed, are there any other copies in this or other editions that *are* signed? How do they compare in quality and price? (Signing of prints was not widely practiced until the late nineteenth century.)

Not every question will be applicable to every piece, and not every applicable question must necessarily be put to the seller; some facts you may be able to determine for yourself. The inability of the seller to answer some of these questions should not necessarily prevent you from buying. But the more you learn about a potential purchase (and the more you learn about the seller's professionalism and knowledge by the way he handles your questions), the better equipped you will be to make an intelligent decision.

It is wise to get in writing, on the bill of sale, as much of the above information as you can. This way, you will have a better chance of pressing your claim (through the courts, if necessary) if you later discover that you have been misled (more on this in Chapter 7). Certain contemporary print workshops—Gemini G.E.L. in Los Angeles and Tyler Workshop in Bedford Village, N.Y., for example—routinely supply detailed written documentation for their prints; purchasers should request copies of such documentation from the sellers of contemporary prints. Six states—California, Illinois, Maryland, Hawaii, Oregon and New York—have "print disclosure statutes" that require sellers to supply certain key facts about the prints they sell. Provisions differ from state to state, but each law requires disclosure of at least some of the following: name of artist, year printed, size of edition, workshop where printed, information about whether the plate has been destroyed, whether the print is from a posthumous edition, whether it is a restrike and whether the plate was reworked. In those states, you have a legal right to receive such information (and the seller has a legal right to disclaim knowledge of these facts if he himself does not have them). New York also has a law making it a misdemeanor for sellers to use the word "signed" to describe prints that are only signed in the plate. (In such prints, the signature is merely printed on the paper, rather than personally signed in pencil by the artist.)

What Kind of Condition Is It In?

The physical condition of a work of art affects its beauty, its durability and, consequently, its price. In 1978, the Metropolitan Museum of Art consigned to auction at Sotheby Parke Bernet, New York, a large, badly damaged painting by Benvenuto di Giovanni. According to Brenda Auslander, SPB's old-masters expert at that time, the painting (*The Assumption of the Virgin,* 1498) might have sold for as much as $500,000 if it had been in perfect condition. But looking much the worse for a badly bungled "restoration" attempted some twenty or thirty years before, the painting was knocked down to a New York dealer for only $67,500. Similarly, SPB's print specialist, Marc Rosen, noted that a fine impression of the fourth state (each time the artist makes alterations in the plate, another version, or "state," is created) of Rembrandt's *The Three Crosses* that was offered at auction in 1980 would probably have sold for $300,000, if it were not for one important defect: around 1800, someone took it upon himself to cut down the size of the print on each side. "Quite a bit was lost from the top," according to Rosen. This and other defects were noted in the sale catalogue and the print actually fetched $44,000.

Unfortunately, not all damage to art works is as easy to detect as it was in these two instances. Although auction houses often sell works in whatever condition they receive them, dealers and collectors sometimes have works restored to make damage less obvious. There is not necessarily anything sinister about these activities. Almost every painting over a hundred years old has had some touching-up by a restorer, and almost everyone in the art world, museum officials included, feels that a certain amount of restoration is desirable (to allow a viewer to experience a "whole" work without being distracted by areas of damage) and even necessary (to preserve the physical integrity of the work

How one painting was restored
(*Deborah Hall* by William Williams):
Top left: Before restoration
Top right: During restoration, after lining,
cleaning and filling lacunae
with gesso before retouching
Left: After restoration

and prevent future deterioration). What *is* frowned upon is "restoration" that violates the artist's intention or that may do physical damage to the work (as occurred with the Metropolitan Museum's consignment to SPB). There is still great controversy, however, as to what specific conservation practices are acceptable (more on this in Chapter 8).

Before buying a work of art, every collector should ask the seller what kind of condition the work is in and to what extent it has been restored. By looking closely and asking questions, you will eventually develop some expertise of your own and be able to detect certain types of restoration. But the field of conservation is so complex (and sometimes, so deceptive) that even the most experienced of collectors—Norton Simon, Paul Mellon and Edward Carter among them—occasionally consult outside experts.

"Condition is important, but it is not an absolute," according to Stanley Moss, the old-masters dealer. If you stripped the pictures at the Metropolitan Museum of the paint applied by conservators, "you would be in for quite a surprise. A certain amount of wear and tear is considered normal in paintings that are four to five hundred years old. . . . You shouldn't be afraid to get a picture that's essentially there."

Detecting Restoration: How do you know how much is "there?" One way of detecting restoration in old masters is to examine closely the crackle pattern in the paint. "If you see cracks," said Moss, "bless their little hearts. That means the paint is original. Where they disappear [or where the pattern abruptly changes], you are looking at an area that has been filled in." Also sometimes visible to the informed eye are variations in the surface texture and tonality; these too may be signs of restoration. "The restorer will not use exactly the same materials and brushstrokes as the artist," noted conservator Lawrence Majewski. One small but valuable investment, according to Moss, is an inexpensive ultraviolet light (available from lighting or scientific supply companies, from about $30 up). If requested (and surprisingly few collectors *do* request), many dealers and auction-house specialists will bring out their own ultraviolet lights to aid your examination of their wares. When paintings are examined in a dark room under ultraviolet, areas of restoration usually show up clearly as dark spots. A white glow can also indicate restoration, according to Moss. "If a painting is restored with a paint that is a lead compound, you don't see the restoration but you see a whiteness that means the painting has been 'souped up.' It's a dishonest restoration," one meant to deceive potential purchasers. Similarly, dealer Richard Feigen noted that there are "ultraviolet-inhibiting varnishes" used by dishonest restorers to make detection of

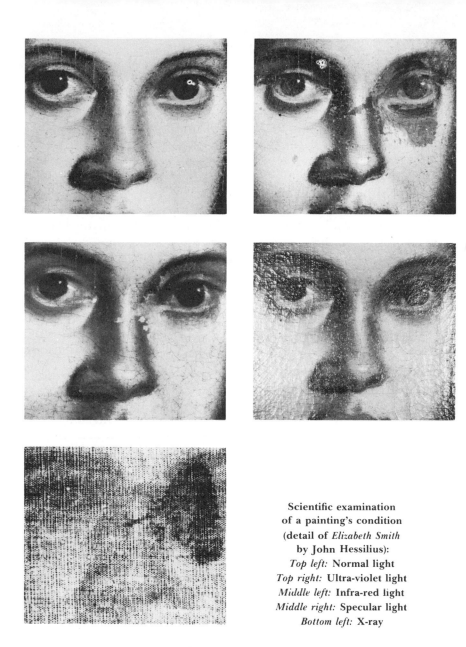

Scientific examination
of a painting's condition
(detail of *Elizabeth Smith*
by John Hessilius):
Top left: **Normal light**
Top right: **Ultra-violet light**
Middle left: **Infra-red light**
Middle right: **Specular light**
Bottom left: **X-ray**

restoration difficult. "I don't think a collector can tell condition if the restoration is subtle," Feigen said. "I find it difficult myself."

There are, of course, many other scientific tools available to aid detection of "subtle" restoration. At the *ARTnews* conference, Majewski gave a rundown of some of the most commonly used techniques: specular illumination—light that hits the painting at a slight angle—makes it easier to detect variations in surface texture; infrared photography reveals what lies beneath a dirty surface and penetrates thin layers of restoration; X rays show painting losses, repairs to sculpture, and the extent to which corrosion has penetrated ancient bronzes; close examination under a microscope can reveal even the most subtle changes.

Relining: Relining of paintings—affixing a fresh, new canvas to the back of a worn, fragile one to give it needed support—is also a subject of great concern to many collectors, because of its possible effects on condition and value. If the back of an old painting looks relatively fresh and clean, it has probably been relined. You can also detect relining by looking at the edge of the canvas on an unframed painting: you will see two layers of canvas if the painting has been relined. (On some paintings, you may have to scrape away some cloth or paper tape at the edge of the stretcher in order to see the two layers.) "Some collectors will buy only unrelined pictures," noted Christopher Burge of Christie's. "The European view was not to reline unless you had to because of damage or danger of paint loss. The American view was to do it as a matter of course if a painting was of a certain age." The danger of relining is that it may alter the way a painting looks. If the canvas is drawn too tightly or pressed down too strongly, it may alter or flatten the surface texture and cause the painting to lose some of its freshness; if a wax-resin lining (in which wax-resin is used to make the lining adhere to the original canvas) is used, it may darken the colors. "There is a great deal of bad lining done in the world," noted John Pope-Hennessy, consultative chairman of the Metropolitan Museum's department of European paintings. But he also observed that more difficult and dangerous than relining is providing a new support for an old-master painting that was originally on wood panel. "When a painting is transferred from panel to Masonite or canvas, there is almost always a significant loss," he noted. Such transfers cause a permanent change in the surface texture of the painting and should not be undertaken unless absolutely necessary, according to old-masters expert Brenda Auslander. Dealer Eugene Thaw observed that any picture that has not been relined and is in good condition is more pristine and desirable than one that has been relined. If a painting is on its original stretcher, with its original label, you know that it has been well taken care of and "hasn't been through the grinder," Thaw observed. He added, though, that almost all pictures eventually need relining.

Cleaning: Similarly, almost all pictures eventually need cleaning and, here again, there is great controversy over when and how this should be performed. Paul Mellon says that one of his main concerns about a potential purchase is when it was last cleaned and by whom. "Commercial restorers," he said, "have often damaged pictures by overcleaning or over-inpainting." So strong are his feelings on this subject that in 1978 he called a temporary halt to all cleaning of paintings at the National Gallery of Art, where he is chairman of the board, because "none of the trustees had been told they were going to start work on *The Mill,* one of the most important pictures in the world, let alone the National Gallery." The cleaning of *The Mill,* a highly popular painting traditionally attributed to Rembrandt (although some now question that attribution), removed the dark varnish that gave the work a gloomy atmosphere considered by many (including British painter J. M. W. Turner, whose friend had once owned the painting) to be one of its most endearing qualities. The ensuing controversy caused a reevaluation of the museum's conservation policies. Now, according to Mellon, the trustees are kept closely informed of everything to be done by the conservation department.

Many collectors and dealers are delighted to buy dirty pictures: "If it has not been cleaned or fiddled with lately, it may be an advantage," observed Mellon. A dirty painting may be cheaper to buy than a cleaned one, he noted, and the buyer is then free to have the necessary work done by someone in whom he has confidence. (It is possible, before buying, to get an idea of how a painting will look once it is cleaned by consulting a conservator or by wiping it carefully with white spirits, a liquid that temporarily brings out the underlying colors. Application of white spirits by an amateur is extremely risky, however. It can ruin paintings that have a certain type of varnish, no varnish, or a blistered, dry paint surface.) Overzealous cleaning may reduce the value of a painting by removing not only layers of dirt and varnish that the artist never put there but also the glazes and paint that he *did* apply. (Glazes are translucent materials that alter the tonality of the layers of paint beneath.) A "skinned" Impressionist painting (one in which the glazes have been cleaned away) is worth 30 to 40 percent less than a comparable pristine one, according to dealer Stephen Hahn. "If a picture is overcleaned," he said, "it looks thinly painted and you can see the preparation of the canvas [the "ground," usually white] coming through the sky. In an overcleaned Renoir, the transparent colors of the skin are gone."

In examining the condition of works on paper, it is wise to ask that they be removed from their frames so that you can look carefully for possible tears, folds, discoloration and repairs. Posters, in particular, are often in damaged condition; they were made on cheap paper and were not originally intended for long life.

Inherent Weaknesses: In addition to examining the current condition of a potential purchase, you may well want to investigate what its condition is likely to be years hence. Many art works have "inherent vice"—something about the materials or the way they were put together that makes it likely that the works will seriously deteriorate despite your most conscientious efforts at preservation. This should not necessarily prevent you from buying a work if you like it, but you should at least be aware of the dangers. If prints, photographs or watercolors are on acidic paper or are mounted with materials that are not acid-free, they will eventually discolor (like old newspapers). It was not until about the middle of this century that the harmful effects of acidity were recognized, and many nineteenth- and twentieth-century prints were made of, or mounted with, unstable materials. (Earlier prints—on handmade paper made from rag, rather than machine-made paper made from wood pulp—usually are acid-free.)

Modern techniques have also created potential condition problems for paintings and photographs. In many modern works, according to conservator Majewski, the artist used materials and combined them in ways that insure that they will fall apart. "If the artist is living," he said, "you should ask how he proceeded in making the work of art." Many contemporary paintings, he noted, were done on unprimed canvases that are very difficult to clean. Many color photographs are almost impossible to preserve. Their colors may seriously fade within about ten years, if exposed to any light. There are processes (e.g., dye transfer) for making color photographs that are thought to be essentially permanent in the dark, but they are more expensive and artists do not use them as widely as the other, less permanent processes. Experts differ on the question of whether color photography is a suitable field for collecting: at a photography seminar sponsored by *Art in America* magazine in 1975, dealer Harry Lunn, Jr., said, "I personally much prefer black-and-white. You can't sell something that is going to self-destruct."

Where Did It Come From?

As already mentioned, an art work's provenance—its history of ownership—may be an important aid to assessing its authenticity. It may also influence the selling price: some people will pay more for a distinguished provenance that seems to enhance the importance of a work. The simplest way to find out about the history of a piece is to ask; most sellers will happily tell you if a work has a desirable provenance. You may then want to ask what documentary evidence the seller has to support this history. Certain books (such as catalogues raisonnés) may publish the ownership record of certain works, and certain works may be accompanied by letters, bills of sale, labels or other documentary evidence of their past history. As previously mentioned, however, it is relatively simple to manufacture a wonderful provenance and provide the "documents" to back it up.

"The provenance of paintings is usually known by looking at the labels on the back," said old-masters dealer Stanley Moss. The labels may indicate which dealers have previously had the works in their inventories, which auction houses have sold them, which museums have exhibited them. (Further details may then be tracked down by contacting these dealers, auction houses and museums and by examining their catalogues.)

In the case of a relatively recent work, it is often possible to verify its early history by contacting the artist, the artist's heirs or the original dealer. Nineteenth-century French paintings, according to dealer Stephen Hahn, are "all recorded somewhere." He often verifies a work's authenticity by checking it against the records and photographs of the original seller in Paris (whose identity can often be learned from a label on the back of the painting). Even if the gallery is no longer in operation, its files may have been kept intact for reference purposes.

For a twentieth-century work, it should be possible to trace its history back to the artist or artist's estate. Dealer Sidney Janis says that "on every piece we get from an artist, we get an authenticated photograph [signed by the artist] that we keep in our files. We give the buyer a facsimile of the authenticated photograph. If you can't get that kind of documentation, I would hesitate to buy." In the case of a deceased artist, "the estate has records and the collector should insist on those records," according to Janis. If the dealer cannot supply satisfactory documentation, the collector can send a photograph directly to the administrators of the estate, asking them to authenticate it. The dealer can tell you how to contact the estate. However, there have also been cases where misinformation has emerged from artists' estates. Some top New York dealers, for example, are convinced that the widow of a famous modern master recently passed off some posthumous forgeries as genuine.

In many cases involving older art, the seller honestly does not know the complete history of a work, or, if he knows, he may not tell you.

"You should ask a dealer about a work's history, but don't ask him where he got it from," said Carl Crossman of Childs Gallery in Boston. He noted that dealers are often willing to tell you if they obtained a work from a private collection, but they are less eager to reveal that they bought it from another dealer or at auction. They may, in fact, resent a collector who tries to push them to reveal their sources. "It is the height of naïveté to ask a dealer where he got something," said dealer André Emmerich. "In some cases, he will be glad to tell you— if it is deaccessioned by a museum (aithough you may wonder, 'If it's so good, why did they sell it?') or if it has a wonderful history. But a dealer is not going to tell you, 'I got it from a retired diplomat who smuggled it out of Egypt in a diplomatic valise,' or 'I bought it at auction for much less than what I'm asking.' " Similarly, collector Paul Singer observed that "if a dealer can give you a desirable provenance, he will state it. But if he bought something at auction, he's hoping you haven't studied the auction catalogues so you know what he paid for it." He said that one dealer had offered him seven Chinese art objects from the David David-Weill Collection for $150,000, more than ten times what Singer knew the dealer had paid for them just a few years earlier at a 1972 auction at Sotheby Parke Bernet, London. (Singer declined to buy, but added that the dealer would probably be able to get his price, given the increased demand for such objects.)

Auction houses often do not tell where they get their wares, in deference to the many consignors who wish to remain anonymous. If the consignor agrees to be identified, the lot will be described in the catalogue as "the property of [name]." Often, if several items in a row are from the same owner, the identification will appear only over the first item; you are expected to assume that all subsequent lots come from the same source, until you come to a new designation (e.g., "property of various owners," or "property of another owner"). If the owner is not identified for a particular work, the provenance listed for it in the catalogue is incomplete; it does not include the name of the most recent owner who consigned it for sale. However, in such a case you may ask the auction-house specialist after you buy the work if he can tell you the name of the last owner. Sometimes the consignor will identify himself to the new buyer.

Export Restrictions: Some of the stickiest questions about a work's history come up in connection with antiquities and other works coming from those countries that place legal restrictions on the exports of works considered to be national treasures. If an object has been illegally removed from its country of origin, you will almost certainly not be told, and some dealers and collectors feel that this should not concern you. "The important thing," according to Emmerich, "is that a piece is authentic and legitimate and that its presence on the market here is not in contravention of American laws." In most cases, with the exception of certain Pre-Columbian objects, works can be legally imported into the United States even though they were exported contrary to the laws of their countries of origin. Works that were actually stolen from public or private collections *cannot* legally enter the United States, but some countries define "stolen" more broadly, to include all antiquities removed from their soil. (They consider these to be the property of the nation, even though they are not owned by any individual or institution.) The United States has a special arrangement with Mexico providing for the return of cultural property illegally exported from that country after February 1971, and a 1972 law prohibits import into the United States of Pre-Columbian monumental or architectural sculptures or murals that left their countries of origin illegally. A 1979 decision by the U.S. Court of Appeals in the case of *United States* vs. *McClain,* which involved Pre-Columbian artifacts, opened up the possibility that those who knowingly buy or sell objects that were illegally removed from their countries of origin may not only risk confiscation of those objects; they may also risk going to jail. (Those who were sentenced to jail in this case, however, were not collectors; they were people involved in a smuggling network.) The principles stated in that decision could technically apply to objects removed illegally from *any* country, and while preliminary enforcement efforts have focused on Mexican objects, many U.S. museum officials are concerned that Turkey, Peru, Egypt and other countries will lay claim to antiquities in public collections, based on assertions that the objects were removed contrary to those countries' laws, according to Ashton Hawkins, vice-president, secretary and counsel of the Metropolitan Museum of Art. While objects in private collections are less visible and therefore less likely to be targets of patrimony claims, it is still prudent for a collector of antiquities to ask sellers whether their offerings left the countries of origin legally. Particularly in the case of Mexican Pre-Columbian pieces, it is a good idea to ask whether the objects left Mexico before 1971.

More than forty-five countries are now party to an international agreement to return illegally removed objects to their countries of origin, but the United States is not, at this writing, among them. The agreement—the UNESCO Convention on the Means of Prohibiting and Preventing the Illicit Import, Export and Transfer of Ownership of Cultural Property—was promulgated by UNESCO in 1970 and ratified by the United States Senate in 1972. But efforts in Congress to enact the legislation needed to implement the convention have repeatedly bogged down in controversy between the proponents, who feel that action is needed to put a stop to the pillage of cultural monuments and archaeological sites, and the opponents, who maintain that the pillage will go on anyway (with the trade in antiquities shifting from the United States to other art-buying countries) and that the countries of origin themselves have not done enough to police their own treasures. In an article appearing in the October/November 1978 issue of *The Art Gallery* magazine, André Emmerich suggested that the art market has actually helped to save objects found at sites that are being rapidly destroyed due to advancing industrialization, construction and governmental neglect. "All we can do," he wrote, "is to encourage the preservation of those objects that miraculously survive the inevitable depredations of our advancing contemporary civilization. In the real world —as distinct from the utopia of which some academics dream—this is best done by endowing such objects with sufficient monetary value to ensure their preservation."

Collectors of antiquities—including Paul Singer and Norbert Schimmel—often express an ambivalence about these issues. "It is horrible what happened to the sculpture in caves" in China, Singer observed. "People knocked things from the wall and nobody gave a damn." But he noted that such objects were "shipped out with the country's permission. Then they were highly esteemed, cherished, studied and put in museums and collections where they were kept in perfect condition. It gave the world an idea of the greatness of Chinese art." (China has since adopted strict controls on the export of cultural objects; virtually nothing over a hundred years old is allowed out.) Singer also noted that since almost all Chinese antiquities were stolen from tombs, the background that a collector can receive about their origins is often sketchy or nonexistent. Some dealers will say that an object came from a certain place, when they really don't know, he said. One of the great tasks of scholarship, he added, is to try to determine the true sites of origin of antiquities.

Norbert Schimmel says that he now generally does not buy objects that were once attached to buildings. Gesturing towards paintings displayed in his Manhattan apartment that had been hacked out of an Egyptian tomb, he said he was now "ashamed I bought these." He added that he does not like to buy objects that left their countries of origin after the effective dates of laws banning their export, "but when

I see a nice object, I believe it left before. Sometimes I ask. In Europe, everybody buys and they don't ask any questions." Like Singer, Schimmel noted that even if you ask questions, you are unlikely to get illuminating answers. "Dealers never tell you exactly where something was found. They say, 'Anatolia,' and then they tell you all their stories. John Cooney [the Cleveland Museum's curator emeritus of ancient art] once said, 'Only buy the object; never buy the stories.' "

Antiquities are not the only types of art affected by export restrictions. A number of countries in Europe and elsewhere have laws restricting exports of other cultural properties regarded to be of national importance. Italy, as previously noted, has particularly strict and far-ranging export laws (which are routinely flouted by smugglers). Great Britain, a major art-market center (which, in 1978, sold far more art to the United States than to any other country) has what many consider to be one of the more enlightened art-export policies. If an object more than a hundred years old is considered of national importance by a special reviewing committee, its export can be temporarily embargoed to give a British public institution the chance to raise funds to match the export price. If such funds are not raised, an export license is granted.

Clearly, if a collector is contemplating an important purchase from a source in a foreign country, he must inform himself about that country's art-export laws. (A somewhat sketchy rundown on the statutes of more than a hundred countries is provided in *The Protection of Cultural Property: Handbook of National Legislations,* compiled by Bonnie Burnham and published in 1974 by the International Council of Museums.) The United States takes an extremely liberal attitude toward the import and export of art: art is generally allowed to enter the country free of customs duties, and the only law protecting national treasures concerns antiquities (i.e., Indian artifacts) found on U.S. government-owned land.

Once you are able to answer the questions about whether a work is really what it is represented to be, what its condition is and where it comes from, you will be better equipped to make an intelligent decision about whether to buy an object to which you felt a strong initial attraction. An unfavorable or inconclusive answer to one or more of the questions does not necessarily mean that you should walk away. But you should be able to say that you still like and want to own the piece after you have subjected it to this rigorous analysis. The more experienced you become, the easier and less time-consuming it will be for you to answer these questions to your own satisfaction.

Chapter 7

———◆———

THE GRAND GOOFS

Despite all your careful examination of an art work—your detailed questions, patient research, and thorough analysis—you will probably acquire at least one art object that you will later wish you had passed by. Almost every collector, whether a brilliant connoisseur or a Saturday-afternoon gallery-hopper, has at some time had the misfortune to see his "grand goût" result in some grand goofs. One of the grandest was the much-heralded purchase by the Cleveland Museum of Art—one of the richest and best-run art museums in the world—of a painting of St. Catherine of Alexandria which, according to the museum's original announcement, was thought to be by the sixteenth-century German master Matthias Grünewald. Three years after the 1974 purchase, the museum revealed that its staff had begun to suspect that the painting was a twentieth-century forgery, and their suspicions were confirmed by the research of the museum's chief conservator, Ross Merrill. The New York dealer (not identified by the museum) who sold the painting to Cleveland agreed to refund its full (undisclosed) purchase price, thought by some observers to be more than $1 million. The refund was to be made mostly in cash, but partly with a late fourteenth-century Italian altarpiece by Spinello Aretino. The Cleveland Museum's highly respected director, Sherman Lee, declared that the dealer had "acted in an honorable and courageous way in handling this matter and was as much taken in by the forgery as we were. He is a reputable art dealer with whom the museum has worked in the past and will continue to work in the future."

If a major museum and major dealer can make such a mistake, so can you; it's part of developing your eye and your collection. "Anybody who hasn't bought a fake," according to dealer-collector Ben Heller, "hasn't bought enough." But if you one day discover that a work of "fine art" is not quite as fine as you had imagined, you have many other options besides burning it or banishing it to the attic. One possibility is to keep it—it may not be a Rembrandt, but it's still beautiful to you. However, if your masterpiece manqué seems to be leering at you, there are many ways to unload it and still recoup at least part of your investment.

The simplest and most obvious approach is that of the Cleveland Museum—send it back where it came from. Many dealers, as previously noted, are willing to give exchanges or, sometimes, cash payments to customers who have merely tired of certain works. In the case of a work that is a proven fake, you should not hesitate to ask for a refund. A dealer-member of the Art Dealers Association of America, according to the group's brochure, "stands unreservedly behind every object he sells." Dealer Klaus Perls, a former president of the association, noted that "those of us who regularly buy and sell sometimes make mistakes. To protect yourself, you should buy from a source who you have reason to believe will be financially able to reimburse you if a mistake is made." Similarly, if you buy at auction, you will be better protected if you deal with the major houses that, at least to a limited degree, stand behind the goods they sell. Even if your purchase is not technically covered by the terms of an auction house's guarantee, you may, as previously discussed, sometimes get satisfaction if you present a persuasive case that shows you were seriously misled by the auction house's representations.

For obvious reasons, going back to the seller does not always work. The seller may refuse to acknowledge that he sold you a piece that was forged or misattributed. He may not want to admit and pay for his mistake, or he may honestly believe in the authenticity of what he sold. He may also maintain that you bought the item at your own risk and that you should have known that attributions of centuries-old objects are subject to revision based on new scholarly and scientific research. In some cases, the threat of a lawsuit may cause such sellers to make concessions. In others, you may have to back up your threat with legal action. Under the Uniform Commercial Code and other laws of various states, you may be able to sue successfully even if the seller made a written declaration that "all warranties, express or implied, are hereby excluded." The UCC says that "any description of the goods which is made part of the basis of the bargain creates an express warranty that the goods shall conform to the description. . . . It is not necessary to the creation of an express warranty that the seller use formal words such as 'warrant' or 'guarantee' or that he have a specific intention to make a warranty," according to the UCC. If you paid a Rembrandt price for a forgery, you may be able to argue successfully that the seller's attribution of the work to Rembrandt had formed "part of the basis of the bargain" and was, therefore (under the terms of the UCC), covered by an express warranty. In a case like this, the seller cannot rely on having made a general statement disclaiming all warranties; he has to specifically disclaim making any warranty with regard to *authenticity* to satisfy the requirements of the UCC. Under the code, the seller can be liable to you even if he had no intention of misleading you and honestly thought that his attribution was correct. The seller is *not* legally responsible, however, for mere expressions of opinion about his wares: you are unlikely to win a lawsuit in which you charge that a seller exaggerated a work's importance or aesthetic merit.

Sellers sometimes may argue (probably unsuccessfully, in a court of law) that even statements about the authorship of most works of art are mere expressions of opinion, since no one can be certain about the history of works executed long ago. To clear up such ambiguities about the application of the UCC to sales of fine art, two states—New York and Michigan—have enacted laws that specifically create an express warranty of authenticity out of any written description of authorship provided by an art merchant to a buyer who is not himself an art merchant. In a 1978 case under the New York law, an art collector, Joseph Dawson, successfully argued that a New York dealer, Gerald Malina, owed him a refund (with interest) on certain Chinese art objects purchased by Dawson in 1974. Dawson argued that refunds were due to him on five objects which, he said, were not from the periods ascribed to them by Malina; U.S. District Court Judge Dudley Bonsal ruled that only three of Malina's attributions were without "reasonable basis in fact at the time that those representations were made." No refund, he said, was due on the other two. This decision, according to some art-law experts, may have weakened the express-warranty protection under the New York law: it seems to absolve sellers from liability if advances in art scholarship yield unfavorable reattributions. New York has two other art-related laws that provide buyers with recourse against sellers of fraudulent art. The laws make it a criminal offense to alter any object so that it "appears to have an antiquity, rarity, source or authorship which it does not in fact possess," or to issue false certificates of authenticity for works of art.

Although you are unlikely to consider the possibility of future legal action when you decide to buy an art work, you should protect yourself by getting as much information as possible about the work *in writing* from the seller. Catalogue descriptions and notations on a bill of sale can be important evidence in court if a dispute arises. If you do decide to sue, how much should you sue for? In cases involving the purchase of a copy of an authentic work, or in cases where the seller did not have the right to convey to you the title in an authentic work (i.e., if the work was stolen from its previous owner, who then discovered its where-abouts and asserted his ownership rights), you may be able to convince a judge that you should receive not just the original purchase price (plus interest) but the present (and, possibly, greatly appreciated) mar-ket value of the genuine work. This argument was successfully pursued by the purchaser of an authentic Chagall painting that turned out to have been stolen from a Belgian couple by German invaders during World War II. In a 1969 court case, the purchaser, Albert List, was awarded $22,500 for a painting he had bought for only $4,000 in 1955 from dealer Klaus Perls. The Chagall was returned to its previous owner, Erna Menzel, and Perls was required by the court to pay List the full amount of the work's appreciated market value, even though Perls, who had bought the painting from a Paris dealer, had known nothing about its unusual history. (The judges felt that a person in Perls' position should have been able to determine whether he was getting good title. If a dealer cannot obtain "reasonably reliable infor-mation as to the status of title," according to the judges, he should himself refuse to buy the work or at least inform his clients of the uncertainty about title.)

In the case of a fake that is a mere fabrication in the style of a known artist (rather than a copy of an authentic work), it may not be possible to sue for the work's appreciated market value. The question of how much the work's market value would have appreciated if it had actually been by the artist is almost impossible to answer. "To ask this ques-tion," according to Franklin Feldman and Stephen Weil in their book, *Art Works: Law, Policy, Practice,* "is to conjure up a phantom art work." No one can know what a particular painting would have been worth had it been by Degas, because Degas never did (and never would) actually paint that picture. "To value a painting that has never existed," accord-ing to Feldman and Weil, "would seem an exercise so speculative that restitution [refund of the purchase price] would seem the proper rem-edy." Such was, in fact, the remedy sought in another court case in which the purchaser of a fake "Raoul Dufy," Arthur Weisz, sued Parke-Bernet Galleries (the New York auction house's name before it was acquired by Sotheby's of London), where he had bought the work in 1962 for $3,347.50. Parke-Bernet, relying on the disclaimer of warran-ties of authenticity that were published in its catalogue, denied having any legal responsibility. The auction house won the case on appeal.

If your case seems weak, or if you are daunted by the prospect of spending time in court, you may still be able to recoup at least part of your investment, even if the seller is unwilling to make a refund. Some museums, including the Fogg Art Museum in Cambridge, Mass., and the Minneapolis Institute of Arts, maintain study collections of fakes; if you donate an object to one of these collections, you can take a tax deduction for your charitable contribution. But the amount of the allowable deduction is equal only to the work's fair market value *as a fake,* not (as many collectors and even dealers mistakenly believe) the price that the collector paid when he believed that the work was genuine. Many museums, of course, do not accept donations of fakes, and those that do accept only objects that interest them for study purposes.

There is one other time-honored but dishonorable way to dispose of fakes: trying to pass them off as the real thing. If you try this and are found out, you will lose not only your investment in the objects but the esteem and trust of the professionals on whom you must continue to rely if you are to collect successfully. For this reason, collectors who try to sell fakes usually do so through the relatively impersonal process of auction rather than through consignment or sale to gallery owners with whom they must deal intimately. Good relations with an auction-house expert, while helpful, are not as essential to buying well as are good relations with a dealer who can decide whether or not he wants to sell you a desirable item. An auction-house expert may unmask a fake and refuse to sell it, he may merely have doubts about it and give it a qualified attribution (e.g., "style of . . . ," "school of . . .") or, in the rush of organizing a large sale, he may be as much taken in by the fake as the collector was. One collector interviewed for this book rationalized his disposal of fakes at auction by noting that other pieces he had consigned for sale had received qualified attributions from the auction-house experts, even though, in the collector's view, the pieces were perfectly genuine. "I've lost a great deal of money because of their [the auction-house experts'] lack of knowledge," he maintained. "They make many mistakes against the seller." The same collector said he had sometimes also sold his mistakes to dealers who spoke little or no English; transactions with such buyers are not complicated by discussions of attribution or authenticity.

Rather than make another buyer the victim of their own errors, some collectors donate their problem pieces to nonprofit institutions, but do not disclose their doubts about the works. They then take tax deductions for their "charitable contributions" equal to the supposed fair market value of the works at the time they were donated. According to William Speiller, associate professor at Rutgers University School of

Law, "a person who wishes to dispose of a work of questionable attribution would be more likely to donate the work than sell it." In an article about "The Favored Tax Treatment of Purchasers of Art" that appeared in the *Columbia Law Review* (March 1980), Speiller observed that "buyers would be more likely to check the authenticity of a work than [would] the beneficiary of a gift"; any doubts among potential buyers, he noted, would reduce the price at which a work could be sold. "Consequently," wrote Speiller, "the taxpayer who cannot prove the authenticity of a particular work may well profit more by donation than by sale." (More on the tax consequences of art donations in Chapter 9.) Donations of fakes that are not recognized as such by the donee may not financially victimize anyone (except the taxman), but they cloud and confuse the public's understanding of art. A fake that is studied or exhibited as genuine by a respected institution distorts art history and may impair the vision of future generations of collectors and connoisseurs.

Chapter 8

PROTECTING
YOUR TREASURES

Owning an art work makes you a custodian of culture and entails certain responsibilities. You have the obligation of trying to keep the work in no worse (and possibly in better) condition than it was in when you acquired it. You have the moral obligation of sharing your treasures, if asked, with a wider public through loans to museums and galleries (provided, of course, that you are satisfied with the measures taken to insure the safety of your possessions). You must take adequate precautions against fire and theft, and you may want to get an insurance policy that covers your collection against these and other perils. Your first responsibility, beginning the moment your new acquisition leaves the place where you bought it, is to provide it with the physical environment best suited to insure its good health and longevity. No one who has invested time, passion and money in the pursuit of fine art wants to see that investment diminished by any of the multifarious forms of deterioration or damage to which it may be subject. Yet many collectors, whether through ignorance, laziness or neglect, make it virtually certain that such harm will eventually occur. The papers, textiles, pigments, metals and other materials from which art is made are vulnerable to attack from heat, moisture, light, pollution and human carelessness, but much can and should be done to decrease these risks. It is far better (and less expensive) to keep works of art in good condition than to try to restore them once the damage is done.

Conditions for Display and Storage

The greatest protection you can provide for your works of art, according to conservation expert Lawrence Majewski, is to keep their environment constant. Ideally, the temperature should be 65° to 75° F and the relative humidity 50 to 65 percent ("preferably a constant 55 percent"). Speaking at the 1980 *ARTnews* conference, Majewski noted that "in the average New York apartment where there is no humidity control, the humidity reaches 10 percent in winter and 90 percent in summer. Almost no organic material [e.g., paper, canvas, wood, ivory, leather] can take that." Humidity can be measured with a hygrometer and controlled with humidifiers and dehumidifiers. Temperature control is accomplished by heating and air conditioning. Controlling temperature and humidity also means not hanging art against a building's outside walls (especially if those walls sometimes get cold or damp) or over radiators, heat vents or that most favored of all display areas—the fireplace. Majewski suggested that collectors who do not conscientiously control the temperature and humidity in all rooms containing art should at least maintain control in one room, where they can keep their most fragile objects.

Wide fluctuations of temperature and humidity may cause the various constituents of a painting—canvas, stretcher, priming, paint, varnish—to expand and contract at different rates, resulting in cracking, blistering and flaking. Excessive humidity can cause varnishes to turn an opaque white (called "bloom") and can cause the surfaces of works on paper to become dotted with brownish stains from mold growth (called "foxing"). Metals may rust or corrode when exposed to moisture and air pollution, and some iron sculpture and excavated bronzes should be kept at a humidity level below 30 percent, according to conservator Elisabeth Batchelor in her essay for the *Collector's Handbook* published by the Cincinnati Art Museum. "You can achieve this," she said, "by keeping the object in a case with silica gel to absorb excess moisture."

Two other environmental factors can be great art destroyers: light and pollution. The less you expose paintings and, especially, works on paper to light, the less risk there will be of discoloration and fading. Ultraviolet rays are the most harmful: you should not hang art in direct sunlight or under fluorescent light, which has a higher ultraviolet content than incandescent light. "If you choose individual picture lights," according to conservator Caroline Keck in her book *How to Take Care of Your Paintings,* "make sure the bulb will not be so close that the heat from it will tend to bake the surface of the painting. . . . Any form of attached light should be used only as needed; turn it on for given occasions and don't forget to turn it off." Works that are particularly fragile and vulnerable to light can be covered by textile curtains, to be opened only when someone wants to view them.

S. F. B. Morse, *Fitz-Greene Halleck:* **Showing bloom on the varnish**

Everyone knows that airborne dust and dirt can darken and partially obscure an art work; it is best to keep works away from air vents and other areas where exposure to soot and dirt is apt to be particularly great. But other invisible pollutants can also attack certain works in less obvious and more dangerous ways. Sulfur dioxide becomes sulfuric acid when absorbed by paper and causes discoloration, brittleness and, eventually, disintegration of the paper fibers, according to Francis Dolloff and Roy Perkinson in their booklet *How to Care for Works of Art on Paper.* The acid, they say, also reacts with and destroys certain pigments used in watercolors and oils, and it continues its harmful work even after the paper has been removed from contact with the gas. And severe brown stains caused by sulfuric acid are, they indicate, often seen on framed pictures that have been partly or entirely exposed to the air by lack of adequate backing.

Proper mounting and framing can do much to minimize environmental hazards, while improper practices can create hazards of their own. Works on paper should be matted and framed behind glass. The back of the mat protects the entire back of the picture (extending beyond its borders), while the front, which has a rectangular picture window cut out of its center, keeps the protective glass from touching the face of the art work (which might lead to mold growth or other damage to the surface). The two mat boards are usually hinged together along one edge with gummed cloth tape. Dolloff and Perkinson stress that all mats should be acid-free, and preferably of four-ply or eight-ply thickness (the latter for pastels, collages and very large works). All-rag matting board, sometimes referred to as "museum board," is "composed not of actual rags but of high-grade cellulose obtained from cotton fibers," according to Dolloff and Perkinson. It is totally acid-free. The use of acidic mats, or even mats with acid-free surfaces but acidic cores, will eventually cause staining of your art work. Dolloff and Perkinson note that aesthetic considerations are also important in choosing an appropriate mat: "A well-proportioned mat should reflect the dimensions of the picture, and its lower margin should be slightly greater than the upper." They advise further that "A space of at least 1/8 inch should be allowed around all sides of the image or plate mark," the mark caused by the pressure of the edges of a printing plate on paper. A good rule to follow, they add, is that

a picture should not have to compete for attention with its surroundings. This does not mean, however, that the basic colors in the picture should be repeated in the mat. The glowing brown tones of a bistre drawing, for example, lose their effect if surrounded with a mat of a tan or umber tone. A cool slate blue or olive gray provides a visual complement to the color of the drawing and enhances its appearance. Using complementary colors in this manner is often the key to presenting a picture with its full aesthetic effect.

As a general rule, the off-white color of the all-rag matting board is sufficient for etchings and engravings. Simple, colored mats look well on watercolors, and mats more elaborately decorated with color, ruled lines, and perhaps a narrow strip of gold paper ('French mats') are often effective on drawings. Bear in mind that the simplicity of a mat's appearance is the key to continued enjoyment of the picture.

There are several simple variations on the standard procedures for matting, to accommodate special circumstances or preferences.

Materials that should *never* be used to attach art works to their mats include Scotch tape or any other pressure-sensitive tape, gummed brown wrapping tape, rubber cement and synthetic glues.

Such materials discolor works on paper and are difficult to remove. Prints should never be attached overall to their mats with paste or glue. Prints that are mounted in this manner, described as "laid down," almost always suffer impairment of condition and value. Works on paper are best hinged to the backboard of their mats with high-quality gummed paper or Japanese mulberry-fiber paper. The best adhesive for the latter is starch paste, made with wheat or rice starch and water. The hinge itself is a narrow strip of Japanese paper, cut to whatever length is necessary to support the size and weight of the picture. It is folded in half along its length so that one half can be attached to the back of the art work at its upper margin, and the other half can be attached to the backboard of the mat. (There are several variations on the standard hinge, to accommodate special circumstances or preferences.) Two hinges are generally used (unless the work is very large) and the picture hangs freely, which "permits the paper to expand or contract without stress as the atmospheric conditions vary," according to Dolloff and Perkinson. There is some controversy over the best way to attach photographs to their mats. Some experts recommend Japanese paper hinges and starch paste; some recommend dry mounting (the use of a specially prepared dry-mounting tissue that becomes sticky when heated between the print and the mat); some prefer use of small triangular corner envelopes, into which the four corners of the photograph are inserted. The advantage of the last method is that no adhesive touches the photograph and it can be easily removed from its mat. Dry mounting, on the other hand, is difficult to reverse; the attachment of the photograph to a particular mat may be permanent.

Framing of all pictures (including those on canvas as well as those on paper) should include a strong cardboard backing to protect the reverse side from dirt and damage. Framers should never cut down a picture (or even cut the margins of a work on paper); this diminishes the work's value and distorts the artist's intention. Glass or acrylic plastic should always protect the surfaces of framed works on paper. Acrylic plastic (e.g., Plexiglas) is unbreakable and is available in a variety which filters out ultraviolet rays, but "it scratches easily and has a tendency to collect dust because of its static electricity, which also rules out its use on unfixed pastel or charcoal drawings or paintings with flaking or powdery pigments," according to Dolloff and Perkinson. Nonreflective (usually frosted) glass is not generally considered a good choice because it tends to obscure or distort a picture's appearance. (A new type of nonreflective glass, called "Denglas," works very well, but is quite expensive.) Paintings on canvas may also be protected by glass, but their surfaces are less fragile than those of works on paper and are often protected with varnish; most experts feel that the dangers of damage to the unshielded surfaces of most works on canvas are far outweighed by the disruptive effect that glass can have on the viewer's experience of the works' colors and textures.

The frame itself should be large enough to receive a painting and permit it to be keyed out (stretched tighter if the canvas has gone slack), according to Caroline Keck in her book *How to Take Care of Your Paintings.* "It should also be in sound condition; the painting should not be expected to hold the frame together. . . . Under all circumstances, a painting is framed correctly (from the physical standpoint) only when it is placed in a true plane, without warp, strain, or pressure, and firmly held." Keck recommends the use of screws and mending plates (metal straps with holes for the screws at each end) to attach the wood of the frame to the wood of the painting's stretcher. The customary practice of nailing paintings to their frames increases the likelihood of damage, because "it takes hammering to put nails in and wrenching to pull them out, and at best they are none too permanent under strain." Wooden frames are potentially damaging to works on paper, because resins from the wood can migrate and stain the paper. Proper matting lessens this danger; the use of aluminum frames eliminates it.

Just as a painting should be mounted in a sturdy frame, so should a sculpture be mounted on a sturdy base—heavy enough to make toppling unlikely. Cases can be used to protect particularly fragile objects. (More detailed information on climate control, lighting, mounting and framing is available in the books on conservation and those on collecting prints and photographs, listed in the Bibliography.)

One way of increasing the longevity of your art works is rotating them—putting only a portion of your collection on display at one time while the rest is stored under conditions that minimize exposure to light and dirt and fluctuations of temperature and humidity. Periodic changes of display have the added benefit of helping you to see your collection in a fresh perspective. "One of the great pleasures of collecting art works is to rearrange them, to have a new hanging," observed Richard Brown Baker. Similarly, in an interview for an article (Dec. 15, 1974) in the *Los Angeles Times' Home* magazine, Norton Simon said that he "shuffle[s] the paintings to different places because I'm always searching for a better relationship to the art. The more a painting is moved about, the more I discover in it, and the more I can share a particular artist's vision."

Art works that are not on display should be stored in an area that is cleaned and dusted regularly and kept at a relatively constant temperature and humidity. In her book, Caroline Keck recommends that paintings be stored on sliding screens constructed of metal or heavy mesh. As an alternative, she suggests construction of a series of wooden or metal slots in varying widths and heights into which you can slide paintings, which must be separated by rigid sheets of strong cardboard, Masonite, or Homosote.

Works on paper are best stored in Solander boxes (sturdy, hinged containers specifically made for storing unframed documents and works on paper) or metal storage drawers and cabinets. They should be stored unframed but matted, with a thin cover tissue of clear cellulose acetate or Mylar. (You may instead use an envelope of cellulose acetate or Mylar to enclose the entire print.) For long-term storage, a cover sheet of acid-free lining paper, Permalife paper or Japanese vegetable paper is preferred, according to Cecile Shapiro and Lauris Mason in their book, *Fine Prints: Collecting, Buying and Selling.* "Cellulose acetate," they say, "has the defect of attracting electricity and therefore dust, thus becoming more harmful than helpful." Pastel and charcoal can also be picked up by statically charged cellulose acetate, making it an unsuitable material for storage of works in those media. Such works should not be stored or displayed where they will be subjected to strong vibrations (such as from a door slamming shut), because the powdery pigments can be shaken off. Fixatives that are sometimes sprayed on pastels to prevent such losses can undesirably alter their appearance.

To prevent the growth of mold on stored works on paper, keep the relative humidity in the storage area below 65 percent. Small sachets or dishes of thymol (a fungicide in crystal form) can be used to kill mold that has already caused foxing (the brownish stains on paper): The affected art work is stored for two or three days in a closed container with thymol crystals that are vaporized by the heat from an incandescent light bulb of more than 40 watts. The fumes from the crystals penetrate the paper and attack the mold.

Do-It-Yourself Conservation

Despite your most conscientious efforts at proper display and storage, chances are that at least a few of the works in your collection will have condition defects that need attention. The science and art of treating these defects and of preventing new ones from occurring is what art professionals call "conservation." Defects may be present

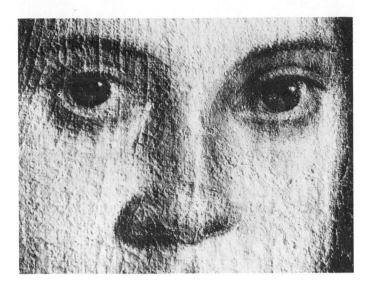

Raking light (detail of *Elizabeth Smith* by John Hessilius)

when you buy the work, they may occur suddenly due to accidents or mishandling, or they may develop slowly over many years of ownership. The only way to know when works need special attention is to become condition-conscious. While the experts disagree about how much, if anything, you should do yourself once you discover certain condition problems in your collection, everyone agrees that collectors should carefully monitor changes of condition and that corrective action should be taken whenever such changes threaten a work's physical integrity. You should carefully examine (and preferably note down in writing) a work's condition at the time of purchase, making periodic check-ups to assure yourself of its continuing health. Things to look out for when examining paintings include: *surface ripples and bulges* (which occur when a canvas is too loosely stretched or is being pushed out from behind by, for example, a knot of excess picture wire or an accumulation of debris in the space between the canvas and the bottom of the stretcher); *age cracks* (especially when the paint is curling along the cracks, the back of the canvas is puckering, or you can see the canvas through the cracks in the painted surface when you hold the painting up to the light); *flaking of paint* (which may sometimes occur if age cracks are left untreated). Your discovery of such defects will be aided by examining your paintings under "raking light"—a beam that is cast almost parallel to the surface of the painting and that consequently throws any irregularities into sharp relief. A gooseneck lamp or a folding Tensor light can easily be adjusted to the necessary angle. Problem areas can then be further examined under a magnifying glass. For works on paper, danger signals include *discoloration, fading* and *brittleness and disintegration of the paper.*

Another condition defect, less damaging to a work's physical integrity than those mentioned above but no less disruptive to the viewing experience, is dirt. You may be able to get some idea of how dirty a painting is if you remove it from its frame. There may be a small border that the frame has shielded from dirt, giving you some notion of what the true colors once were. Collectors who are disturbed by the muddiness of once-vibrant colors are often tempted to take matters into their own hands. They ambitiously attack their paintings with cleaning preparations and cotton swabs and, in their misguided zeal, often cause serious damage or ruin. Many experts strongly caution against collectors' undertaking any sort of do-it-yourself cleaning, although they usually make an exception for light dusting of the surfaces of paintings and sculpture with a soft-bristled (camel-hair or badger-hair) brush. (A frame can be vacuum cleaned, if care is taken not to disturb a painting's surface. Protective glass can be cleaned with a window cleaner, but this should be sprayed on the wiping cloth, never on the glass itself.) Majewski advocates superficial dusting but flatly asserts that collectors should "never use water or solvent in cleaning." Keck, recognizing that some impetuous collectors will be moved to clean their own paintings no matter what the experts say, provides (in *How to Take Care of Your Paintings*) some detailed instructions on how best to go about it. Noting that the success of various methods depends on many variables ("the kind of medium used by the artist and its current condition; the nature and state of the varnish, if any; the chemical or physical deterioration of the structure"), she makes no guarantees and issues a firm warning: "Clean your paintings at your own risk." Particularly dangerous territory for the novice is the painting that is badly cracked or unvarnished. When you scrub off the dirt, the paint may come with it.

For those who are aware of but undaunted by the risks of do-it-yourself cleaning, Keck recommends use of

a mixture of equal parts of rectified spirits of turpentine and petroleum naphtha or use [of] one of the white cream furniture polishes that consist of a wax emulsion in water. (Make certain the cream polish you buy is for use on furniture only and *not* to remove tough stains from porcelain.) . . . You may also use a noncaustic soapless detergent powder, many of which are on the market. These should be mixed with water in a proportion of 100 to 1, that is, a 1 percent solution. . . . If you have employed the wax-emulsion type of cleaner, after the job is done and the excess wiped dry, the slight film of wax left on the surface of the painting can be polished with a clean silk cloth or with a clean soft brush of the kind used to shine shoes. Do this very gently, making sure the supports are still behind the canvas to protect it from the strain of the brushing pressure. When either the naphtha-turpentine mixture or a detergent solution in water has been used, the cleaned surface is often dull in appearance and will need an addition of varnish to make it look pleasing again.

Before the cleaning is begun, the canvas should be supported from behind with flat, regular blocks of plywood or built-up cardboards, and the cleaning solution should be applied with cotton swabs that are squeezed almost dry. The first application should be on an unimportant area along the edge of the painting, and you should stop immediately if something goes wrong. Clean small areas at a time, changing the cotton swabs frequently and using dry swabs to wipe off all the dirt and cleaning solution immediately after an area is cleaned. Cleaning works on paper is a still trickier matter because of the fragility of the surface and the absence of protective varnish. Keck says that "minor smudges of dirt can be removed with soft gum erasers—be careful if these are over pencil or color. Serious dirt should always be cleaned away by a professional."

Less risky or dramatic than cleaning the front of a painting is cleaning its back. For this, Keck recommends that

> if your painting shows no rip, if it isn't separated from its stretcher, if the paint isn't curling off or the canvas dried out to paper brittleness, you may clean the reverse with the soft brush attachment of your vacuum cleaner. Should you have any doubts, *don't* do it! But if it seems perfectly safe, go ahead and remove the dirt before it gets smeared about the front surface. Pass the little round brush back and forth lightly across the exposed part of the reverse. You will be able to mark the extent of your progress by the change in the appearance of the canvas threads as they get cleaned.

You can also clean out the dust and debris that may have accumulated between the canvas and the lower edge of the stretcher by turning the painting upside down with its back facing you, slanting the edge now on top towards you, and tapping that edge. A flat spatula can be used to ease out any remaining objects or dirt. Keck also gives instructions on removing and replacing frames (paintings should be removed from their frames for all cleaning tasks), removing bloom from varnish, revarnishing, removing dents and bulges from a canvas, and "keying out" a painting (to stretch the canvas more tightly, removing surface ripples). Collectors planning to undertake cleaning or any other do-it-yourself tasks should carefully assess the condition of their art works and study Keck's detailed directions before daring to proceed.

Consulting Professional Conservators

Most serious collectors feel it is best to consult professionals about condition problems, especially if those problems involve works that are valuable or fragile. If a work exhibits one or more of the changes that can threaten its physical integrity (curling or flaking paint, puckering canvas, disintegrating paper, etc.), a visit to a professional conservator is probably in order. But some experts maintain that collectors and conservators are frequently overzealous about restoration and can conserve an art work to death. "I feel that the less that's done to any work of art, the better," said John Walsh, Jr., of the Boston Museum of Fine Arts, "as long as the thing is reasonably sound and not deteriorating and as long as it bears some reasonable resemblance to what we can imagine the artist's original intention was." Similarly, Marc Rosen, the print specialist at Sotheby Parke Bernet, New York, said that he regards conservation as "an occasionally necessary evil. . . . So many things are cleaned and overcleaned. Collectors seem to have 'foxing on the brain.' It is true that you must make sure your prints are not falling apart, but in so many instances a print that is a few hundred years old, with a teeny brown spot, will be sent to be laundered and ironed and made to look like a piece of stationery. This does violence to a piece of history: it will not look the way it did. There are only a few people who are specialists in the field, who will know what the coloration of a Rembrandt should be and will say that you shouldn't have this done."

Finding the right person for the job is crucial because, as Walsh observed, "there are a lot of quacks around and the damage they do is irreparable. . . . It is a field where the hazards are very numerous and the number of qualified people is small relative to the mass." He added that collectors should "choose conservators by the work they've done. You should see it and have someone you trust look at it. You should not fall for personalities. You should be inclined to go on the recommendation of a qualified professional who has constant dealings with conservators and restorers, such as a curator who has a sophisticated understanding of the field." Collector Paul Mellon stressed the importance of picking a conservator who has a firm background in art history, as well as in the scientific and practical aspects of conservation. "There have been many occasions," he said, "where a conservator with a thorough scientific training may not have had enough understanding or appreciation of art history or may not have known the work of the artist whose pictures he was cleaning. This may have led him to put a slant on a picture that was different from what the artist intended."

The best starting point for advice on picking a good conservator is, once again, your local museum. A staff member from the conservation department or the appropriate curatorial department will usually give you a list of three recommended conservators and tell you to shop around, according to Majewski. The names of several top paintings conservators were mentioned repeatedly by those interviewed for this book: Gertrude Blumel, Marco Grassi, Gabrielle Kopelman and Mario Modestini, all in New York. Keck provides a list of thirty-two recommended conservators in the appendix of *A Handbook on the Care of Paintings* and Shapiro and Mason provide a list of twelve in *Fine Prints: Collecting, Buying and Selling.* You may also write to the American Institute for Conservation of Historic and Artistic Works, a national professional association of conservators (see Appendix) for its directory, which lists its members, fellows and honorary fellows. Membership in AIC is no guarantee of professional competence, but fellows must have five years of practical experience beyond their period of training and must pledge to abide by AIC's standards for professional conduct. An application for membership must be endorsed by five AIC fellows. Applicants' knowledge, skill and experience are reviewed by the group's membership committee. Honorary fellows are persons recognized by AIC for outstanding contributions to the field. Also available from AIC is a list of "certified paper conservators."

You may yourself attempt to assess a conservator's qualifications and experience by asking how long he has practiced, whether he has had substantial experience treating art works similar to your own, who some of his past clients have been (including museums), and what kind of training he has received. There are, at this writing, only three degree-granting programs for conservation in the United States: the Cooperstown (N.Y.) Graduate Program (run by Caroline Keck and her husband, Sheldon), operated jointly by the State University College at Oneonta and the New York State Historical Association; the Winterthur Program in Conservation, operated jointly by the Winterthur (Del.) Museum and the University of Delaware; and the program of the Conservation Center of New York University's Institute of Fine Arts, New York City. In addition, the Center for Conservation and Technical Studies of Harvard University's Fogg Art Museum runs a highly respected internship program for conservators. (Another training program, run by Oberlin College, Ohio, was recently phased out.)

Many top conservators feel that a practical apprenticeship under a master conservator is more important than all the scientific and theoretical training an institutional program can provide. In an interview for Sylvia Hochfield's *ARTnews* article, "Conservation: The Need Is Urgent" (February 1976), Jean Volkmer, chief conservator at the Museum of Modern Art in New York, stressed that experience is the best teacher, and described several unusual conservation techniques she had developed, based on her intimate knowledge of modern paintings. She "is a firm believer in the value of on-the-job training; she thinks the chemistry can be assimilated in the course of practical work." Volkmer got much of her on-the-job training in an apprenticeship with the Kecks before they founded the Cooperstown program.

The professional standards set by AIC provide useful guidance on how to assess a conservator's practices. According to AIC, conservators should compile detailed records and reports on their progress and findings, and should provide copies of these to the owners of the works: an *examination report* should document any alterations or deterioration that the conservator finds in the work; a *proposal for treatment* should outline what the conservator intends to do to correct these conditions (and the owner may be asked to agree in writing to the proposed treatment before it is begun); a *report of treatment* should detail the exact materials and methods used by the conservator to correct defects and to provide new protection. It should be accompanied by photographs showing: condition before treatment; condition after the work has been "stripped down" (cleaned of dirt, discolored varnish and paint applied in previous restorations); condition after treatment. Additional photographs may also be taken to provide more information about the work's structure and the conservator's methods of treatment. AIC stipulates that a contract between the conservator and the owner should spell out the requirements for reports and photographs, and should set forth the exact work to be done and its estimated cost. The conservator should also estimate how long the treatment will take.

The most difficult but, perhaps, most crucial part of your assessment of a conservator is evaluating the appropriateness of his proposed treatment. "We spend a lot of time with our restorers, making judgments about how far to go, what should be left alone, and what to work on," said dealer Eugene Thaw. "There are a lot of questions about just cleaning a picture and about whether to touch it at all. People are fools if they just say to a restorer, 'Here's my picture.' " The problem is that few collectors know enough about conservation to make an informed judgment about different methods of treatment, and even the experts often disagree about what should or should not be done. There are strong differences of opinion, for example, about methods of relining, inpainting (filling in cracks and losses with new paint), and the extent to which art works should be cleaned. (A group of art lovers once picketed the Metropolitan Museum over the last issue, asserting that many of the museum's old masters had been insensitively scrubbed. But discussions with the museum's then new conservator, John Brealey, left the group more optimistic about the future course of conservation at the Met.) The conservation of contemporary paintings presents new and, to some extent, unresolved problems because many are unvarnished and some were done on unprimed canvases, making them very difficult to clean. The artists wanted these paintings to have a mat, unshiny look, but any damage to or soiling of their surfaces is very difficult to repair without destroying the desired effect of an even, undisrupted surface texture. If the artist is alive, he can sometimes be prevailed upon to solve the problem by repainting an entire picture for the owner. The late Ad Reinhardt, for example, once repainted for the Museum of Modern Art one of the works from his black period (paintings with very soft, mat surfaces that look all-black at first sight but, on closer examination, are seen to consist of squares of several very dark colors). "I said to him, 'What am I going to do when you're gone?' " recalled Volkmer of MOMA. "But he felt that this reflected our times. Everything has built-in obsolescence." Caroline Keck recommended that "unless paintings finished mat are kept behind glass or in dirt-controlled atmospheres, it is wise to compromise on their appearance and protect the surface with a thin, quick-drying dull varnish." But she conceded that the question of whether or not to varnish remains a subject of great controversy.

Certain principles, however, are widely agreed upon by most professional conservators (although they are sometimes ignored by less skilled or less scrupulous practitioners). The "principle of reversibility," as set forth by AIC, stipulates that conservators should not do anything to art works that cannot later be undone. Needs for future conservation or wishes of future owners may make it desirable to return a work to its unrestored state or to employ different methods of treatment, and this cannot be done if a conservator uses materials or techniques that are "so intractable that their future removal could endanger the physical safety of the object," in the words of AIC's Code of Ethics. The conservators' association also stipulates that its members should have a "firm previous understanding" with the client (and with the artist, if living) about the nature and degree of restoration to be performed on a given work, and that such restoration cannot ethically be carried "to the point of modifying the known character of the original." What this means to most responsible conservators is that while they can legitimately fill in areas that have been lost from an art work, they cannot obscure or "improve" in any way the work of the original artist. There is great controversy, however, over the question of just how the losses from art works should be filled in. At one extreme are the purists who feel that losses should be painted white or with a flat tone that harmonizes with the surrounding tones; this makes clear to the viewer which areas are the original work of the artist and which are not. At the other extreme are those who feel that where there are no firm clues about what the artist intended for a lost area, the conservator is free to invent something that seems appropriate. In choosing a conservator, you may well want to ask whether he uses materials and methods that are reversible, whether he ever sees fit to paint over an artist's original work, where he stands on the question of how best to fill in losses, and, specifically, how he proposes to treat losses from your art work.

Also a subject of controversy is when and how to reline a painting. "No one method of lining is best. It depends on the problems of a particular painting," said Majewski. He noted that a wax-resin lining (in which wax resin is used as the adhesive) helps to reattach badly flaking paint, but may darken the colors and change their relationship to each other. A wax-resin lining is often ironed onto the back of the old canvas, which can cause a flattening of the painting's surface. To prevent this, a device called a "vacuum hot table" may be used instead of lining irons, particularly for paintings that have marked impasto or brushwork. A glue-paste lining is sometimes used when the conservator or owner doesn't want to risk any changes in a painting's tonality, but this type of lining contains moisture that may cause further condition problems in the future. A white-lead lining may expand and contract so much that the surface of the painting is ruined; Keck strongly advises against this type of lining and further notes that white-lead adhesive is so strong that it is almost impossible to remove without causing damage. In choosing a conservator, you may want to ask whether he thinks your painting should be relined, what method of relining he proposes to use and why. If you have any misgivings about his answers to your various questions, seek a second opinion, just as you would for serious questions about your own health. According to AIC's standards, your consultation with another conservator "should not be regarded [by the first conservator] as evidence of want of confidence and should be welcomed."

Lending Art

The risks to an art work's condition are greatly multiplied when it is sent out on loan, and many formerly generous owners have sharply curtailed their art's travels because of past damage. "We lend art to museums, and nine times out of ten it comes back damaged," said Arnold Glimcher of Pace Gallery at the 1979 New Museum panel discussion of contemporary art dealers. Many artists, he said, no longer wish to make loans. Similarly, collector Ralph Colin said that he no longer makes frequent loans because of the damage sustained by his works. "One Dubuffet I lent came back completely wrecked," he said. "I won't lend to anyone in Italy and I will only lend to the most responsible museums and dealers, not to museums in small towns." At the 1979 New Museum panel of contemporary art collectors, Barbara Schwartz observed that "it's very risky to lend. We've had a lot of damage to paintings." But Richard Brown Baker said that while he is not enthusiastic about lending, he feels a responsibility to lesser-known artists to make available good examples of their work for retrospectives or other shows, "to increase their visibility."

Whether motivated by altruism, vanity or greed (museum exhibitions of privately owned works may enhance a collector's reputation and boost the market value of his collection), many collectors accede to loan requests and some actively encourage them. Loans can also benefit you by providing your collection with some helpful attention from a museum's conservators and researchers. As a custodian of culture, you should be willing to share your treasures with others, but only if you can assure yourself that all due care will be taken to minimize the risks. The first step is to make a thorough assessment of the condition of prospective loans: fragile works should not be subjected to the strains of packing, shipping and public display unless a conservator can first restore them to travelworthiness. If you judge a work to be fit for travel, your careful assessment of its condition, documented in writing and backed up with photographs (with copies sent to the borrower), will help you, the borrower and the insurance company to verify the nature and extent of any damage that occurs during the loan period. You may want to ask the borrower to prepare a written "condition report" on your loans as soon as they arrive at the borrowing institution and again just before they leave.

Once you have determined that your art objects are fit for travel, consider whether the prospective borrower is capable of caring for them properly, particularly if you are dealing with a small institution of uncertain reputation. Ask about building construction (especially fire resistance), security, fire protection, climate control, lighting and availability of experienced art handlers. Some museums prepare formal "facility reports" to respond to such queries. The borrower should sign a written agreement specifying the duration of the loan, the nature and amount of the insurance coverage and the borrower's obligation to exercise the same care for your works as for works in its own collection. As a lender, you have a right to control the circumstances of the loan, and you should ask for the provisions in a museum's loan agreement to be changed if they don't suit you. New provisions may also be added. You may, for example, want the right to withdraw your works from the borrowing institution at any time—a provision that is not likely to appear in any standard museum loan agreement.

The borrower should pay for packing and shipping, but the manner in which works are packed and shipped is generally up to the lender. The borrower may make suggestions and recommendations about packing and shipping, and you are free to ask for advice. You may do the packing yourself or employ a commercial packer (preferably one with fine arts experience). Art works are generally shipped in specially constructed solid wooden crates. Keck recommends wrapping a work in tightly sealed glassine, surrounded by a cardboard carton and further cushioned by crepe-paper-filled padding (such as Kimpak), aircap plastic sheeting, plastic or rubber sponges, thick sections of hemp (such as undercarpeting) or webbed sisal, or blocks of polystyrene foam that have been cut to fit the exact shape of the object. One commonly used cushioning material, excelsior, is "by far the worst," according to Keck, because it can scratch surfaces and "is both a fire-hazard and a retainer of moisture." In her book *Safeguarding Your Collection in Travel,* Keck observes that "when you have finished packing an object inside a crate, you should be able to jar the crate and observe no evidence (or sound!) of movement. . . . Whatever is loosely packed is not safely packed." The outer wooden crate, according to Keck, should be lined with strong waterproof paper that is stapled in place (with the staples covered by masking tape, to prevent their coming loose and damaging the art work). The top of the crate should be attached with screws, rather than nails, to minimize risk to the art work and to make it easy for the borrower to open the crate and to reuse it in returning the work. (You should conspicuously label the side that should be opened.) Canvases should never be rolled unless absolutely necessary, since this may cause cracking and chipping. If a painting is so large that it must be rolled for shipment, it should be rolled with the painted side out, on a rigid drum of light wood or strong fiberboard, with a sheet of glassine paper protecting the surface. Commercial packers, if used, should be carefully supervised, particularly if they are not art specialists. Outside of New York City, according to John Buchanan, registrar of the Metropolitan Museum, it is difficult to find good commercial packers who have experience with art. Speaking at a 1976 workshop on art loans sponsored by the Smithsonian Institution, Buchanan said that commercial packers should be asked to "come to your premises, or, if they do it at the packing house [you should] go there and watch every step of the way."

Shipping can be by truck, railroad, airline or steamship line. Certain companies—Seven Santini Brothers (which has a fine arts division) and Hahn Brothers in New York, for example—specialize in packing and shipping fine art and can be expected to provide more expert handling than conventional shippers. When dealing with most carriers, your instructions on the crate (such as "Fragile" or "This Side Up") provide no guarantee that your treasures will not be subjected to the same rough treatment afforded all other cargo. If you are shipping a particularly valuable or fragile work, the only way to guarantee careful treatment is to travel with it yourself or insist that the borrower send a courier to accompany it (something that is likely to be done only for extremely important loans). Buchanan recalled that the presence of a courier some years ago in Jacksonville, where a shipment of paintings from the Met was being unloaded, saved the museum's cargo from being thrown out of the hold to the ground, about ten feet below. Despite the risks of mishandling, crates should never be labeled "Valuable Art Works"; this can only serve as an invitation to theft.

Insurance coverage for loss of or damage to art loans is almost always provided and paid for by the borrower. Such coverage should be wall-to-wall—protecting the work from the moment it leaves your premises until the moment it returns. The dollar amount of the coverage is arrived at jointly by the borrower and the lender and is specified in the loan agreement. The agreement usually requires the lender to state that, in the event of loss or damage, he will accept the amount paid by the insurance company as full compensation for his claim. (If you feel that the value of your object has increased during the time of your loan, you should contact the borrower to have the loan agreement amended; you will only receive the value set forth in the loan agreement in the event of a loss.) The lender has a great deal of influence in setting the valuation of his art for insurance purposes—an influence that museum officials complain is exercised unfairly by certain collectors who may try to use museum-sanctioned appraisals to establish high market values for their works. Several years ago, for example, the Met was asked to accept a lender's appraisal of nearly $1 million for an object by an artist whose prices at auction had never exceeded $250,000, according to Buchanan. Museum officials usually try to spot questionable appraisals and urge lenders to accept more realistic ones, but sometimes museums must accede to lenders' wishes in order to get desirable loans. If forced to accept an inflated appraisal, the museum may insist on reimbursing the borrower for his cost in insuring the loan under his own insurance policy rather than the museum's policy. This way, if a loss occurs and an insurance company is faced with an inflated claim, the museum's standing with its own insurance company is not impaired. Under some circumstances, a lender may prefer to have his loan covered under his own policy—if he thinks, for example, that his own coverage is better than that provided by the borrower. You may request the borrower to reimburse you for the cost of insuring the loan yourself, if you feel your coverage is superior. Huntington Block, a Washington, D.C., broker specializing in fine-arts insurance, observed that some lenders may prefer coverage under their own policies because, in the event of a claim, they can deal with their own regular insurance people.

Buying Insurance

In shopping for your own fine arts insurance, you should look for coverage that is "all risk" (insuring all losses except those that are specifically excluded in the policy) and, if you expect to lend works frequently, wall-to-wall. Usually excluded from coverage are losses due to wear and tear, gradual deterioration, moths, vermin, inherent defects, war, nuclear damage, and damage resulting from conservation work. Some exclusions are negotiable (although you may have to pay a higher premium to get them removed): breakage of fragile objects, damage by flood or earthquake, and mysterious disappearance (where an object is missing, but the reason for its disappearance is not known), for example. It is wise to get a "valued at" policy; under this type of coverage, the insurance company agrees to accept the appraisals that you have provided in advance and to pay you the full amount of those appraisals in the event of a total loss. Otherwise, if you suffer a theft, the insurance company may insist that the object was really worth less than the amount of the appraisal and may refuse to pay you the full amount (even though you have been paying insurance premiums based on the higher value). Some owners of very large collections have been able to get even more favorable treatment than "valued at" coverage: they pay premiums based on recent appraisals, but the insurance company agrees to pay their claims based upon full market value at the time of the loss, rather than at the time of the appraisal. Even if you have "valued at" coverage or coverage based on current market value, a dispute may still arise over how much the insurance company should pay you in the event of a partial loss (where the object is damaged but not destroyed). You should discuss in advance with your insurance company the method to be used to settle possible disputes: the usual practice is for the insured and the insurer to select one appraiser each; if those appraisers disagree, they jointly select an umpire to resolve the issue.

Many policies will automatically cover your new acquisitions, provided that you report them within a specified time (usually ninety days) and pay the added premium retroactive to the time of acquisition. Another provision to ask for is an option to claim either a total or a partial loss if one or more items from a pair or set of objects is totally destroyed or stolen. Many "pairs and sets" clauses stipulate that the insurance company will pay the full amount for the entire pair or set in the event of such a loss; the company will then assume ownership of all of the remaining objects in the set. You may want the option of receiving partial payment and retaining ownership of whatever remains. You may also want a "loss buy back" clause that gives you the right to repurchase stolen property that may be recovered by the insurance company.

Relatively small art collections can be scheduled on the personal property floater of your regular homeowners policy. The disadvantage of such coverage is that art losses may eat up an unacceptably large portion of your total coverage for personal property. In an article on "How to Protect Your Valuables" (August 1980) *Consumer Reports* magazine suggested that separate coverage be purchased for art and antiques if such objects account for 50 percent or more of one's personal-property coverage under a standard homeowner's policy. Broker Huntington Block recommends that owners of collections valued at $25,000 or more take out a separate fine-arts policy. Most collectors can do this through their regular insurance brokers or by shopping around among various local brokers for the best coverage and rates. Owners of multi-million-dollar collections, however, are likely to receive more favorable coverage and rates by dealing with the handful of brokers around the country who specialize in fine-arts insurance (see Appendix). At this writing, annual rates for a collector's fine-arts policy generally range from 10¢ to 50¢ per $100 of value. (Rates are usually lower for major museums, higher for dealers and artists.) As the collection grows, the rate per $100 generally declines. Fine arts insurance specialists sometimes offer special premium-reducing options to multi-million-dollar collectors: Such collectors may be allowed to insure only a fraction of the value of their collection and apply that coverage to any portion of the collection, up to the amount insured, or they may be able to buy their insurance in "primary and excess layers." "Primary insurance," which may cover the first $1 million in losses, is paid at the regular rate; excess coverage, paid at a lower rate, takes effect only after the million-dollar coverage is exhausted. (The rate is lower because the insurer regards a loss in excess of $1 million as unlikely.)

Losses and damage should be reported promptly to your insurance company; if the object is valuable, it is a good idea to ask for an insurance adjustor who has had previous experience with art-related claims. Thefts should also be immediately reported to the police. If an art work is damaged during shipment, the carrier should be immediately notified by phone, with a follow-up letter; the crate and all packing materials should be saved for inspection by the carrier and the insurance companies. If you have a total loss, your claim should be for the entire replacement value of the object, as established by a recent appraisal (which, if you have "valued at" coverage, has already been accepted by the insurance company). If the loss is partial, you should claim not only the cost of restoration but also the amount by which the value of the object has depreciated as a result of the damage. (A damaged and restored object is never as valuable as it was in its undamaged state.) Your conservator probably will not give you a dollar estimate of the depreciation suffered by your object, but he will tell you the percentage by which he thinks the value has been decreased. By applying this percentage to your appraisal of full value, you can determine how much to claim for depreciation. Most experts agree that appraisals of art for insurance purposes should be updated every three years and, perhaps, more often in areas where the market is particularly volatile. (More on how to obtain reliable appraisals in Chapter 9.)

Insurance proceeds are taxable. If you originally paid $1,000 for a work and you receive $5,000 for it from your insurance company, your $4,000 profit is subject to taxation. In most cases, collectors' profits from insurance proceeds are taxed at capital-gains rates. But if you received the insured work as a gift from the artist, or if you have not owned it for the one-year holding period required for long-term capital-gains treatment, you will have to pay the higher rates that are applicable to ordinary income. (The rule is that if you would have owed ordinary income tax had the work been sold, you have to pay at those rates on any profits from insurance proceeds. More on the tax ramifications of art transactions in Chapter 9.) There is a legal way of avoiding any tax on insurance proceeds, however: if you use the proceeds to buy similar property within two years after the end of the tax year in which the insurance proceeds were paid. To satisfy the "similar property" requirement, it may not be enough merely to buy another art work. A 1981 Internal Revenue Service letter ruling indicated that taxation of insurance proceeds can be avoided only if the collector replaces the lost works with other works in the same medium (i.e., lithographs should be replaced by other lithographs, paintings by other paintings, etc.).

Some collectors decide not to insure their collections. They don't want anyone (including their insurance company) to know what they own, they would prefer to spend their money on conservation and security precautions rather than on insurance premiums, and they reason that if they do suffer a loss, they can deduct it from their taxes. It is true that casualty losses (i.e., sudden damage or loss due to fire or theft) are tax-deductible. But the size of the deduction is limited to the *lesser* of the following, minus $100: the work's fair market value at the time of the loss, or its "adjusted cost basis." The adjusted cost basis is the original purchase price (or the work's value at the time of acquisition by other means, such as inheritance) plus the cost of any repairs or improvements (such as framing or cleaning). If the value of a work has appreciated substantially, a tax deduction based on the original purchase price will be small compensation for its loss. If its value has remained fairly constant, self-insurance becomes an attractive alternative to paying insurance premiums (which are usually not tax deductible), particularly if the collector is in a high tax bracket. The fact that deductions are only allowed for losses that are sudden has led, according to New York attorney Eugene Vogel, an expert on art-related tax issues, to "some learned discussions about whether termites attack overnight or gnaw for years."

Security Precautions

Preferable to receiving either insurance proceeds or tax deductions for losses is preventing those losses in the first place. A conscientious program of "risk management," as a loss-prevention strategy is called, can also help to reduce your premium if you do decide to insure. Some companies will not even insure a big collection unless it is protected by an alarm that reaches the police department. Many insurance companies now also ask for smoke detection devices, which are not expensive to install. In her essay on "How to Buy Art Insurance" in the Cincinnati Art Museum's *Collector's Handbook,* the museum's then associate registrar (now associate curator), Anita Ellis, recommended that collectors present prospective insurers with a detailed list of the steps they have taken to reduce the risk of loss. Such a list should include details related to: *conservation* (climate and lighting control, display and handling, regular examinations); *record-keeping* (documentation of all acquisitions, including photos and appraisals, kept in a safe-deposit box); *fire prevention* (ionization detectors, smoke detectors, portable fire extinguishers, sprinkler system, storage in fireproof vaults, proximity of fire hydrant or fire station); *theft prevention* (guard dogs, noise alarms, silent alarms hooked to police department, lighting of house, past theft history) and *structural safety* (fire-resistant construction; good insulation, electric wiring, plumbing and heating; regular procedures for controlling termites and other insects; unlikelihood of extreme weather conditions or natural catastrophes such as hurricanes, tornadoes, floods, earthquakes). Providing an insurer with such a list may help to convince him that you are a good risk and deserve special consideration on rates. Broker Huntington Block said that a general summary, rather than a detailed list, "will usually do just fine, and the insurance company will insist on its own inspection in any case."

A bewildering variety of simple and sophisticated devices to prevent and detect fire and theft is available from a large assortment of companies with varying degrees of integrity and expertise. Security experts generally advise collectors to avoid overly complex security systems that can be costly and difficult to install, maintain and operate. A typical residence where valuables are stored should have a perimeter alarm system, which protects points of access to a building or apartment, as the "primary line of defense," according to Detective James King, an art thefts investigator with the Montgomery (Md.) County Police. "Normally an interior alarm system [which detects the thief after he has entered] is not needed. But if one is desired, a logical choice is an extension of the perimeter system to interior doors and other openings." Writing in the May 1979 issue of the *Art Theft Archive Newsletter* (now called the *Stolen Art Alert*, published by the International Foundation for Art Research), King advised that

> the components of any system should be Underwriters Laboratories (U.L.) approved to insure the purchaser of equipment standards. Any internal wiring should be installed in accordance with local electrical codes.

Before purchasing any alarm system, obtain written estimates from two or more companies. Before deciding on a particular company, check its history of service and performance. Company employees who enter your home or business should be bonded, and the company should be willing to furnish a list of nearby customers who can be contacted for references. It is also advisable to check the company's reliability with a local Better Business Bureau, consumer protection office or police agency.

After a company is selected, read the contract thoroughly. It should list the points of protection and itemize the equipment to be installed. The contract should include a guarantee of equipment and workmanship as well as a maintenance agreement.

Alarms function by responding to certain changes that an intruder causes in electrical currents, physical vibrations, acoustic waves, thermal rays, or magnetic, electromagnetic or electrical fields. The most commonly used perimeter protection devices include *magnetic contact switches* that set off an alarm when a window or door is opened; *metal foil tape,* glued around window edges, that sets off an alarm when a window is broken; *hidden electrical wires,* built into walls, ceilings, floors and doors, that set off an alarm when they are broken; *vibration detectors* that are activated by the vibrations caused when an intruder attempts to break into a building or apartment. Experienced burglars can sometimes recognize and thwart this first line of defense, leading some collectors to adopt various measures of interior protection: *step mats* (also called contact mats, pressure-sensitive mats or carpet detectors), hidden under carpets or doormats, that set off an alarm when an intruder steps on them; *motion detectors* (microwave or ultrasonic) that are activated by the movements of an intruder; *photoelectric systems* that set off an alarm when an intruder interrupts an invisible infrared light or laser beam; *passive infrared devices* that are sensitive to the heat radiated from the body of an intruder; *audio detectors* that are sensitive to the noise produced by an intruder; *capacitance alarms* that detect an intruder's approach within a certain distance of a particular object; various switches and sensors (many relatively inexpensive and easy to install), affixed to or installed under an object, that are activated when the object is moved. The trouble with some of these systems is that they are very sensitive and can sometimes be activated by inconsequential happenings: fluttering curtains, scurrying mice, variations in temperature, air movements, etc.

Once activated, theft-detection devices can signal the presence of an intruder in two ways: by *local alarm* (loud noises or flashing lights that are set off in the home) or by *silent alarm* (a signal sent to a neighbor, a commercial alarm-monitoring company or the local police department). The latter type, also called a central station alarm or remote alarm, "provides the security force or the police with a better opportunity to apprehend the burglar or thief and possibly to solve other cases," according to *Museum Security,* a publication of the International Council of Museums, by Robert Tillotson, chairman of ICOM's International Committee on Museum Security. The local alarm, according to Tillotson, "has the advantage of frightening the burglar and perhaps preventing theft or vandalism." Many security systems incorporate both types of alarms, and are linked with a fire-detection system that also sends both local and remote alarms.

Two types of smoke detectors are commonly used in residences: *ionization detectors,* which respond to fast-flaming fires, and *photoelectric detectors,* which are sensitive to smoldering fires. Other devices for fire protection include *sprinkler systems,* which react to heat (and which may cause water damage to art works); and *hand-held fire extinguishers.* Extinguishers using water or dry chemicals are recommended by Tillotson, who notes that dry-chemical extinguishers containing ammonium phosphate are suitable for all types of fires (those involving ordinary combustibles, grease, or electrical equipment) and are more efficient than all other extinguishers of equal weight. A dry-chemical extinguisher "leaves a powdery residue but does not damage an object," according to Tillotson. More thorough discussions of the various protection devices are contained in Tillotson's book and in *The Fine Art of Art Security* by Donald Mason, retired senior investigator of art crimes for the Federal Bureau of Investigation (see Bibliography). Mason's book lists thirty-four manufacturers of security equipment.

While assessing all of the sophisticated hardware on the market, collectors should not lose sight of certain simple time-honored devices and practices that are basic to home security: strong, pick-resistant locks on doors; window locks; lighting of rooms in an unoccupied house (preferably with timers that turn lights on and off); lighting of the house's exterior (to make it harder for intruders to escape notice); reliance on the watchful eye of a friendly neighbor (particularly when you will be away for an extended period). If you are going to be away from home for a very long time, such as an entire summer, you might consider storing your most valuable works off premises. Some museums provide summer storage space for friendly collectors, and some companies (such as Hahn Brothers and the fine arts division of Seven Santini Brothers in New York) specialize in shipping and storing works of art. In choosing security devices that are best suited to your needs, you may be able to receive expert guidance from your insurance agent or the local police department.

If, despite all your precautions, a theft does occur, you should immediately report it to the local police and your insurance company (which will ask you for the police report number). You should not disturb the scene of the crime until after the police have investigated. Thefts of art valued at more than $5,000 should also be reported to the local office of the Federal Bureau of Investigation. You may also wish to notify the FBI's Art Squad, 201 E. 69th St., New York, N.Y. 10021, and its Interstate Transportation of Stolen Property Desk, J. Edgar Hoover Building, Washington, D.C. 20535. Interpol, the Paris-based international organization for cooperation among law-enforcement agencies, also promotes the recovery of stolen art and can be notifed c/o U.S. Department of Justice, Washington, D.C. 20530. Since much stolen art eventually winds up in major art-market centers like New York City, you may also want to notify the Property Recovery Squad of the New York City Police Department, 1 Police Plaza, New York, N.Y. 10038. Notification of these law-enforcement agencies does not necessarily mean that they will actively pursue your case. But it does mean that they can disseminate the descriptions and photographs of your stolen art to dealers, auctioneers and others who may be approached to buy or dispose of your works. In addition, if the works are eventually recovered (perhaps as part of a larger case involving a major theft operation), your report to a wide variety of agencies will greatly increase your chances of being identified as the owner to whom the works should be returned.

Two private groups also function as clearinghouses for information about stolen art: the Art Dealers Association of America and the International Foundation for Art Research (see Appendix for addresses). Both organizations publish regular art-theft bulletins that include descriptions and photographs from international sources. You will not be charged for inclusion of your stolen works in their reports, and, if you wish, your identity will be kept in confidence. (ADAA does require publication of the name and address of someone to be contacted with information about the theft, but you may use the name of your insurance agent or local police investigator for this purpose.)

Your ability to make a meaningful report to investigators and others will depend upon how conscientious you were, prior to your loss, in keeping thorough and accurate records about your collection. Law-enforcement officials are frequently exasperated by collectors who expect them to find and identify stolen works on the basis of vague descriptions such as "a landscape with a lake and trees." They stress that collectors should keep a file of photographs of all their works, and these photographs (along with descriptive information and appraisals) should be kept in a safe-deposit box or some other off-premises location. On-premises records may be destroyed along with your collection in the event of fire, or may be stolen by a thief, for whom your appraisals may serve as a handy guide to the most valuable works in your collection.

Chapter 9

WHEN ART COLLECTOR MEETS TAX COLLECTOR

When art collector meets tax collector, the result is often a skirmish. Every art transfer—whether a sale, exchange, donation or bequest—has tax consequences that are often either imperfectly understood or willfully disregarded by the participants, and the Internal Revenue Service has become increasingly vigilant in pursuing "artful" tax-dodgers. Collectors whose primary concerns are aesthetic should nevertheless be aware of the financial side of their activities; that means learning not only about the market but also a little about tax law. Collectors whose primary concerns are investment-oriented have an obvious interest in minimizing their taxes to maximize their profits. Complicating this task is the problem of getting reliable, well-documented appraisals for works that show up on tax returns as gifts, donations or bequests. The IRS subjects such appraisals to skeptical scrutiny, aided by its Art Advisory Panel—a group of up to twelve outside experts who meet periodically to review taxpayers' appraisals of higher-priced art works (usually only those valued at $20,000 or more). The very fact that there *is* such a panel—a highly unusual review procedure for the IRS, which ordinarily relies on its own staff appraisers—underscores the fact that some very special tax questions are raised by the ownership of art, questions that collectors ought to be able to answer knowledgeably and convincingly when the IRS auditor comes to call. The following is a general guide to the tax consequences of art transactions, but only a personal tax advisor can map out the best art-related tax strategy for a particular collector. It should also be noted that Congress makes frequent changes in the tax law, so consultation with a tax advisor is essential for the most up-to-date information.

Sales, Swaps, Depreciation

The most obvious and, usually, simplest instance of an art-related tax is the tax payable on sale profits. In most cases, a collector's profits from art sales will be taxed at long-term capital-gains rates, which are considerably lower than the rates for ordinary income. (At this writing, the maximum capital-gains tax is 20 percent, compared to the maximum income tax of 50 percent.) Under the law that is in effect at this writing, art is eligible for long-term capital-gains treatment if it is held for more than one year and is *not* any of the following: 1) part of the seller's business inventory (as would usually be the case if the seller were an art dealer); 2) a work created by the seller (i.e., the artist); or 3) a gift from the artist to the seller. The last restriction is the one most likely to affect collectors, many of whom are unaware of the tax pitfalls of accepting artists' gifts or are unconcerned about them because they never intend to sell their friends' creations. But even the least mercenary of collectors may be dismayed to discover that accepting a gift from an artist creates adverse tax consequences not only if the work is sold (in which case the profits are taxed according to ordinary income rates rather than capital-gains rates) but also if it is donated to a museum or other nonprofit institution (more on the tax implications of donations later). The standard (but misguided) advice to collectors wishing to avoid such pitfalls is to pay the artist something for his work, even if it is only one dollar. But art-tax experts point out that if you pay an artist substantially less than the true market value for his work, the IRS may regard the transaction as a "bargain sale." In such a case, a fraction of the art work's value—equal to the fraction that represented a gift from the artist—will get ordinary-income treatment rather than the more favorable capital-gains treatment when the work is sold or donated by the collector. For example, if a collector pays an artist only one-quarter of the market value for his work three-quarters of the work's value at the time of its sale or donation will be treated as ordinary income, provided that the IRS discovers that a bargain sale did, in fact, take place. If a collector pays what appears to be a reasonable amount (rather than just one dollar or a token amount) for a work by an artist-friend, and does not tip off the IRS that a bargain sale took place, he may succeed in getting full capital-gains treatment at the time of donation or sale.

Another tax-related question that may arise from a sale is just how much of the proceeds are taxable. A collector is permitted to deduct his expenses related to maintaining an art work from the taxable profit.

In other words, a collector who buys a work for $10,000, spends $2,000 over the years for its framing, conservation, storage, appraisals, insurance, etc., and sells it for net proceeds of $20,000 (after commissions paid to the gallery or auction house that arranged the sale) owes taxes not on the $10,000 difference between the sale proceeds and the purchase price, but only on the $8,000 profit after expenses (the $20,000 sale proceeds, less the $10,000 purchase price *and* less the $2,000 in expenses for framing, conservation, etc.). Keeping careful records of expenses is, therefore, an important tax-saving strategy for collectors who may eventually sell their art. But although they can deduct expenses from taxable sale proceeds, most collectors cannot treat art-related expenses as business deductions (even if they buy art partly as an investment), nor can they use losses from the sales of art works to offset taxable gains. (More on this in the next chapter.)

Art that is hung in business offices generally cannot be depreciated like office equipment or furnishings, because depreciation deductions are allowed only for items that have an expected useful life of a specifiable number of years. Since art works that are hundreds of years old continue to be collected and displayed, there is no known limit to the expected useful life of fine art. However, the IRS does allow depreciation deductions for mere office decoration—pictures that are not considered "art" and that a company might reasonably be expected to discard after a certain length of time. Thomas Hartnett, chief of the art valuation group in the IRS's national office and chairman of its Art Advisory Panel, says that he uses the following criteria in deciding whether an object is "art" or "mere decoration": "Is it by an identifiable artist? Was it bought by an art-knowledgeable person in the firm? After a specifiable number of years, will the company really throw the object out of the building and into the garbage?" But even works that clearly qualify as art rather than decoration are frequently depreciated by business firms, without arousing objections from the IRS—the taxman never finds out about it. Depreciation deductions for art are frequently lumped together with a company's other depreciation deductions (for office furniture, machinery, etc.) and are therefore not readily apparent to tax auditors. If a firm's overall depreciation deduction seems reasonable, an auditor may fail to detect improper deductions for art. In his article on "The Favored Tax Treatment of Purchasers of Art," William Speiller said that his interviews with members of ten large accounting firms suggested that most art objects used in a trade or business are depreciated. None of those interviewed knew of more than one or two clients who segregated art works on their books and chose not to take any depreciation. Several told of valuable works that were depreciated. Three even admitted that their own firms owned decorative art objects that were being depreciated under a furniture-and-fixture account.

Another tax-related prohibition that is often ignored bars collectors from making any tax-free exchanges of works of art, unless, as discussed in the next chapter, the exchanging collectors are deemed "art investors" by the IRS. Most collectors who swap art are legally required to pay tax on the difference between the fair market value of the property they acquire and the basis (the original purchase price plus expenses) of the property they give up. Swapping art for other goods or services is also a taxable event. In a 1979 revenue ruling, the IRS stated that in a situation where an artist gave one of his works to an apartment-building owner in exchange for six months' free rent, the building owner had to report the work's fair market value as part of his gross income. Similarly, the artist was required to report the rental value of the apartment as income. But in his article on taxing art, Speiller observed that "it is generally believed that most taxpayers do not report gain" on art swaps, and the IRS is likely to be none the wiser. In the long run, though, collectors who fail to report swaps of contemporary art to the IRS may be outsmarting themselves. At the 1981 Practising Law Institute seminar on "Representing Artists, Collectors and Dealers," New York art-tax attorney Ralph Lerner said that if the artist whose work was acquired through a swap becomes well known and the collector wants to donate the art work, it may be treated by the IRS as ordinary income property (i.e., as a free gift from the artist, which is not eligible for a full charitable deduction) if the collector cannot prove that he purchased it, whether in cash or in other property or services.

Tax Deductions for Donations

According to Lerner, the charitable deduction for donations of art was, prior to changes in the tax law effective Jan. 1, 1982, one of the best tax shelters available in an era of tightening loopholes. The large benefits available from such deductions led Speiller, in his article, to conclude that "as a group, purchasers of art are not now bearing their [fair] share" of the national tax burden. The abuses cited by Speiller still exist, but the reductions in capital-gains and income-tax rates passed by Congress in 1981 have greatly reduced the financial attractiveness of donating art to nonprofit institutions. Subject to certain requirements and restrictions (to be discussed below), art collectors can deduct from their taxable income the full fair market value of works that are donated to appropriate nonprofit institutions, such as museums. When a work greatly appreciates in value, the donor gets to deduct the appreciated value, not just his original cost in purchasing the work. Before the 1978 reduction of capital-gains tax rates to a maximum of 28 percent, which was followed by the 1981 reduction of capital-gains rates to a maximum of 20 percent and the 1982 reduction of income-tax rates to a maximum of 50 percent, this frequently meant that collectors in high tax brackets were financially better off donating a work than selling it (which requires the payment of sales commissions, capital-gains tax and any applicable state income taxes). Some taxpayers may still realize greater financial benefits from donations than from sales—if they exaggerate the values of donations in order to obtain larger (and legally unwarranted) tax deductions. Such ploys (which were in use even before capital-gains rates were reduced) can tip the financial scale in favor of giving rather than selling; they can also, if found out, greatly complicate one's relationship with the IRS. As of 1982, taxpayers who overvalue their donations can be charged a penalty ranging from 10 to 30 percent of the additional tax due because of the overvaluation. (The exact rate depends upon the degree to which the value was, in the IRS's view, inflated.) In addition to this, donors claiming inflated values who are found out by the IRS must pay the regular interest rate that is charged on all types of tax underpayments. As of 1982, that rate was raised to equal the prime interest rate (the rate that banks use as a basis for setting interest rates for the most creditworthy corporate borrowers).

The crux of most art-related tax problems is determining just what "fair market value" means when that term is applied to art. IRS regulations define fair market value as "the price at which the property would change hands between a willing buyer and a willing seller, neither being under any compulsion to buy or sell and both having reasonable knowledge of relevant facts." But, as attorney Lerner observed in his article for the 1981 PLI seminar, "when trying to place a value on a unique collection, these guidelines do not offer much help. . . . The contemplated 'retail market' rule . . . is an attempt by the Internal Revenue Service to formulate a simple rule where one does not fit." Art can be sold in many different markets—through galleries and auction houses and from collector to collector; the price in each case may vary substantially. Setting a fair market value for an unusual work of a type that rarely appears on the market is particularly difficult, since data on recent comparable sales may not exist.

Assuming that a collector can arrive at a figure for fair market value that is acceptable to the IRS (more on how to go about this later), he can deduct from his taxable income the work's full fair market value at the time of its donation, provided that the following four requirements are met:

1) The donee is categorized by the IRS as a "public charity" rather than a private foundation. (Most art museums, schools and hospitals qualify as public charities.)

2) The donated art is "capital-gain property," rather than "ordinary-income property." Capital-gain property is property that, if sold, would give the seller a long-term capital gain. Art is not capital-gain property if it has not appreciated in value, if it has not been held by the taxpayer for more than one year, if it was a free gift to the taxpayer from the artist, or if it is part of the taxpayer's business inventory (as in the case of a dealer).

3) The donee's use of the donated art must be related to the purpose or function for which the organization received its tax exemption. This "related-use rule" means that a collector who donates art to a museum for exhibition or study is eligible for the full fair-market-value deduction; however, a collector who donates art to be sold for the benefit of the museum has not met the related-use rule. In the latter case, the collector can only deduct from his taxable income a sum equal to fair market value *minus* 40 percent of the work's appreciation in value. (This limitation also applies to art donated to any of the many charity auctions held to benefit nonprofit institutions.) According to IRS regulations, the related-use rule is satisfied if, at the time of donation, it is "reasonable to anticipate that the property will not be put to an unrelated use by the donee." In other words, if a museum accepts a donated painting, but later decides to sell it, the donor's charitable deduction will probably not be jeopardized. "If the museum recipient were to immediately sell the work, it would cast doubt on the full market-value deduction," according to New York attorney Robert Anthoine, speaking at the 1981 "Arts and the Law" conference sponsored by Volunteer Lawyers for the Arts and the Committee on Art Law of the Association of the Bar of the City of New York. "But most museum administrations have a policy of keeping any donated work in the collection for a period of time," Anthoine noted. Lerner advises donors to make sure that the related-use rule is met by getting a letter from the museum stating how it will use the donated property.

4) Deductions for contributions of capital-gain property, such as art, must not exceed 30 percent of the donor's adjusted gross income.

A collector may elect to increase this to 50 percent, but he will then lose the chance to take deductions equal to the art works' full fair market value. Instead, he will only be able to deduct an amount equal to fair market value *minus* 40 percent of the works' appreciation in value. In other words, a collector who originally paid $10,000 for a painting that has appreciated in value to $30,000 may donate the painting and take a tax deduction for the entire $30,000 if his adjusted gross income is $100,000 or more. If his adjusted gross income is $50,000, the maximum deduction he can take in one year for his donation of the painting is $22,000: the painting's fair market value of $30,000, minus $8,000 (40 percent of the work's $20,000 appreciation in value). A collector making a donation that exceeds 30 percent of his adjusted gross income might do better (unless he is very infirm or elderly) by taking advantage of the "carryforward" provision of the law. This allows the amount of the charitable deduction that could not be used during the first year (because of the 30 percent limitation) to be apportioned among up to five succeeding tax years. In the above example, the collector with the $50,000 adjusted gross income could donate the $30,000 painting and take a deduction of $15,000 (30 percent of his adjusted gross income) in each of two succeeding years. If he had elected the 50 percent option, he would have had a one-time deduction of $22,000 and would have lost the remaining $8,000 in deductions that the work might have afforded him.

Major collectors and their advisors have developed various ingenious techniques for maximizing the financial benefits from donations. One popular device is the "snowballing fractional interest": instead of donating the entire art work to a museum, a collector may donate just a fraction of his interest in the work, with his remaining interest to be donated over several succeeding years. This strategy is not only useful in getting around the 30 percent limitation (since a large tax deduction can be spread over many years) but can also result in a much larger total deduction than could have been realized had the entire work been donated at once. A collector who gives a museum a 10 percent undivided fractional interest in a $100,000 painting can take a $10,000 tax deduction (10 percent of the painting's fair market value) for the year in which the donation is made. If the painting then increases in value to $110,000 during the following year, he can give another 10 percent interest to the museum and take a tax deduction of $11,000 (10 percent of the appreciated fair market value in the year during which the second donation is made). The total of tax deductions for partial donations that are spread over a period of time will come to much more than the maximum $100,000 that the collector could have deducted had he donated the entire painting in the first year. (It will also, however, come to much less than the deduction he could have taken had he held onto the painting and donated his entire interest at the highest appreciated value.) Another advantage of giving a fractional interest is that the donor does not have to part with his treasure forever. If he donates a one-third interest, for example, he can keep the work for two-thirds of the year, letting the museum have it for only one-third of the year (an option that gives traveling collectors a convenient, secure repository for valuable works when they are not at home to care for them). Most museums will accept a fractional interest only on the understanding that they will eventually acquire complete ownership of the work, either by future gifts during the collector's lifetime or by bequest.

Another donation-related strategy is a bargain sale to a museum, which significantly reduces the bite of capital-gains taxes that would be due if a work were sold for its full fair market value: if a collector sells an art work to a museum for less than full value, he must still pay capital-gains tax on the sale proceeds, but the reduction in price is treated as a tax-deductible donation to the museum. If, for example, a collector buys a painting for $1,000, holds it until it is worth $4,000 and sells it to a museum for $2,000, he is deemed to have sold one-half of the painting and his taxable gain is $1,500—his proceeds from the sale ($2,000) minus one-half of his original cost in buying the painting ($500). Meanwhile, he receives a $2,000 income-tax deduction for donating one-half of the painting.

Yet another widely used strategy—the "buy low, donate high" scheme—has come under increasing scrutiny by the IRS. For several years, investors have been making bulk purchases of art (particularly print editions) at heavily discounted prices, for the express purpose of later donating the art to nonprofit institutions. At the time of donation, these investors claim a tax deduction equal to the art's supposed retail value—usually several times their original cost. These "buy low, donate high" schemes have been the subject of several IRS revenue rulings that have disallowed the deductions on three grounds: 1) The bulk acquisitions and the "frequency and continuity" of the taxpayer's donations make him "substantially equivalent" to a dealer; dealers are not eligible for full fair-market-value deductions when they contribute works from their inventory. (As previously explained, full deductions are granted only for capital-gain property, and a dealer's inventory is deemed to be ordinary-income property.) 2) The donations were not made after "a period of accumulation and enjoyment" of the contributed property; instead, the property was bought expressly for the purpose of creating a charitable deduction. 3) The best evidence of the true fair market value of the donated property is the price that the donor (and others like him) recently paid for it, not "some artificially calculated estimate of value" that is greatly in excess of the price at which sales have actually taken place.

The first two arguments (embodied in Revenue Ruling 79-256, which deals with donations of lithographs, among other things) have been strongly criticized by tax experts, who argue that there is no legal basis for classifying big donors as dealers, or for applying an "accumulation-and-enjoyment" test to donations. More recent revenue rulings (80-69, dealing with an assortment of gems, and 80-233, dealing with an edition of Bibles) and recent comments by IRS officials indicate that the third approach—the fair-market-value test—is likely to be the one emphasized in future IRS attacks on "buy low, donate high" schemes. A collector can still legitimately claim a charitable deduction that is many times his original cost, provided that he can convincingly prove (with sales data from arms-length transactions) that the claimed charitable deduction is truly the work's current fair market value. According to attorney Robert Anthoine, a collector can successfully claim a high deduction "if you make a genuine bargain purchase and, at the time you make the donation, the same work is being sold by an established gallery at an established [higher] price."

The IRS is likely to be very skeptical, though, of bulk-purchase schemes in which works are held just long enough (more than one year) to receive capital-gains treatment and are then donated at values that greatly exceed the collector's cost. In its policy statement on "Valuation of Donated Property" (Publication 561), the IRS declares that "unless you can show the existence of unusual circumstances, it will be assumed that the increase or decrease in value of your donated property from your cost will have been at a reasonable rate." The IRS frequently requests taxpayers to report what they originally paid for their donated works, and if the taxpayer does not cooperate, the IRS may do its own detective work. In a 1968 U.S. Tax Court case involving an art collector named Samuel Silverman, the IRS uncovered a large number of U.S. Customs records (including purchase invoices) relating to Silverman's importation between 1957 and 1965 of paintings that he had bought in France for (in most cases) less than $100 each. He later donated these paintings to museums and universities at much higher values (ranging from $200 to $1,200). Silverman's total claimed deductions came to $100,525; his cost for the donated paintings was only about $13,600. The court reduced his allowable deduction to $30,500 and observed that the appraisals obtained by Silverman from New York dealer Victor Hammer (brother of collector Armand Hammer) appeared to be "highly inflated." In the words of the decision, Victor Hammer "rendered a 'package' service, appraising the paintings in the first instance and then arranging for and carrying through the making of the gifts. . . . For his services in connection with each such gift, Hammer received a further fee equal to a percentage of his valuation of the paintings donated. . . . An example of his conduct which troubled us was the request that he made of some donees that they include in their letter of receipt a statement reading, 'We have had these paintings professionally appraised as follows,' and then to set forth Hammer's appraisal of the items involved. Any such letter of acknowledgement would be highly misleading, in that it would raise a reasonable, but false, inference that the donee had obtained an independent appraisal."

The Silverman case notwithstanding, dealers can often be very helpful in arranging legally acceptable donations for collectors who lack contacts at museums. With their extensive art-world connections, dealers are likely to know which museums will be most receptive to particular types of art works. Ivan Karp of O. K. Harris Gallery, for example, said that he had helped arrange donations of thirty-five works to museums in one year. John Walsh, Jr., of the Boston Museum of Fine Arts said that his institution probably accepts less than 10 percent of the works offered for donation. He added that whether a particular museum accepts a particular gift is not necessarily a function of the greatness of the museum or the greatness of the art work. It is a question of how the work would fit into the museum's collection. "The main question we ask ourselves is, 'Do we want to exhibit it?' If the answer is, 'Not all the time,' then we ask ourselves what contribution it might make to the museum's other functions, such as teaching people about art by keeping a reserve available, and lending works to other institutions. If we don't need a work for exhibition, we may try to get the collector to donate it to a smaller museum, a historic house, a library or a hospital. We try to suggest specific ones." Walsh also emphasized the importance of advance discussions with curators of any proposed bequests. "All a will can do is offer a work of art to an institution. The institution then decides whether to accept it. If you do leave works to a museum, it is a good idea to supply your lawyer with an alternative or two in case the museum turns them down." If a bequest is rejected, the heirs are left with the problem of finding another recipient for the art works or paying estate taxes on works for which no donee can be found. (More on estate taxes later.)

Tax Shelters in Print Publishing

Perhaps the most endangered art-related tax dodges are tax-shelter schemes involving the publication of prints. Such arrangements, designed to benefit those in the highest tax brackets, began to blossom in the late 1970s but have since been trimmed back by tax-law changes and IRS enforcement efforts. As New York attorney Gregory Marks observed at the 1981 Volunteer Lawyers for the Arts–New York City Bar Association conference, the IRS is "on the warpath" against print tax shelters, and investors in such schemes are dealing with "a potential time bomb."

A typical tax-shelter deal was outlined in a 1979 revenue ruling (79-432) in which the IRS disallowed most of the tax deductions claimed by an investor. "In 1979, the taxpayer, an individual, purchased an 'art tax shelter' from a sales promotion corporation. For a stated consideration of $200,000, the taxpayer received: 1) an original master lithographic plate made by a specified artist, 2) the right to 300 limited-edition prints (created from the master pursuant to the supervision of, and signed and numbered by, the artist who created the master), and 3) all common law and statutory copyrights in the master and in images therein, including the exclusive right to use, manufacture, sell, distribute, promote, advertise, and license the master, prints therefrom, and images therein for any purpose whatsoever [i.e., commercial spin-offs such as posters, greeting cards, ceramic plates, etc.]. ... The stated consideration of $200,000 was paid at closing by delivery of $30,000 cash and a note described as a partial recourse note in the amount of $170,000. The note states that it is recourse [meaning that the taxpayer is obligated to pay it off] to the extent of $70,000, but is nonrecourse [meaning that payment is due only if there are sufficient proceeds from the sales of prints and related products] to the extent of $100,000 and the entire interest on the note. ... The note is secured by the master, products derived therefrom, and associated copyrights. ... In the event of default or at the time the note and accrued interest are due, the taxpayer may require the note holder to accept any unsold prints, posters, or other products utilizing the image from the master in satisfaction of the remaining indebtedness to the extent of 65 percent of a formula value of such products. The formula value of each class of products will be the average retail price at which the items of such class have been sold in the last five, or all if less than five, bona fide retail sales."

Under such an arrangement, the investor would ordinarily try to claim tax deductions for depreciation of the lithographic plate based on the entire $200,000, even though his cash outlay was only $30,000. He would also have claimed an investment tax credit of $20,000—10 percent of the $200,000. In its revenue ruling, the IRS asserted that the fair market value of what the taxpayer had purchased was only $30,000, rather than $200,000, and that no more than $1,000 could be attributed to the lithographic plate. (The effect of the latter assertion is to knock out the opportunities for substantial depreciation deductions and investment tax credits, since these benefits are based on the value of the plate, not the prints themselves.) According to the IRS, the "primary item of value purchased by the taxpayer" was the right to the three hundred prints, and "the value of an edition, as a package, is not determined simply by projection of retail price of a single print multiplied by the number of prints in the edition, but reflects other considerations: 1) the fact that some prints in the edition may not be sold or may be sold only at a reduced price; 2) the time period over which the prints will be sold, and the present value of the expected proceeds; and 3) the cost of marketing the prints. Based upon the above facts and circumstances, it is concluded that the fair market value of the items purchased by the taxpayer is $30,000." The IRS also concluded that the entire $170,000 note was really nonrecourse, because the taxpayer was allowed to pay off the $70,000 "recourse" portion by merely returning prints or other products made from the image. "Thus, if the taxpayer can make a few initial sales at relatively high prices, any personal liability can be discharged by returning the remaining prints even though they are of little, if any, value." The extent to which a note is deemed "recourse" or "nonrecourse" by the IRS is important because of a 1978 change in the tax law that allows investors in shelters formed after Dec. 31, 1978, to take tax deductions only up to the amount that the investor has "at risk." (Only real-estate shelters are exempt from the "at risk" rule.)

In yet another move against print tax shelters, the IRS formed an Art Print Advisory Panel, a group of outside print-market experts (including dealers and museum professionals) that met for the first time in January 1981 to help determine whether the values of specific tax-shelter schemes were legitimate or inflated. According to the Sept. 15, 1981, issue of *The ARTnewsletter,* the panel downgraded the values of every one of the first 350 print tax-shelter schemes it examined. An IRS official told *The ARTnewsletter* that the panel generally reduced six-figure valuations to four- or low five-figure values. Despite the discouraging effects of IRS enforcement efforts, print tax shelters have been vigorously promoted in recent years. One of the most widely publicized ventures was the tax shelter promoted by Jackie Fine Arts (one of the biggest operators in this field) involving the production and sale of limited-edition copies of five hundred Picasso works inherited by Maria Picasso, the late artist's granddaughter.

Some tax-shelter promoters, searching for weaknesses in the 1979 revenue ruling, have questioned the IRS's assertion that almost all of a shelter's fair market value must be attributed to the prints rather than to the lithographic plate. Attorney Gregory Marks, who has advised some artists on tax-shelter schemes, noted that the revenue ruling does not have the force of law. It is the official interpretation of the IRS's national office, but it is not definitive and there have been no court cases providing guidance on this subject. "We will not know exactly what the status of art tax shelters will be for some time to come," Marks observed, "but we are on notice that the prognosis is not good." He noted that the IRS is almost certain to disallow tax shelters "which do not necessarily have any economic purpose" except to help investors avoid taxes. Similarly, attorney Ralph Lerner commented that investing in a tax shelter is a "big mistake" if the shelter's "sole purpose is to create losses. . . . It has to have true economic reality" (i.e., a real chance to realize the profits on which the claimed value of the tax shelter is based). Marks noted, though, that some investors may feel that postponing their tax obligations until the IRS gets around to taking decisive action is "sufficient justification" for participating in art tax shelters. (The stiffer penalties for overvaluing donations also apply to tax-shelter overvaluations, however, making the postponement of tax obligations much less attractive than it was formerly.)

Artist-participants see tax-shelter financing as a new source of income to support their work. Among the well-known artists who have accepted such financing are Alex Katz, Robert Rauschenberg and James Rosenquist. Other artists and dealers, though, feel that tax-shelter financing debases an artist and his art and they say that prints made for tax shelters are generally of inferior quality. The proliferation of tax-shelter prints can only hurt the market by flooding it with mediocre goods, in the view of some established print dealers; the Art Dealers Association of America went so far as to issue a statement urging all galleries and artists to shun tax-shelter deals. Dealer Sylvan Cole, Jr., who supports the association's stand, opposes tax shelters because they "pay off the artist to become a party to a scheme that has nothing to do with art. . . . In the long run, these deals can be damaging to the artist. They require large editions of works, sold at high prices. If more prints are introduced into the marketplace than it can absorb, there may be a drastic reduction of prices for the artist's work." Supporters of tax shelters assert that dealer-opponents are simply worried that an alternate method of print marketing may siphon off some of their business.

Estate Taxes

At the opposite extreme from the investor who participates in art-related deals solely to avoid taxes is the serious collector who gives so little thought to the tax consequences of his activities that he leaves his heirs with a giant estate-tax problem. This can occur even though the tax law passed by Congress in 1981 has done much to reduce the bite of estate taxes: Effective Jan. 1, 1982, there is no estate tax on bequests (no matter how large) to one's spouse, and the amount that can be bequeathed tax-free to others will be gradually increased from $175,-625 to $600,000 by 1987. The new law also lowers the maximum tax rate on estates from 70 to 50 percent by 1985. Still, art works that have appreciated greatly in value can create a very large tax liability if bequeathed to someone other than the collector's spouse, because art in a collector's estate is taxed according to its fair market value at the time of the collector's death—a value that may be many times the amount that the collector originally paid. The heirs' problems are compounded if the collection constitutes the estate's chief asset. Works must then be sold to raise enough money to pay the taxes. Charitable bequests, or gifts made during the collector's lifetime to noncharitable beneficiaries (e.g., family members or friends) can substantially reduce an estate's tax bill. Bequests to charitable organizations create estate-tax deductions equal to the fair market values of the works at the time of the collector's death. In order to qualify for the full fair-market-value deduction, bequests do *not* have to meet the same stringent rules that must be met by lifetime donations: the related-use rule (requiring the donee's use of the donated property to be related to the purpose for which the organization received its tax exemption) does not apply, the donees can be private foundations as well as public charities, and there is no limitation on what percentage of an estate can be donated.

A collector can also reduce his taxable estate by making annual gifts of art, during his lifetime, to family members and friends. Effective Jan. 1, 1982, the law allows individuals to give away, free of any gift tax, $10,000 a year. In addition, a married person can give away, tax-free, his spouse's $10,000. Also as of Jan. 1, 1982, a married person can make unlimited lifetime gifts to his spouse completely tax-free, thereby reducing the size of his estate. In his article on the taxation of art, Speiller noted that art objects are "particularly attractive" as tax-free gifts, because "by undervaluing art objects, the donor may be able to keep gifts within the annual exclusions. . . . In this way, substantial amounts of art can be passed from one generation to the next free of transfer taxes. . . . Taxpayers have little to fear by undervaluing gifts that they claim to be nontaxable due to the annual exclusion. . . . No gift tax returns are required for gifts within the annual exclusion; thus, no appraisals need be obtained and there will be no audits. Further the [Internal Revenue] Service concentrates its gift tax audits primarily on returns that show gift tax payable."

Sales of inherited art works are subject to capital-gains tax but, under current law, only the appreciation in value from the time of the collector's death (not from the time that the collector originally acquired the work) is subject to taxation when a work is sold by an heir. There have been recent attempts (which may be revived) to change the law so that heirs would have to pay tax on the entire appreciation of value from the date that a work was acquired by the deceased—a much heavier tax burden requiring careful record-keeping by collectors to document the original purchase prices of all their holdings. According to IRS regulations (Section 20.2053-3,d,2), selling expenses (gallery commissions, advertising costs, etc.) are deductible from either estate or income taxes (but not both) if the sales are "necessary in order to pay the decedent's debts, expenses of [the estate's] administration or taxes, to preserve the estate, or to effect distribution" of the estate. To insure that such sales are deemed "necessary" by the IRS, a collector might specifically direct in his will that particular art works be sold or that certain unspecified works be sold in order to accomplish the objectives set forth in his will (such as to fund a trust that will yield a reasonable income for the beneficiary).

Appraising the Appraisers

Perhaps the single greatest subject of contention between art owners and the IRS is the accuracy of art appraisals. Appraisals are needed for works that are charitable donations (in order to determine the size of the tax deduction), noncharitable gifts (to calculate the gift tax) or bequests (to calculate the estate tax). Collectors may also need appraisals for other reasons—for example, to determine how much insurance coverage to buy, or whether a seller is asking a fair price. Since there is no single "right answer" to the question of how much an art work is worth, a good appraiser will be able to tailor his valuation to the purpose for which it is made, and will be able to back up his appraisal with solid factual documentation.

"Different types of appraisal seek different levels of value," noted C. Hugh Hildesley of SPB. When donating a work, for example, a collector is interested in obtaining the highest possible valuation, so that he can take the highest possible tax deduction. The opposite is true for bequests and gifts; a lower appraisal means a lower estate or gift tax. For insurance purposes, the collector's interests are best served by getting an appraisal at the high end of a work's probable replacement value—the amount that the collector would have to pay to buy a similar work if his own were lost. While a somewhat generous insurance appraisal (updated periodically) will help keep insurance proceeds in line with art-market inflation, a highly inflated appraisal will unduly increase the costs of insurance and may cause problems for the collector's heirs if the IRS looks at insured values in determining the art's value for estate-tax purposes. Although the IRS says that all tax-related appraisals must report an object's "fair market value," the ambiguity of this term when applied to art allows some room for creativity on the part of an expert appraiser who has the collector's best interests at heart.

Any good appraisal should be based partly on sales data for comparable works, but an appraiser may use data from high-priced gallery sales to establish high values for donated works, or from less expensive auction sales or private sales between collectors (where no gallery commission is charged) to establish lower values for gifts or bequests. Where a higher valuation is desired than that suggested by comparable sales data, the appraiser and taxpayer may argue (but only if convincing proof can be offered) that the donated work is superior to anything that has recently appeared on the market. Where a lower valuation is desired, the appraiser and taxpayer may argue that the work in an estate is inferior to those recently on the market or that recent prices were artificially inflated (by public-relations hype, an anomalous bidding duel between two stubborn buyers, or an effort by dealers to make the market seem stronger than it really is).

If an appraisal deviates greatly from readily available market data, the appraiser's supporting documentation must be particularly exhaustive and convincing. An appraisal that is unsupported or only flimsily supported by fact is likely to be questioned by the IRS, even if it is presented as the informed opinion of an "expert." In its Revenue Procedure 66-49, the government has set forth exactly what it requires in an appraisal; any collector seeking an appraisal for tax purposes should see that his appraiser has a copy of these guidelines and follows them. The following elements should be included:

- A summary of the appraiser's qualifications.
- A complete description of the object, indicating the size, subject matter, medium, name of artist, date, etc.
- The cost, date and manner of acquisition.
- A history of the object, including proof of authenticity such as a certificate, if one exists.
- A photograph of a size and quality fully identifying the subject matter, preferably a 10-by-12-inch or larger print.
- A statement of the factors upon which the appraisal is based (e.g., sales of other works by the same artist, particularly on or near the valuation date; prices in dealers' catalogues for the artist's works or for works by comparable artists; the economic state of the art market at the time of the valuation; a record of exhibitions at which the work was displayed; a description of the artist's standing in his profession).

Taxpayers are not required by law to obtain expert appraisals for all art works that appear on their tax returns. For donations, the taxpayer is required only to state the method by which he has arrived at his determination of fair market value (which may or may not be an appraisal). For estates, appraisals are required only if the value of household and personal effects exceeds $3,000. But, as Speiller pointed out in his article, even if an appraisal is not required, it is probably the most practical way to substantiate one's claim for the IRS. Some taxpayers even go so far as to obtain two or more appraisals to support their claims, but this extra trouble and expense are not usually necessary; IRS officials say that one well-documented, professionally prepared appraisal is sufficient.

How does one find the people who are best qualified to make such appraisals? The best policy is to avoid the generalists and to seek an expert—usually a dealer or auction-house specialist—who is closely involved in the market for the particular type of work that you want appraised. "As a general rule," according to Gilbert Edelson of the Art Dealers Association of America, "an appraiser who claims to be able to appraise everything may not be able to appraise anything. People with considerable knowledge of old-master paintings are highly unlikely to have the knowledge to appraise contemporary works."

Thomas Hartnett of the IRS has suggested that collectors ask the following questions in trying to assess an appraiser's qualifications: Do you have comprehensive, well-organized records of relevant private sales and auction sales (including subscriptions to the catalogues of local, national and European auction houses)? Do you subscribe to any secondary sources (i.e., newsletters, books) that report on the results of sales? How do your education, training and experience qualify you to authenticate and value a work by this artist in this price range? Hartnett added that taxpayers should be wary of appraisers who make "vague claims" to having the requisite knowledge because they have "sold works of art for thirty-five years. . . . The world of big-ticket art appraisal is amazingly inefficient, ineffective or bad," he said, because of the "absence of a well-established art appraisal profession. There is no such thing as a true accreditation of appraisers. . . . Membership or nonmembership in professional appraisal societies such as the Appraisers Association of America or the American Society of Appraisers is not conclusive."

In his 1979 talk to the New York Society of Security Analysts, C. Hugh Hildesley of SPB said that an appraiser should be willing to provide prospective customers with a list of satisfied clients, and should be prepared to discuss his "failure rate" in dealing with the IRS. "Any appraiser who is not willing to support his appraisal through the conference and appellate level with the IRS is somebody you should look out for very carefully," according to Hildesley, "because any major appraiser must, for his fee, be prepared to follow up and support his appraisal to the Supreme Court, if necessary."

To locate a qualified appraiser, the IRS (in its booklet on "Valuation of Donated Property") suggests that collectors should seek advice from an art historian at a nearby college or the director or curator of a local museum. The major auction houses and dealers are obvious sources of appraising expertise. SPB and Christie's both offer a wide variety of appraisal services ranging from a free oral appraisal of what an object might bring at auction to formal written appraisals of entire collections. The cost for the latter type of appraisal at Christie's, at this writing, is $1,500 a day per appraiser, plus travel expenses. The fee is refunded if the appraised objects are consigned to Christie's within a year of the appraisal. The fee at SPB varies depending upon the value of the collection. For collections valued at under $100,000, the fee, at this writing, is $1,000 a day for the first appraiser and $250 a day for each additional appraiser, or 1.5 percent of the appraised value, whichever is less. For collections valued at $100,000 to $250,000, the fee is $2,000 a day for one appraiser and $1,000 a day for each additional appraiser. For collections valued at more than $250,000, the fee is negotiable. Travel expenses are extra and the appraisal fee is *not* generally refundable if objects are consigned to auction. A written appraisal at SPB or Christie's of just a few objects can be considerably less expensive—sometimes as low as $200 to $300 for several works that are brought to the auction house's premises. Free verbal appraisals are made only if the objects are brought to the auction house (by appointment) or if photographs of the objects are sent there. Recipients of such appraisals are under no obligation to consign their goods to auction (although the auction houses offer this free service in the hope of obtaining new merchandise). The big-two auction houses also periodically run special appraisal days around the country when, for a small charge (typically $5 per object), their experts give oral valuations of objects brought to them by area residents. Oral appraisals are useful as rough guides to an object's value, but only formal, written appraisals are acceptable for tax purposes.

Smaller auction houses also provide appraisals, often for smaller fees. According to a survey in the Aug. 3, 1981, issue of *The Gray Letter* (a weekly newsletter focusing on the antiques market), appraisal rates at auction houses around the country may range from $50 to $100 an hour, $250 to $500 a day or 1 to 1.5 percent of appraised value, with minimum fees anywhere from $75 to $300. Like SPB and Christie's, many of the smaller houses give free oral appraisals and relatively inexpensive written appraisals for objects that are brought to their premises.

Many dealers provide free appraisals for their clients; others charge a fee or request that a contribution be made to the foundation operated by the Art Dealers Association of America. Individual dealer-members of the association provide appraisals for estate-tax and insurance purposes and for a collector's general information, but the association has a special procedure for appraising works to be donated to nonprofit institutions: Such appraisals are made by a panel, composed (when possible) of three dealers who are experts in the appropriate field. The names of the panelists are not disclosed to the collector unless their appraisal is challenged by the IRS, in which case the association stands ready to defend its appraisal before the IRS and in court, if necessary, without charge to the collector. (The American Association of Dealers in Ancient, Oriental and Primitive Art offers a similar appraisal service.) In rare instances, where an important collection is involved, the ADAA also provides a panel to appraise works for estate-tax purposes. The fees for ADAA appraisals, at this writing, range from $50 for works appraised at up to $2,000 to $750 for works appraised at $75,000 to

$99,999. For works appraised at $100,000 and over, the fee is 1 percent of the first $250,000, 0.5 percent of the second $250,000, a flat $4,000 on the excess up to $1 million and a flat $5,000 on the excess over $1 million. In his article, Speiller suggested that ADAA dealers may tend to set relatively high valuations for donated works. "Doing so," he wrote, "is good for the donors, who want maximum charitable deductions; good for the museums, which are hungry for gifts; and good for the dealers themselves, who want to please their clients and at the same time establish high prices for future sales." Speiller also says that ADAA appraisals seem to stand a better chance with the IRS than other appraisers' valuations for charitable donations.

Other appraising groups include the American Society of Appraisers and the Appraisers Association of America (see Appendix for addresses), each of which issues a directory of its members. ASA includes a wide variety of appraisers, who handle everything from real estate to personal property; AAA is more art-oriented. Senior members of ASA must pass a qualifying exam and must have five years of experience as full-time appraisers. AAA members take no exam but must have five years of experience, and must submit references and sample appraisals when they apply for membership.

There are two basic methods of charging for appraisals: the flat-fee method, based on the amount of time spent by the appraiser, and the percentage method, based on the appraised value of the object. Either way, the cost of appraisals for tax-related purposes—charitable donations, gifts, or estates—is tax-deductible. In its August 1980 article, *Consumer Reports* observed that "percentage fees can tempt a dealer to overvalue an item in order to obtain a higher fee. The American Society of Appraisers, in fact, discourages percentage fees. A percentage fee is fairer when it is calculated on a sliding scale, with a lower rate for higher valuations." According to Philadelphia attorney Norman Donoghue II, the IRS may look more favorably on flat-fee than on percentage arrangements for donation-related appraisals, because the appraiser is not compensated for giving a higher figure. He added that donors should choose appraisers who are truly objective and independent, to avoid raising eyebrows at the IRS; an appraiser who is closely associated with the donor or donee is more apt to be accommodating in providing an overly high appraisal, in the IRS's view.

IRS Review Procedures

The art of second-guessing the IRS and trying to determine in advance what will pass its inspection is a major preoccupation of many tax attorneys and art collectors. In its policy statement on "Valuation of Donated Property," the IRS has announced that it "does not give recognition to any appraiser or organization of appraisers from the standpoint of unquestioned acceptance of their appraisals," nor does it approve appraisals in advance, before the actual filing of the tax return. There is, then, no way to determine beforehand whether an appraisal will breeze through the review process or get mired down in challenges. Even engaging a prestigious appraiser with strong art-world credentials is no guarantee of clear sailing. Adolph Posner, an ophthalmologist, learned this in 1976, when the Tax Court upheld the IRS in disallowing $10,000 of a $15,000 deduction taken by Posner for donation of a painting by Antonio Zanchi, a seventeenth-century Venetian artist. Posner's appraiser was Clyde Newhouse, the prominent New York dealer who has served both as president of the Art Dealers Association of America and as a member of the IRS's Art Advisory Panel. Posner also enlisted the expert testimony of Michael Milkovitch, a specialist in Italian painting who was director of the art gallery of the State University of New York at Binghamton (to which Posner had donated the painting), and Gustine Scaglia, another specialist in Italian art and professor of art history at Queens College, New York. In the face of this expert testimony, the IRS still prevailed, even though the expert who testified on the government's behalf, New York dealer Victor Spark, admitted in court that he had never heard of Antonio Zanchi until he was called upon to value the painting. The court was impressed by the fact that the only evidence offered by either side of a comparable sale of an authentic Zanchi was a $2,592 auction sale in 1971. (Posner's donation was made in 1969.)

As the Posner case illustrates, the IRS and the courts often give strong weight to auction prices in determining an art work's fair market value. Therefore, if a collector's valuation of art on his tax return differs substantially from recent auction prices, he (or his appraiser) ought to be able to give very convincing proof that the collector's work differs significantly from the recent auction offerings, or that the prices at auction were not a true reflection of the overall market. The staff appraisers who handle art-related tax returns in the district offices of the IRS are usually specialists in other areas (often real estate) who have very little knowledge of art and the art market. Unable to make judgments on quality or authenticity, they rely heavily on published auction prices for the same or roughly comparable works. The district offices handle some of the most difficult art valuation cases—those involving works of relatively low value by little-known artists, for which little or no market information exists. Works valued by the taxpayer at $20,000 or more are automatically referred to the national office in Washington, where a different, more sophisticated review process is employed (more on this later).

Despite the importance of auction prices in the IRS review process, engaging the appraisers with the most intimate knowledge of auction prices—the auction-house specialists—is no guarantee of a trouble-free audit. Joseph Sataloff, a Philadelphia surgeon, found that out when the IRS said that a Russian candlestick he had donated to the Smith-sonian Institution was worth only $15,000 to $18,000, instead of the $130,000 he had claimed as a deduction. His claim was based on an appraisal for that amount by SPB's experts. Sataloff sued the auction house in 1981 for $6 million, claiming that the emotional upsets he had suffered after the IRS challenged the appraisal had rendered him "unable to practice surgery." (The suit is still pending at this writing.)

The candlestick, having been assigned a value of more than $20,000 by Sataloff on his tax return, was referred to the national office of the IRS, where a group of staff experts (who have greater art-related expertise than those in the district offices) review taxpayers' appraisals and refer those that look particularly doubtful to a special Art Advisory Panel—a rotating group of up to twelve dealers, museum professionals and art historians who meet periodically in Washington to help the IRS determine the fair market values of high-priced works that appear on tax returns. The panel members serve without pay and are chosen by the IRS (with recommendations from previous panelists) in such a way that a wide range of specialties is represented. Created in 1968 to combat valuation abuses by taxpayers and to make up for the IRS's lack of art expertise, the panel often makes recommendations that are unfavorable to taxpayers: in 1980, for example, the panel reduced about half of the valuations for donated works that it acted upon and increased nearly half of the valuations for gifts and bequests.

Panel members are not told who the taxpayers are or whether a given work is being valued for estate, gift or donation purposes; the IRS does provide each panelist with a photograph and descriptive information for each work and with recent auction prices of comparable works, when available. Panel meetings are closed to the public and panelists' discussions are completely confidential. Although every member of the panel is invited to give his opinion on each object being considered, decisions are often largely based on the judgment of the one or two experts in the relevant field. Sometimes a disagreement among the panelists cannot be resolved, and the IRS staff is presented with a range of values for a particular work. Sometimes the panelists feel that they do not have enough information about the work to reach a decision; they then ask the IRS staff to go back to the taxpayer for more facts. Art-tax attorneys say the panel usually takes about six months to a year after getting a case before it hands down a decision. Its determinations are not legally binding on the IRS, but, as a rule, the IRS abides by the panel's judgments unless new evidence is presented by the taxpayer.

Taxpayers who are not happy with the panel's decisions assert that even the experts cannot possibly make accurate determinations of value (and, especially, of authenticity) from mere photographs; some also charge that the dealer-members of the panel have a built-in conflict of interest because of their financial stake in establishing high prices for works in their fields of specialization. Defenders of the panel maintain that art professionals, in the course of their work, regularly render accurate judgments about art from photographs and that dealers must be on the panel because of their substantial market expertise. In his art-tax article, Speiller criticized the panel for being too lenient with taxpayers; he maintained that

> a review of the detailed records of the Panel meetings disclosed that adjustments [for donated works] were made primarily in cases where the items were *greatly* overvalued. [Speiller's emphasis.] Examining the 53 cases [in 1977] of overvaluation, the Panel recommended adjustments in only eight cases where overvaluation appeared to be less than 40 percent and in only 15 cases where overvaluation appeared to be less than 100 percent. It therefore seems reasonable to conclude that the works whose values were not adjusted may well have been overvalued by significant amounts.

Speiller added that donors of very valuable works probably stand a good chance of getting away with extreme overvaluation:

> For example, who is to say whether a great and rare work is worth $2 million or $3 million? Since the most valuable works are likely to be appraised by highly knowledgeable and reputable dealers and since there is no regular market for such works, it would, indeed, seem presumptuous for the Panel to second-guess the appraisers. In such a case, the power of the appraisers seems awesome; they in effect have the ability to grant an extra $1 million of charitable deduction to the donor.

Taxpayers who are unhappy with the decision of the panel or the IRS staff can (and frequently do) appeal. The first step in preparing an appeal is to request a written statement from the IRS setting forth its decision and the reasons for it. The next step is to request an informal conference with the appraisal staff, followed (if necessary) by a formal hearing with the conference staff, a formal hearing with the appellate staff and, if all else fails, a trial in Tax Court, District Court or the Court of Claims. Few cases ever go to court, however, and IRS officials concede that if a taxpayer persists up to the appellate stage, he can often get a break: the IRS is not eager to get involved in the complexities of a court trial, unless the amount of tax at issue is great. One reason the IRS does not like to go to court is that it has difficulty getting experts to testify on its behalf. (Important art-world figures who *have* been willing to appear in court for the IRS include Alexandre Rosenberg of Paul Rosenberg & Co., the New York gallery; Eugene Thaw; Ralph Colin; and Kenneth Donahue, former director of the Los Angeles County Museum of Art.) Instead of working through the appeals procedure, a taxpayer can sometimes simply request reconsideration by the Art Advisory Panel—if he can provide significant new information that the panel may not have adequately considered the first time around. Attorney Ralph Lerner recently proved the value of the second hearing by getting the panel to accept a deduction of $300,000 for a portrait of George Washington by Joseph Wright that the panel had originally valued at only $35,000. Lerner and his client submitted a new appraisal (confirming the previous one) and included additional information about the artist and a historical analysis according to which the work's rarity and value were greatly enhanced by the fact that Washington had himself posed for the portrait.

Because of the secrecy surrounding it, its reliance on commercially oriented experts and its attempts to put fixed values on unique works whose prices may vary depending on circumstances and the subjective judgments of potential buyers, the Art Advisory Panel will probably be the subject of art-world controversy for as long as it exists. There is occasionally talk of abolishing the panel, since most other IRS appraisals are handled by the government's own staff rather than by outside experts. Collectors who have received unfavorable decisions from the panel might welcome its demise, but review by unknowledgeable IRS staff members might prove even more unfavorable: some staff members in the district offices are convinced that the art professionals on the panel are overly sympathetic and lenient to their collector colleagues (who are often the clients or patrons of the panel's members). The panel's chairman, IRS senior appraiser Thomas Hartnett, concedes that "in a perfect world, we would get appraisals from people who were both knowledgeable and isolated," but he defends the panel as the best available means of dealing with a complicated problem. Like most IRS employees, he is resigned to unpopularity. "We disagree [on valuations] with most people most of the time," he observed. "There is no possible way to make friends."

Chapter 10

"ART APPRECIATION"— COLLECTING FOR PROFIT

In a development that gives new meaning to the term "art appreciation," many investors have begun to view art and other tangibles as attractive alternatives to stocks and bonds. The New York brokerage firm of Salomon Brothers has, for several years, compared the compounded annual rates of return from various types of conventional investments with the return from various types of tangibles and, until its 1981 report, repeatedly concluded that the confrontation between tangible and financial assets was "won decisively by tangibles." The annual rate of return from stocks between 1970 and 1980 was 6.8 percent, compared to 6.4 percent for bonds, 13.4 percent for old masters and 18.8 percent for Chinese ceramics. (In 1981, however, stocks joined the "elite group" of inflation-beating investments.) In 1979, on his television program "Wall Street Week," Louis Rukeyser reported that "American landscapes are selling at six times their 1970 prices. Traditional European paintings— once viewed with similar disdain and widely available for about $1,000 each—have been even more profitable. On average, they cost twelve times what they did in 1970. . . . Drawings of all sorts are now selling—by conservative estimate—at five times their 1970 prices." In the chapter on "Art as an Investment" in *The Deskbook of Art Law,* Professor Leonard DuBoff of Lewis & Clark College's Northwestern School of Law reported that art prices had multiplied eighteen times during the period from 1950 to 1970, while stock prices had merely quadrupled.

The statistics sound impressive but are unreliable. There is no accurate way to measure the art market's rise and fall. Many art transactions, carried on privately, never get reported, and the profitable transactions are much more apt to come to light than the unprofitable ones. Even the auction houses (which are the source of most statistical infor-

Vincent van Gogh, *Le Jardin du poète, Arles*

mation about the art market, since their prices are public) tend to exaggerate their successes and play down their failures. Unsold works are almost never mentioned in the auction houses' publicity releases and are omitted from their after-sale price lists. With such incomplete data to work with, no statistician can accurately gauge the dynamics of the art market.

Nevertheless, isolated examples of extraordinary appreciation are easy to document and, when reported by the press, are certain to excite the avaricious imagination. Ben Heller bought Jackson Pollock's *Blue Poles* in 1956 for $32,000 and sold it in 1973 for $2 million, for a compounded annual rate of return of 28 percent; Vincent van Gogh's *Le Jardin du poète, Arles* sold at auction in 1958 for $372,000 and was auctioned again, by Henry Ford II, in 1980 for $5.2 million, a 13 percent compounded annual rate of return; Mr. and Mrs. Burton Tremaine bought Jasper Johns' *Three Flags* in 1959 for $900 and sold it in 1980 for $1 million, an incredible 40 percent compounded annual rate of return. Less well publicized examples also illustrate art's investment potential: The $3-million price for Picasso's *Saltimbanque Seated with*

Above: **Jasper Johns,** *Three Flags*
Left: **Pablo Picasso,** *Saltimbanque*

Arms Crossed at SPB's 1980 Garbisch sale was widely reported, but the price the Garbisches paid for it in a private 1971 transaction with Wildenstein & Co. was not. According to Harry Brooks, president of the gallery, the earlier price was $875,000 (a compounded annual rate of return of 15 percent). Nor is it always necessary to hold onto an art work for many years to register impressive gains. Dealer Sidney Janis said that the person who sold a polished bronze *Fish* by Constantin Brancusi for $400,000 at Christie's, New York, in October 1978 had bought it from his gallery for half the price less than a year previously. Print dealer Sylvan Cole, Jr., said in 1980 that prices for George Bellows' fight scenes had doubled in one year and that Mary Cassatt's prints had quadrupled in price as a result of new levels set at a single 1980 auction at SPB, New York. Also at SPB, a Massachusetts couple paid $29,000 for a carved and painted wood figure of a racetrack tout at a 1979 folk-art auction and resold it at another SPB auction the following year for $53,000, setting a new auction record for an American folk sculpture.

Aroused by such stories, investment-minded buyers have increasingly flocked to the galleries and auction houses, undeterred by the warnings of many art professionals (including some who have benefited from the new investor interest) who regard art investors as philistine and misguided. Even banks and pension funds have gotten into the act. In 1979, New York's Citibank (in conjunction with SPB) began offering art-investment advice to its wealthiest clients (who were counseled to allocate up to 10 percent of their investment capital for art and antiques); in 1974, the British Rail Pension Fund (which provides pensions to railway employees in Great Britain) began a multi-million-dollar art-buying spree, diversifying its investment portfolio with Renoir, Matisse and Picasso, among others. Private art investment groups have sprung up around the country to take advantage of bulk-purchase discounts, and middle-class savers have increasingly sought to salvage their inflation-ravaged capital by joining the "tangibles" cult. In an article titled "Inflation Leads Many Reluctantly to Switch from Saving to Buying" (July 25, 1979), the *Wall Street Journal* reported that one man had recently bought "four LeRoy Neiman prints at $1,000 apiece and a Norman Rockwell lithograph for $2,000, nearly emptying the family's savings account," in hope of getting a better return on his money than his bank's 5.25 percent.

While Neiman and Rockwell are popular names today, some experts feel that their appeal may be too transitory to qualify them as "investment-quality" artists. Finding art that is of true "investment quality" is not easy because many art owners know a good inflation-hedge when they have one. They are not selling their finest works. "None of my clients wants to sell," lamented dealer Richard Feigen, who added that he had "never had this problem before." When asked if they would be willing to convert their treasures to cash, Feigen's

Attributed to Charles Dowler, *Race Track Tout*

clients have replied, "What do you want me to do with those green pieces of paper? They're useless." Nevertheless, Feigen has tried to solicit new business from investment-minded buyers through ads in financial publications: "In 1961 we sold a client this Picasso painting for $45,000. In 1973 we sold it for him for $500,000." (Other Feigen ads substitute Tanguy or Kandinsky for Picasso, with twelve-year appreciations of, respectively, $93,000 and $224,000.)

The Advantages of Art Investment

As an investment, art has certain advantages that no stocks or bonds can match. The intangible rewards—aesthetic pleasure and, sometimes, social prestige—that accrue from art collecting are, for some, a sufficient hedge against possible financial loss. For the more pragmatic, there is a material hedge: the possibility of big tax deductions for donations of art that might be unsalable or salable only at a substantial loss. In his article on the tax treatment of art, Professor William Speiller noted that many collectors overvalue the art that they donate to non-profit institutions and succeed in claiming tax deductions based on those inflated values. The owner of art that has decreased in value, he noted, may be tempted to donate it and claim a tax deduction equal to the original purchase price, even though the legally allowable deduction—equal to the work's fair market value at the time of donation—may be substantially less. "The investor in art will be familiar with the charitable deduction and know of the possibilities for overvaluation," according to Speiller. "Thus, he is given an unusual opportunity for investment gain at relatively low risk. If the values of the purchased objects skyrocket, he is a winner; if they nose-dive, he is protected from severe loss. In effect, the charitable deduction acts as an insurance policy on his investment." In an interview with the *New York Times* for an article on "investibles" (May 13, 1979), Robert Salomon, Jr., a partner in Salomon Brothers, described another tax-related reason for art's appeal as an investment: the fact that some very profitable art transactions probably go unreported to the IRS, particularly when the transactions are between private collectors. "No one can put a figure on the money involved," said Salomon, "but it is a sizable subterranean or non-taxpaying economy—non-taxpaying in that the profits often elude the tax collector, unlike the gains on securities."

Yet another tax advantage (and one that is legal) is available to those few art buyers who qualify as "investors" in the eyes of the IRS. An ordinary art collector—one who buys art primarily for pleasure rather than profit—cannot take tax deductions for the expenses involved in forming and maintaining a collection and cannot deduct capital losses resulting from unprofitable sales. But a buyer who can convince the IRS that his *primary purpose* for collecting is investment is entitled to take deductions for selling losses as well as for the costs of insurance, conservation, storage, art books and magazines, advisors' fees and other collection-related expenses. It is not easy to obtain these benefits, though, because the IRS is not easily convinced that an art buyer is truly a cold-blooded investor. In the landmark 1970 decision on the subject, the U.S. Court of Claims found that Mr. and Mrs. Charles Wrightsman, noted collectors of French eighteenth-century art and furniture, did not qualify for investor status because their personal lives revolved around their art interests and most of their collection was "on display or in use" in their New York apartment and Palm Beach home. This, the court concluded, was clear evidence that "personal pleasure," rather than investment, was the Wrightsmans' "primary purpose in acquiring and holding works of art." To prove otherwise, a buyer would have to treat art transactions in the same serious, businesslike way in which he would treat any other investment: maintain accurate, detailed records and inventories; keep well informed on the state of the art market (perhaps even charting it); buy and sell regularly; become an expert in a particular field or retain expert consultants; buy works according to their investment potential rather than personal preferences. To prove definitively the absence of the pleasure motive, an investor might store his works without even looking at them. Such behavior will undoubtedly make one richer in deductions but poorer in satisfaction.

The Risks

Despite the opportunities it offers for profit, pleasure, prestige and tax avoidance, art has many disadvantages in relation to other forms of investment: Stocks pay regular dividends and bonds pay regular interest, but art (unless, as in rare instances, it is leased) produces no income. The collector does not realize any financial gain from his investment until he sells or donates it. Far from generating income, an art portfolio creates expenses that are unknown to the stockholder: costs of conservation, storage and insurance. Art does not have the liquidity of stocks: You can always sell a share of AT&T, but if you consign a work to a dealer or auction house, you will probably have to wait several months for the sale to be transacted, or you may find out, after waiting all that time, that no one wants to pay your price. If you need quick cash, you may be able to sell to a dealer or auction house, but art professionals are not likely to pay you the full market value. "The collector who wants to invest must be aware that a $100 photograph is only worth $50 if he sells at that particular moment," said photography collector Samuel Wagstaff at the dealer-sponsored 1980 seminar in New York on photography collecting. Because of this, and also because works that reappear on the market too quickly are often regarded by potential purchasers as shopworn, most experts feel that art investors must be willing to hold onto their acquisitions for five years or more—another disadvantage of the art market relative to the stock market.

The relative illiquidity of the art market is perhaps even more irksome to the buyer than to the seller. You can always buy a share of AT&T, but you cannot always buy a top-quality work by a particular artist. While one share of a particular stock is as good as any other, this is certainly not the case when one compares different works by an artist. Except in the contemporary field, museums have removed an enormous portion of high-quality art from the market, and many private owners either hold onto their best works or donate them to museums. When a top-quality work (or even a middle-quality one of a type that rarely appears on the market) does come up for sale, it often goes for such a high price that its potential for dramatic further appreciation is questionable. The $6.4-million auction price for a middle-quality Turner, for example, was described by collector Norton Simon as "getting near the heights of tulipomania" (the amazing rise in prices for the coveted bulbs during the seventeenth century, which was followed by an equally stunning fall). The $980,000 auction price for George Caleb Bingham's *The Jolly Flatboatmen* was regarded with similar skepticism by Hilton Kramer of the *New York Times* (June 18, 1978), who noted that "Bingham is a painter I hold in high esteem, but even so, this development strikes me as something absurd, if not actually ominous. Is Bingham really *that* good, even at his best?" He derided as "nonsensical" SPB's claim that Bingham was the "Midwest's Rembrandt," adding that "it is worth pointing out that to be the 'Midwest's Rembrandt' is not quite the same as being Rembrandt." Even an official at SPB, Robert Schonfeld (who has since left the auction house), conceded that his firm had not recommended to its investment clients the Frederic Church *Icebergs* that sold for $2.5 million in 1979. Speaking at the 1980 New York Artexpo, Schonfeld said SPB knew the painting "was going to sell for more than the value for which it represents a good investment in terms of an anticipated series of growth figures discounted back to the present." He added that "the man who bought this painting does not collect American paintings." (To confuse the issue further, Schonfeld's colleague at SPB, C. Hugh Hildesley, maintained on another occasion —a 1980 meeting of the New York Society of Security Analysts, which Schonfeld also attended—that the Church was "a safe bet" as an investment, "because it will remain one of the most important examples of mid-nineteenth-century landscape painting in America.") The scarcity of important examples has caused collectors to turn to less important

George Caleb Bingham, *The Jolly Flatboatmen*

works and to works by previously unsought-after artists, creating a price rise for such works that many observers feel is totally out of proportion to their aesthetic merit or investment potential. In his book *The Economics of Taste: The Rise and Fall of the Picture Market, 1760–1960,* Gerald Reitlinger observed that "the most depressing symptom of the present era [is] the upgrading of journeyman painters. It was due to the plain impossibility for a private individual to obtain works by more inspired masters."

In addition to being much less liquid than the stock market, the art market is much more difficult to analyze. The limited availability of objective data about the art market and the importance of factors that defy quantification (such as taste and fashion) make any technical analysis of trends very tenuous. Some people do compile art charts: A British publishing firm, Art Sales Index Ltd., has produced graphs of auction price trends from 1970 to the present for some 60,000 artists, but these graphs provide no indication about the quality of the works that passed through the auction houses during that period, and they completely ignore private gallery sales.

In the fall of 1981, SPB began issuing "The Sotheby Index"—an attempt to do for art and antiques what the Dow Jones index does for securities. Appearing weekly in *Barron's,* SPB's index purports to track trends statistically in twelve fields (including old-master paintings, nineteenth-century European paintings, Impressionist and Post-Impressionist paintings, modern paintings and American paintings). Aggregate figures show how the market as a whole has fared. But the index is almost entirely based on auction results (so that figures go unchanged for weeks or even months until a relevant auction occurs) and its reliability is limited by the reliability of SPB's specialists, who, having selected a "market basket" of specific art works thought to be typical for each category, try to update the index periodically by estimating what those particular objects would bring on the market.

A German art newsletter, *art aktuell* (which has an English-language edition) has published tables that purport to assess the investment potential of contemporary artists, based on a comparison of their price levels with their "reputation points" (calculated on the basis of representation in important collections, exhibitions and publications). But the vagaries of the art market (particularly in contemporary art) are such that today's hot reputation may be cold by tomorrow.

Trying to buy art exclusively for profit is likely to be self-defeating, not only because many art professionals disdain art investors and won't give them good advice, but also because it is important to be able to appreciate art for its own sake in order to be able to select art that is likely to be a good investment. Contemporary-art collector Eugene Schwartz summed up the paradox that bedevils many would-be investors: "The trouble with thinking of art as investment is that it clouds your eye. Buying art is a strenuous and athletic profession. You have to use the same clarity in buying art as the person who creates the art." While expertise in the communications industry is not a necessary prerequisite to investing successfully in AT&T, a large degree of knowledge and appreciation of art is important preparation for becoming a successful art investor. Investors who do not have this kind of expertise would do well to hire advisors who do.

Although art-related expertise may protect you from calamitous failures, it is still no guarantee of great financial success. To "make a killing" in the art market, you must be able to predict which now-neglected artists or types of art will soon become fashionable. Since fashion does not always coincide with aesthetic merit or art-historical importance, the pronouncements of art experts are not always the best guides to hot investment prospects. This is particularly true in an art market that is starved for important works in traditional collecting areas and is, consequently, foraging in previously overlooked areas to an unprecedented degree. "The art market in the past has followed and been led by art historians and written art history," observed dealer Eugene Thaw at the 1980 *ARTnews* conference. "Today, the art market is provoking revision in art history. Having reevaluated many things that were overlooked or undervalued before, the art market has forced professional art historians to take another look. For example, Klimt and the whole period of Vienna in the 1890s is being reevaluated and looked at in a more serious way. . . . Victorian painting used to be equated with bad taste in any college art appreciation or art history course, but I have undergone a conversion and realize that there is fantasy, excitement and even elegance in some of these products of the nineteenth century." Similarly, in an article on the "New Vogue for Victorian Art" in the *New York Times Magazine* (Feb. 4, 1979), critic Hilton Kramer observed that "painters such as Bouguereau and Gérôme in France, and Watts and Leighton in England—long abominated by successive generations of avant-garde artists and critics and museum connoisseurs—are now winning friends." One such friend was Allen Funt of "Candid Camera" fame, who bought thirty-five paintings by the Victorian academician Lawrence Alma-Tadema during the late 1960s and early 1970s for a total of $264,000 and sold them at auction in 1973 for $570,000. Prices continued to rise subsequent to the sale, so that the record $72,900 fetched by one of Alma-Tadema's paintings at the Funt sale looked paltry compared to the $315,000 fetched in 1980 by the artist's *Caracalla and Geta* at Sotheby's, Belgravia.

As the example of the Victorians illustrates, it is possible to make a good investment buying works that have been generally regarded as "bad art." There are striking examples of this among contemporary artists, some of whom are enormously popular but almost universally scorned by the critics. In an article in the College Art Association's *Art Journal* (Summer 1980), Professor Robert Rosenblum of New York University's Institute of Fine Arts called these popular artists "the Bouguereaus and the Leightons of our time." "No right-thinking museum," he noted, "would ever consider exhibiting" their work, but "if we wanted to ask about prices, we might discover that those commanded by LeRoy Neiman, Simbari, or Bernard Buffet would give pause to museum budgets able to take on those artists, from Rauschenberg to LeWitt, whom we accept in our historical pantheon."

Works by Andrew Wyeth and Norman Rockwell are perhaps the most striking examples of this phenomenon: they are enormously popular, command high prices (which, in Rockwell's case, skyrocketed after his death in 1978), and are generally dismissed by the critics as facile and shallow. Similarly, most contemporary "western art"—paintings and sculpture with cowboy-and-Indian themes—is attacked by purist art critics and collectors "with more barbs than a wire fence," as reporter Beth Nissen observed in a *Wall Street Journal* article (Sept. 21, 1979). And yet, she noted that

> cowboy art appreciates almost as soon as the paint dries. Value of turn-of-the-century Western oils and bronzes has doubled since 1970, and many art prospectors buy the works of promising unknown artists and resell them almost immediately at a 10 percent to 15 percent profit. "The stuff appreciates by 25 percent or more a year, steady," says T. G. Ratcliffe, vice president of finance for LDB Corp. of Kerrville, Tex., a large carpet and floor products company that has a Western art collection valued at about $2 million. "As an investment, the paintings usually beat common stocks, bonds, coins, whatever."

Whether works by popularly acclaimed but critically scorned artists will prove to be good investments in the long run is questionable: perhaps, like the Victorians, they will fall from favor, only to be championed by some twenty-first-century collectors and art historians looking to rediscover neglected merit. In an article on the western art market for *ARTnews* magazine (December 1979), reporter Richard Blodgett wrote that Rudolf Wunderlich of Kennedy Galleries "echoes the warning of a number of other dealers when he asserts that many contemporary [western] paintings and sculptures are not worth the prices being paid. Ultimately, he says, a lot of buyers may be stuck with works they can't resell at anything close to current retail prices."

Ups and Downs

Perhaps the greatest drawback to art as an investment is that it often does not fulfill people's chief expectation of it—it does not always yield big profits, keep pace with inflation, or even appreciate modestly in value. Great art by universally admired artists—touted today as inflation-proof—has historically had its ups and downs in price, influenced by changes in taste, the economy, or the dynamics of the art market itself. According to art-market consultant Robert Schonfeld, formerly of SPB, the art market reached "its historical high quite some time ago" —in the late nineteenth and early twentieth century, taking into account the declining value of the dollar. Schonfeld cited this as evidence that values in the art market now are not overly inflated for would-be investors, but it might just as well serve to prove that art is not necessarily a good investment: some things have declined in value since the beginning of this century, in terms of the purchasing power of the dollar. In a December 1979 study of "Art as Investment," the London Economist Intelligence Unit observed that "the analysis of prices over a long perspective suggests that the years preceding the First World War saw a peak in the prices of pictures and fine furniture which has yet to be equalled." Similarly, in *The Economics of Taste: The Rise and Fall of the Objets d'Art Market Since 1750*, Reitlinger observed that in 1912–13 "almost every category" of art objects, with the exception of pictures, "reached prices that cannot be equalled today." (Reitlinger's book was published in 1963.) He added that "the personal whims of James Pierpont Morgan"—who, according to Reitlinger, may have spent on art the modern-day equivalent of $14 million in 1963 dollars between 1900 and 1913—had as much to do with the art-market rise as the prosperity of the times. Some of the paintings that Morgan purchased "have subsequently reappeared on the market at vastly enhanced prices," observed Reitlinger. "In fact, in the 1930s, when Andrew Mellon was forming his collection, these prices looked extremely low. On the other hand, the objets d'art were bought at prices that have never been repeated since."

As the example of Morgan illustrates, one big spender can cause his own price boom in art, making it difficult for him (and everyone else) to buy at advantageous prices. "I've created, in a way, some of my own problems," conceded Paul Mellon when asked about the rising prices for previously neglected British painters. Conversely, if one or a few big buyers drop out of the art market, they can create their own depression. The market for Chinese export porcelain—pieces created in China to appeal to Western tastes—crashed in 1974, after a ten-year rise, owing to the effect of Portugal's civil disorders on that country's collectors. "The chief Portuguese collector, a rich banker, disappeared into jail for a few weeks," according to an article on the art market in *Fortune* magazine (Nov. 20, 1978). "No one was left to buy in a glutted market."

When a dramatic rise in the market is largely due to an influx of speculators, a dramatic fall is likely to ensue. This makes the recent emphasis on art-as-investment seem slightly ominous. In *The Glorious Obsession*, French auctioneer Maurice Rheims observed,

> For the past ten years or so, capitalists who are anxious to safeguard their wealth and have suffered reverses through injudicious investments have been consulting people like me. Dazzled by rising prices in the art market, they suddenly discover amazing beauty in certain of its wares, though six months previously they couldn't even have told you what they looked like. This situation is really a warning signal in itself;

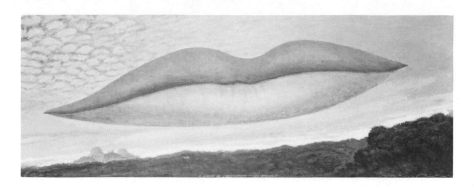

Man Ray, *À L'Heure de l'observatoire: Les Amoureux*

for as soon as speculators who have never previously taken any but a very short-term view, aiming only at a quick profit, begin declaring that art objects are the investor's best friend, there is good reason to suppose that the bell has begun to toll for auction rooms, picture galleries and antique shops.

Surrealist works were touted as "hot stocks" by Harry Brooks of Wildenstein & Co. gallery in an interview for a November 1974 article in *Esquire* magazine. In the same article, John Richardson, then of M. Knoedler & Co. gallery, was quoted as saying that there had been "an enormous boom in the Surrealist painters and there are no indications I can see that they will slack off." But by 1974–75, the wealthy Italian speculators who had fueled much of the Surrealist boom had pulled out of the market. In 1976, dealer Eugene Thaw told the art market conference sponsored by *The ARTnewsletter* that the previously sought-after Surrealist works were "now almost unsalable at a fraction of the price" of the early seventies. The November 1979 sale at SPB, New York, of Surrealist works from the collection of William Copley gave the unsteady market an important boost, setting auction records for several artists (led by the $750,000 price for Man Ray's *À l'Heure de l'observatoire: Les Amoureux,* an auction record at that time for any Surrealist painting). But more than a year later, *The ARTnewsletter* (March 3, 1981) reported that demand for the Surrealists was still uneven: "While the market for works by René Magritte has bounded back and is probably better than ever, there is only minimal interest in the movement's most difficult artists, among them . . . Yves Tanguy," whom Richardson had cited in the 1974 *Esquire* article as particularly hot.

Another example of a market disrupted by speculation was that for Ansel Adams' photographs. In 1978–79, auction prices for his works

—most notably *Moonrise, Hernandez, New Mexico,* his most famous image —kept reaching new heights at each sale. In May 1980, however, the Adams market suddenly collapsed, despite the fact that his work had recently been featured in an exhibition at the premiere showcase for contemporary American photography—the Museum of Modern Art. Many of Adams' works failed to find buyers at the May 1980 sales, and others went for unexpectedly low prices. Prices for a standard-size (16 by 20 inches) *Moonrise* at the various auction houses that May ranged from $9,000 to $16,000 (an auction record); by February 1981, the latest auction "quote" on *Moonrise* was only $6,500. Anne Horton of SPB, interviewed for an *ARTnews* article on the photography market (January 1981), explained that "when the prices for Adams went up so fast, the investment people thought, 'Whew! I never imagined it would go this high—let's sell.' Then too many came on the market at once, and a lot of people didn't buy because of the recession." Pierre Apraxine, curator of the highly regarded photography collection of the Gilman Paper Company, told *ARTnews* that he believed Adams prices had been run up by speculators rather than serious collectors. "If you use the medium as a stock market," he asserted, "you risk falling on your face. That is what has happened now in the case of Adams." Investors' interest in Adams was fueled by the decision of the photographer and his dealers to limit the number of prints he would produce and to raise his prices systematically over a period of time. At the 1980 *ARTnews* conference, which took place before the Adams slump, dealer Harry Lunn, Jr., commented that the Adams marketing scheme (which Lunn had helped implement) had inspired numerous imitators among other photographers and dealers. "People try to order an image before the next price rise takes place," Lunn said. The lesson for collectors: beware of market manipulators; they may cause a temporary run-up in price, but the market will eventually find its own level.

Fickle Fashion

Perhaps the biggest cause of market fluctuations is the most difficult to predict—changes in taste and fashion that may cause even high-quality works to lose their monetary value. The common belief that "masterpieces always hold their value [is] quite untrue," noted auctioneer Maurice Rheims in his memoirs:

> Fashion snaps its fingers at beauty no less readily than at ugliness. People still say "Superb!" to portraits of prominent people by Rigaud, Largillière, Perronneau or Raeburn; nevertheless these portraits now

cost only a fraction of the prices paid by the elegant sitters for having their likenesses taken. It will be objected that the finest modern pictures are like granite steps in the flank of the financial pyramid. Yet the prices of these, too, are giving way. Van Dongen is a case in point: prices for his pictures seem to have halved in less than two years. The beauty of his work is not in question; only its appeal.

Similarly, in *Self-Portrait with Donors,* John Walker observed that a painting by Frederick Childe Hassam entitled *Le Crépuscule* that was unsalable in 1941 at $675 "recently brought $150,000," while a van Dyck that ultimately went to the National Gallery of Art in Washington, *Queen Henrietta Maria with Her Dwarf,* was bought by William Randolph Hearst, the publishing magnate, for $375,000, later sold by Hammer Galleries in New York for $124,998 and, in 1952, bought by the Kress Foundation from Knoedler's for only $82,500. "Its present value," according to Walker (whose book was published in 1969), "would probably be once more about what Hearst paid originally. Thus the price of an acknowledged masterpiece by an artist no longer in vogue has fluctuated widely over the years but has risen scarcely at all; whereas a work by a minor American painter now much in fashion has appreciated staggeringly."

At the 1980 seminar on collecting sponsored by *Antiques World,* dealer Clyde Newhouse noted that eighteenth-century British portraits by such artists as Thomas Gainsborough, Joshua Reynolds, John Hoppner, George Romney and Henry Raeburn were eagerly snapped up in the early 1900s by the American robber barons (who were shrewdly manipulated by that master picture salesman, dealer Joseph Duveen). But by the 1930s, prices for such works had collapsed and some paintings that appeared at auction could not be sold for even one-tenth their previous prices. (Newhouse added that prices for such paintings are again on the rise.) At the same seminar, Carl Crossman of Childs Gallery noted that a revival of interest had recently begun in British turn-of-the-century prints by David Young Cameron, Muirhead Bone and James McBey. In the 1910s and 1920s, collecting such prints was considered chic, Crossman observed, but when the owners of those collections died, "the estates just wanted to dump them. . . . I don't think we'll hit the prices of the 1910s and '20s for another five years."

Economic Influences

Despite some recent claims to the contrary, the direction of art prices is also much influenced by the state of the economy. During

Sir Anthony van Dyck, *Queen Henrietta Maria with Her Dwarf*

the Great Depression, "when the stock market collapsed, the art market disintegrated," observed John Walker in his memoirs. In his book *The Joys of Collecting,* oil magnate J. Paul Getty described the pre-Depression art market in terms that could equally apply to the market in the 1970s:

In the mid and late 1920s, very few works of art of good quality were to be found on the market. The best examples of almost all forms of fine art were in museums, huge private collections, or held by very strong hands.

The United States was enjoying a period of tremendous prosperity, and there were great numbers of extremely wealthy men in Britain and Europe. They bid against each other for whatever came on the market. Prices on those items that were available spiraled completely out of proportion to any reasonable scale of values.

Although I had achieved a degree of business success, I was certainly in no position to compete with collectors of the caliber of the Hearsts, Mellons or Rothschilds. Besides, since my business enterprises were still expanding, I reinvested most of my profits in them. I had only relatively small sums of ready cash at my disposal.

Withal, in the late 1920s, it appeared to me that the days of collecting were just about over. The men who had made their millions and tens of millions before I'd started in business—or even before I was born—swept up just about everything worthwhile that had found its way to the market over the past few decades. The old aristocratic British and European families who still possessed treasure troves of fine art were, for the most part, very well situated financially in those days. And, even if they were not and decided to sell an item or two, they had been conditioned to the idea of entertaining only the most staggering offers for their possessions.

The entire situation changed with awful suddenness. The great panic—the "Crash"—of 1929 shook the art world no less than it did the financial world. The 1930s brought no convincing recovery.

The Depression settled over the United States and spread to Britain and Europe. Now, many of the strong hands that formerly held some of the finest examples of art on the face of the earth were forced to relax their grip. Many choice items became available for purchase, and art prices, like all other prices of the time, dropped to levels which would have been inconceivable a few years or even months earlier.

Here was an opportunity for the would-be collector with comparatively limited means, which could not possibly have been foreseen before 1929. As I became aware of this, my long-dormant urge to collect things of beauty and examples of fine art finally awoke.

More recently, art prices took several years to recover from the effects of the 1974–75 recession, when large numbers of works failed to sell at auction and many newcomers to the art market, including Japanese buyers of Impressionist and modern paintings, abruptly withdrew. "Speculators who once gleefully doubled their money on Matisse in a single year are fleeing," reported the *Wall Street Journal* (Oct. 25, 1974). An article in *Barron's* (Oct. 14, 1974) that appeared just before the disastrous Oct. 23, 1974 Impressionist/modern sale at SPB, New York, listed the reasons for the art world's apprehensive anticipation of that auction: "For one thing, thousands of potential bidders on both sides of the Atlantic are suffering personal liquidity crises. Not only have these individuals lost a bundle in stocks and bonds over the past 12 months, but other investments—including wine and real estate—also have suffered bear markets of their own. Moreover, a basic commodity, money, remains expensive and tight, while the economic outlook at home and abroad is less than sanguine." According to the article, SPB's presale estimates for that sale were more conservative than they had been the previous year, and the auction house had "asked consignors to scale their reserves accordingly. 'Especially in these times,' John Marion, president, told us, 'we wouldn't want to destroy the market by having too many paintings bought in.' " Nevertheless, thirty of the seventy-seven offerings *were* bought in, and confidence in the market was severely shaken.

In evaluating the current art-as-investment theories, it is important to consider the lessons of the 1974 collapse. At his 1979 talk on art investment before the New York Society of Security Analysts, Schonfeld, then of SPB, said that while values of lower-priced objects may be affected by an economic downturn, "the small percentage of objects sold for over $100,000 or $250,000 . . . are, if not totally, certainly very substantially immune from recession." Yet, in 1974, it was (by SPB's own account) the upper end of the market that suffered most. In a November 1974 press release, SPB noted that there had been a "softening of the market in the higher brackets of Impressionist and modern painting and Chinese works of art," and on Oct. 26, 1974, the *New York Times* reported from London that "old masters and Impressionists valued up to the equivalent of $150,000 seem to be holding up well, according to most art-market participants; $500,000 items are harder to sell." SPB's president, John Marion, commented in his company's November 1974 press release that "art commanding prices in five or six figures represents less than one percent of the total volume of items which pass through our galleries. Most of the items we sell are in the under-$50,000 range, and this 'middle market' area has performed well throughout the fall."

Similarly, when the art-investment advocates argue that the fortunes of the art market no longer follow those of the stock market (because investors now see art as an attractive alternative when the stock market goes down), it is instructive to remember that the same theories were being floated before the 1974 collapse. "Until a year or so ago," according to the same *New York Times* report, "the art market —as reflected in the prices paid at auctions—was much stronger than the stock market, because frustrated investors in securities were funneling their money into tangible objects of art whose long-term value seemed assured." In the end, though, the art market did not remain recession-proof; it just took longer than the stock market to feel the effects. The same pattern was seen in 1970–71: the recession hit the art market late.

In the midst of a market boom, it is tempting to believe that the rise in art prices is permanent, and there are many self-interested art merchants who are happy to encourage that belief. But while art-market history may not necessarily repeat itself, it is foolish to pretend that it never will. If and when a shake-out comes, the same merchants who have touted art as an attractive investment are likely to observe approvingly that "overinflated prices" have come down to "more realistic levels," making art a good buy for smart collectors. There were strong signs that this was starting to occur at the beginning of the 1981–82 auction season.

That said, it should also be noted that many observers strongly believe that the character of the art market has changed significantly, making a repetition of the 1974 collapse unlikely. Rightly or wrongly, art is increasingly being seen not just as a pleasant luxury but as a preserver of capital in times of inflation and economic difficulty. In January 1977, SPB issued an art-market study that suggested that "Americans may be 'optimism buyers' of art and Europeans 'pessimism buyers' in their reaction to outside economic factors. Inflation and other negative influences spur Europeans to investing more of their wealth in the rare, beautiful and unique of man's heritage, whereas confidence and prosperity seem to spur Americans to buy, more in the manner characteristic of 'consumers' everywhere." But by 1979, many market observers (including SPB officials) were talking about a "Europeanization" of the American art market, with more people spending "serious" money on tangibles as a hedge against inflation and an alternative to traditional investments. The picture market is now quite closely tied to the markets for real estate and gold, according to Christopher Burge of Christie's, New York. "It is no longer tied to the stock market. It is viewed as an inflation hedge and is therefore related to other inflation hedges." In its report on "Art as Investment," the London Economist Intelligence Unit suggested that an economic downturn might, paradoxically, cause an art-market upturn. Many people would still be very wealthy, the report noted, and, "like a rising tide, money must go somewhere; in a slump everybody knows that it should not be in the bank, or invested in industrial stocks when the factories are falling idle. Thus to the chary investor pictures still look good, and can be expected to look even better as the FT [*Financial Times* of London] and Dow Jones indices sink." The report added, however, that only "big names and important pieces" might fare well in a recession, while under-$4,000 objects might decline in value.

This theory seems to have been supported by the reports of auction houses at the end of the economically uncertain 1979–80 season. C. Hugh Hildesley told the New York Society of Security Analysts in June 1980 that sales at the upper levels of the market had "done extremely well. They have—there's no doubt about it—steadied down in the middle and at the bottom of the market." Similarly, New York auctioneer William Doyle told the *New York Times* (July 14, 1980) that prices for "medium-quality goods" had declined 25 to 60 percent. "I think the good stuff will hold its value, and that's what I intend to offer in sales," he said.

Particularly vulnerable to recession are newly emerging areas of collecting. Speaking at the 1980 dealer-sponsored conference on photography collecting, Anne Horton of SPB observed that there is greater fluctuation in a new field, like photography, than in an established one. "Prices will go up," she said, "but not without occasional setbacks." SPB's Hildesley told the New York Society of Security Analysts in 1980 that folk art was "another example of an alternative field [that] has become more popular . . . because of the high prices of eighteenth-century furniture. . . . I should, however, state that in the current recession, the alternative forms or newer areas of investment have been the first to dip slightly." A weathervane from the Stewart Gregory folk art collection that sold at SPB for $23,000 in 1979 would probably have fetched less had it been sold fifteen months later, according to Hildesley. Another "alternative field," contemporary prints, became popular in the late sixties and early seventies when many collectors were priced out of the paintings market. But, as Cynthia Saltzman observed in an *ARTnews* article on the print market (September 1979), "the mass

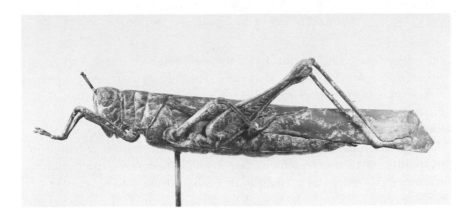

American, 19th century, *Grasshopper Weathervane*

production of prints saturated the market" and, with the 1974 recession, many prints dropped sharply in value while others became unsalable.

The extent to which an object will decline in value during a recession is likely to depend on the length of the recession and the degree to which the price of the particular object was overinflated in the first place. Since the art market usually has a delayed reaction to economic hard times, a quick economic recovery may head off an art-market downturn. People do not usually sell in a short recession, said dealer Stephen Hahn. But if a recession is sustained and the price of a particular art object was inflated beyond its merits during a previous period of inflation and speculation, that object may be vulnerable to the general slump. For this reason, investors are best advised to buy only works of the highest quality, even though, as dealer Sylvan Cole, Jr., observed, "in a period of inflation, everything goes up, even material of very little intrinsic merit."

Art vs. Inflation and the Stock Market

Although art prices generally rise during times of inflation, the validity of the claim that this rise actually outstrips or even keeps pace with inflation is uncertain at best. For one thing, as has already been seen, art prices are subject to taste and fashion and do not always increase, even when the purchasing power of the dollar declines. "Works by Bierstadt and Inness [nineteenth-century American artists] are only now starting to exceed the prices they got in their own time in actual dollars, not even taking inflation into account," according to dealer Lawrence Fleischman. Dealer Eugene Thaw observed that inflation may make "slightly illusory" the seemingly big price increases for certain art works. Works that have doubled in price over a period of time may be worth exactly the same amount in real terms, if you figure in inflation, according to Thaw. In his newsletter *The International Art Market* (April 1980), editor Howard Katzander observed that "there is another way of looking at investment values. To measure the quality of an investment in fine art it is necessary to compare it with more conventional investments made at the same time." He said that Renoir's *La Serre,* which sold for $1.2 million at the 1980 Henry Ford II sale, would have had to fetch $2.14 million to keep pace with more conventional investments. The painting had sold at auction for $200,000 in 1957; Katzander calculated what $200,000 would have yielded had it been invested in securities paying a 6 percent annual dividend (paid out quarterly), reinvested at the same rate. (He also observed that the Van Gogh which Ford sold for $5.2 million would have broken even, using the same investment criteria, at $3.84 million.) However, Katzander also noted that more conventional investments would have been "taxable year after year in the year earned. Only Mr. Ford's tax attorneys can say whether he would have done better on a purely financial basis with one investment or the other."

In its 1979 report, the London Economist Intelligence Unit also compared art with more conventional investments and found that art often comes out second best. The unit analyzed 182 pictures, books and art objects that had been sold at auction twice between 1960 and 1979, and discovered that stocks performed better than 30 percent of the old masters in the study, 44 percent of the Impressionists and 46 percent of the American paintings. (Stock performance was measured by the Dow Jones and London *Financial Times* industrial shares indices, taking into account annual dividends averaging 7.5 percent of the stocks' purchase price, reinvested at the same rate.) Some 25 of the 28 works in the American paintings section of the study were from the collection of John McDonough, which was sold at SPB, New York, in 1978. After that sale, SPB exulted that there could be "no greater evidence of the growth of the market" for American paintings than a comparison of the McDonough prices with previous auction prices for the same works. But the Economist Intelligence Unit found that 11 of the 25 McDonough works did not perform as well as stock-market investments; 4 of them actually sold at lower prices in 1978 than they had at previous sales and another sold for a gain of only $50. Paintings and prints by modern masters were the most successful categories in the Economist Intelligence Unit's survey. All of those sampled (a total of only 13 works) performed better than the stock market.

Choosing Your Investments

If, after knowing all the disadvantages and risks, an investor is determined to take a chance on art, how should he decide where to channel his money? A conservative investor would buy only top-quality works by well-established masters, using his knowledge of value to gauge whether a particular asking price gives him a good chance for future appreciation. A speculator might take a chance on contemporary art by lesser-known artists or works from other periods that are currently out of fashion. Such investments carry the greatest risk but also offer the greatest potential for dramatic appreciation if an undiscovered master later becomes highly sought-after. To be able to pick likely art-market prospects, you have to be able to recognize "art-historical imperatives," according to dealer Richard Feigen; a person with a trained eye and a broad knowledge of art history, he believes, can distinguish those artists who will prove to be important and who will, in the long run, come to be widely admired. The important artists, in Feigen's view, are those who "open other doors," leading art into new directions. Another way to judge an artist's importance, according to Feigen, is to gauge his influence on other artists and the importance of the artists he has influenced. Once you have identified important undiscovered artists, "you should buy them when others are not," Feigen said, "so you will have a choice of works of optimum quality. Then you should pay a premium to get the greatest. The price spread between the least good and the great is narrow for such artists. You have to get there before the Norton Simons do, because you can't compete with their money."

Instead of exploring uncharted territory, some investors look for artists who were previously much admired but have somehow fallen out of favor. "It's worth looking at areas that are currently out of fashion," said David Bathurst of Christie's at the 1980 *ARTnews* conference. "Art history shows that those areas will almost certainly come back." Similarly, dealer Sylvan Cole, Jr., said that he was purchasing prints from periods that "are not 'in' at the moment"—French etchings from 1820–80, Americans from 1900–50 and prints by little-known British artists from the same period. "The art world abhors a vacuum," he commented. "There is no such thing as a forgotten artist. Some are just less well known at the moment."

Like Cole, other dealers are increasingly branching out into new areas. At the 1980 *Antiques World* seminar, Clyde Newhouse commented that "collecting in the eighties is going to be enormously difficult. . . . There is an enormous scarcity of good things. We're going to have to find other routes. Our gallery sold only old masters originally, but we're now also in the Impressionist and American fields because of scarcity. It made us widen our vision and spread out." Similarly, Abbot Vose of Vose Galleries in Boston said that his firm was attempting to satisfy clients seeking paintings priced at $10,000 or less by taking on the estates of American Impressionist painters who are little known today but who won prizes and honors in their own time. (Other areas that some experts feel are overlooked or undervalued are mentioned on pages 7–8.)

In searching for new areas to explore, investors would do well to keep in mind three factors (as set forth by dealer Lawrence Fleischman) that generally determine the prices and appreciation prospects of art works: quality, rarity and demand. If the work of a little-known artist fulfills the first two criteria, demand may ultimately grow and prices rise. Buying quality means paying more attention to the merits of the work than the glamor of an artist's name. As collector Ralph Colin observed, "Picasso painted more good and more bad pictures than anyone." It also means not getting swept up in market fads like Egypto-mania, which swelled during the showing of "Treasures of Tutankhamun" in the United States, but which subsided soon after the show's departure. It also, obviously, means not buying misattributed works or fakes, which are the worst possible investments but which often attract the unwary because they are available at "bargain" prices. Collectors for whom the investment motive is paramount should avoid areas where fakes and misattributions are common, unless they can get very good advice or develop their own expertise. Old-master drawings, for example, may be a profitable area for knowledgeable investors, but it is a difficult field for the uninitiated; many works are unsigned and attributions often change.

Like quality, rarity usually helps to boost an art work's value. *Juliet and Her Nurse*'s $6.4-million auction price was largely due to the infrequency with which a Turner of that magnitude appears on the market. But rarity can sometimes diminish price, if a work is so unusual that it is unfamiliar to most collectors and is therefore unlikely to attract broad interest. Brenda Auslander, formerly of SPB, noted that if such a work does happen to sell well at an auction, "you will begin to see more on the market like it and you will see the beginning of a trend." She added that works that are not typical of a particular artist's output, even if very beautiful, do not usually sell as well as more familiar-looking works by the same artist. Similarly, a very large painting may be rare and important, but it may attract less market interest than a painting that can easily fit into someone's living room. There is one pessimistic school of thought that touts "transportables"—works that can easily fit into a suitcase—as the best possible investments, because they are attractive to big-money potentates in politically unstable countries, who may have to flee their homes at a moment's notice.

Analyzing Market Trends

After picking a field that seems ripe for appreciation, investors should try to analyze and anticipate market trends in that field.

The best approach is to be part of a gossip network. "By talking with other people who are doing similar things, you can begin to spot trends," according to dealer Eugene Thaw. "You must not isolate yourself; you should communicate with dealers, artists and museum people and you should read the magazines." By getting on the mailing lists of museums and galleries, you will receive advance word on important upcoming shows that may stimulate new market interest. "Prices go up as a result of museum shows, gallery exhibitions, book publications or a top collector starting to buy," according to Fleischman.

In its January 1980 publicity release for an exhibition of nineteenth-century American Luminist paintings, the National Gallery of Art in Washington proclaimed that although Luminism was "one of the most inconclusively studied areas of American art, the works are of a quality and interest as high as any in the national school." The increased market interest in Luminism was already obvious a few months before the National Gallery's show, with the $2.5-million auction sale of Frederic Church's huge *Icebergs* in October 1979. After that sale, Stuart Feld of Hirschl & Adler Galleries told Grace Glueck of the *New York Times* (Dec. 6, 1979) that his firm was able to sell "every Church we had—two very, very major ones and a smaller one." Also affected by the sale of *Icebergs* was the price for "son of *Icebergs*," Church's small (10 by 18 1/4 inches) version of the same subject that was sold by the artist's great-grandson in January 1980 at Stalker & Boos, a Michigan auction house, for $225,000—more than four times what it had been appraised at two years earlier.

As the Church example illustrates, major auction sales, like major museum shows, can help create market trends, and when the two work together, the effect can be particularly strong. The auction houses sometimes try to capitalize on this, scheduling major auctions to coincide with related museum exhibitions or art fairs, and emphasizing the connection in their presale publicity. An auction that contains a particularly strong group of works by a single artist or in a particular field often attracts unusually strong interest from collectors and dealers, causing prices to break through previous levels.

In her *ARTnews* article on the print market, Cynthia Saltzman observed that "print prices usually leap to new levels at an auction of a large group of works by a single artist. The famous Nowell-Ustike sales of Rembrandt prints in 1967 and 1968 elevated the market for Rembrandt, much as the Toulouse-Lautrec and Munch sales at Kornfeld [a Swiss auction house that holds important print sales] did for the modern artists." New York print dealer Lucien Goldschmidt told Saltzman that Toulouse-Lautrec prices rose at the 1973 Kornfeld sale "because it was *visible* that there were a whole group of important works and that innumerable people wanted them." Similarly, new price levels were set for van Dyck prints when an unusually large and rare group of nineteen etchings from the collection of Mr. and Mrs. W. Clifford Klenk was sold in 1979 at SPB, New York. "Any time you have a lot of important works in a sale by one master, you have everyone who wants a work by that master competing," commented Andrew Robison, Jr., graphic arts curator at the National Gallery in Washington, after the van Dyck sale. The market for Chinese ceramics got a big boost from SPB's 1980 sale of Song (Sung) Dynasty ceramics and other Chinese works of art from the collection of Mr. and Mrs. Eugene Bernat. Only about one-quarter of the Bernat offerings were considered by experts to be of the highest quality, but the collection had been widely exhibited and the allure of the star lots rubbed off on the rest of the goods. The auction pulled in over $3.3 million—more than twice what the auctioneers had predicted in their published presale estimates.

The Bernat auction vividly illustrated some important axioms of art investment:

• Art works sold as part of a large, coherent collection often attract greater interest and higher prices than such pieces would have commanded individually. "The best things in a collection pull up the rest," observed Eugene Thaw. "In a collection of ten objects of which two are masterpieces and eight are good, the two will carry the other eight along because everyone knows the collector as the owner of the two masterpieces."

• Because of the opportunities for public-relations hype before the sale and multi-buyer competition during it, auction is often the best way to dispose of a collection that contains some high-quality pieces and many of lesser quality. The "souvenir mentality" takes over: bidders vie to come home with at least one object—even if it is a minor one—from a collection that they consider important. James Lally, SPB's Chinese art expert, commented that the spirit of the Bernat sale "was one of absolute determination among bidders to have a piece from the 'Bernat Collection.' People in the room kept setting their sights higher and higher for the objects they wanted." Lally added that "results obtained from the Bernat auction have established a new appreciation and market level for this collecting area." This level was maintained and, in many instances, surpassed by the sale of another important single-owner collection at SPB (Hong Kong and London) in 1980—the Chinese porcelains, ancient bronzes and early ceramics owned by the late Edward Chow, a respected collector and dealer.

• A collection stands a better chance of commanding high prices if it is widely exhibited and published. Works from the Bernat collection had been lent to many museum exhibitions, including those at the Boston Museum of Fine Arts, Los Angeles County Museum of Art and Asia House Gallery in New York. Many that appeared at auction had previously been published in books or articles by China scholars. (The Chow collection was also well known and well published.) According to old-masters dealer Stanley Moss, investment-minded collectors should get to know the scholars who publish works in their field. "Find out who's doing what and let them know about your painting," he suggested.

The trouble with regarding important auction sales and museum shows as bullish market indicators is that they do not always work that way. A sale that is touted as "highly important" by an auction firm's public-relations department may turn out to have a large number of uninteresting, inferior or questionable works, with market-depressing results. Even if an auction appears to set new levels for certain types of works, those levels may not be sustained once the hoopla dies down. *The ARTnewsletter* (Nov. 25, 1980) noted that prices for the finest works in the Bernat sale "were not at all surprising or outrageous [but] objects similar to those in the sale's lower price range will probably bring somewhat less when they appear on the market in the next few years."

Similarly, museum shows are not always the market-boosters that they are assumed to be. It is true that they can give an important lift to reputations and sales, particularly when they draw attention to little-known or insufficiently understood art. But if an artist has already received a great deal of attention, the market impact of yet another museum show (unless it reveals a previously underexposed aspect of his art) may be negligible. According to dealer Leo Castelli, Jasper Johns' work was so well known already that a 1977 show of his work at the Whitney Museum in New York had no effect on the market. He added that, in general, the market impact of a museum show "depends on the consensus about the artist. If there is excitement about the artist, a museum show can have a tremendous effect. But if the general feeling is not around, you can't sell anything." Similarly, dealer Xavier Fourcade noted that "a museum show exposes an artist. When he is good, the museum exhibition shows he is great. But if he is mediocre, it shows that he's mediocre. A museum show can be very dangerous." In his *New York Times* review (Dec. 18, 1977) of the Whitney's Jasper Johns show, Hilton Kramer commented that "retrospective exhibitions on the scale of the Whitney's Johns show are a cruel test for any artist, and for some they are fatal. They have the power to make a small artist seem even smaller, especially when he has the reputation for being 'big.' Johns has the reputation, but he does not have the oeuvre to support it. Hence the boredom. There is simply not enough to look at. Johns's art cannot sustain attention on this scale." (It should be noted that Johns' work does seem to sustain market attention on a grand scale, as the much publicized million-dollar sale by the Tremaines to the Whitney illustrates.)

At the 1980 *ARTnews* conference, Xavier Fourcade proposed a strategy for investing in contemporary artists based on price analysis rather than museum exposure: "If I would have to pinpoint the time at which acquisition of a contemporary work of art represents an investment with a serious chance of a substantial increase within a relatively short period of time, I would say that it takes place at the time when prices for works of a very established artist with a clear and easily verifiable record have started rising seriously. It is most likely that the rise will continue for quite a while, if the general market conditions are favorable, and may become considerable. To give an example from my own business, I would say that acquiring the works of such artists as Gorky, de Kooning or Barnett Newman in the late forties or early fifties would have been purely a love of art, or long-range speculation. To acquire those same works in the late fifties and sixties could already have been called investment. Those artists were already very much recognized, it was easy to check their records, and their prices had reached between $10,000 and $60,000 or $70,000. Those were serious prices, and at that time it was most likely that prices would reach the levels of today, which are between $30,000 or $40,000 and $1 million or more for works of very good quality, depending on their period."

One morbid myth about investing in contemporary art is that works by elderly or infirm artists are good prospects because prices rise when an artist dies. In reality, works by an artist whose reputation was shaky when he was alive may be completely unsalable after he dies. Even in the case of a renowned artist, prices after death may fall if he has left behind a large number of works which may (if the estate is imprudently managed) create a glut on the market. The fear of such an occurrence caused a decline in Picasso's prices after his death in 1973; when it was seen that the works in the estate would probably not be released en masse, the market began to perk up. The death of Alexander Calder in 1976 caused a sharp rise in prices for his highly popular hanging mobiles, but not for the rest of his oeuvre, according to Klaus Perls, who was Calder's dealer during the artist's lifetime.

Sophisticated traders with years of art-market experience have developed their own favorite market indicators and investment strategies. According to Richard Feigen, price trends for paintings by particular artists can often be anticipated by analyzing the trends for drawings by the same artists, because "drawing collectors and curators are five to eight years ahead of those in painting fields." Eugene Thaw commented that astute collectors learn to spot the "category of art objects in every field that is in price limbo." The price of such an art work, he said, is "too much for a dealer to pay to buy it but lower than what he would ask if he owned it and was selling it. This represents a good buy for a collector." Such good buys may come up at auction, he noted, if a work has fallen out of fashion or if a very similar work (or the same work) has recently been on the market.

Another strategy is to vary the location of one's purchases according to where the best buys are. As any traveler knows, a purchase made in a country with a relatively weak currency may be a good buy in terms of a stronger home currency. A Japanese collector visiting the U.S. in 1974 would have spent 294,000 yen for a $1,000 painting, but in 1978 (when the Japanese began to reappear on the U.S. art-buying scene) he could buy a $1,000 painting for only 208,000 yen. Irrespective of foreign exchange rates, certain countries generally provide better buying opportunities for certain kinds of art. For optimum price and selection, it is better, for example, to buy old masters in Europe than in the U.S., according to John Walsh, Jr., of the Boston Museum of Fine Arts. "The auction houses in Europe are a prime source for old-masters dealers," he noted. "New York dealers often buy in Europe and sell here."

Perhaps the best buys are works whose importance no one else has yet recognized—treasures that are sometimes unearthed at garage sales, out-of-the-way antique shops and minor auctions. Seeking such works is an enjoyable but completely unreliable investment strategy; such finds are rare and are usually made by those who have devoted their lives to the quest. For the neophyte, "bargains" are dangerous: a naïve buyer should not assume that the seller is even more naïve. But for the trained eye, such finds can add greatly to the romance and profit of art collecting.

If you don't have a trained eye, you can improve your investment odds by hiring an advisor. But to do this, you should still have at least enough knowledge to determine whether your advisor is competent. "If you want to make money on art," said dealer Feigen, "you should give a 10 percent commission to someone who knows what he's doing, leave him alone and not ask him to buy what you like. I would be happy to do it but, so far, no one has asked me." Unlike Feigen, many dealers (as previously noted) have an aversion to giving investment advice. With them, your best chance at getting such help is to approach the subject obliquely: ask which works they think will maintain their value over the years and which artists they think may be currently undervalued.

A good dealer meets all the criteria for a good investment advisor except one: he has an obvious interest in selling his own goods. The same sort of self-interest taints investment programs that are connected with auction houses. At this writing, the specialists at SPB, New York, serve as advisors for the investment program that Citibank, New York, runs for very wealthy clients. An investment advisory program set up in 1979 by Artemis, the international art-dealing group, died for lack of interest. (Dealers affiliated with Artemis are Eugene Thaw and Xavier Fourcade of New York, Heinz Berggruen of Paris, David Carritt of London, Heinz Herzer of Munich and Robert Light of Santa Barbara.) In the late 1970s, the U.S. Trust Company, a New York–based asset management firm, began an art advisory program for wealthy clients, drawing upon the expertise of a wide-ranging network of specialists. Some groups of investors have formed syndicates to obtain advice and discounts that are available to those who buy in bulk. In 1981, a New York–based doctors' group called the Physicians Planning Service Corporation announced plans to set up a $5-million limited partnership to invest in art, with funds to be provided by participating doctors, dentists and others. Advice was to be supplied by a panel of collectors of American art. Instead of buying into an art-investment plan, it is possible to buy shares in firms that deal in art: SPB and

Christie's are publicly traded on the London Stock Exchange and SPB is also traded over-the-counter in the U.S. Artemis is publicly traded on exchanges in Amsterdam, Luxembourg, Brussels and Antwerp.

When you buy shares instead of art, or when you buy art solely to make money, you are forfeiting art's chief value—the surprise and delight it gives in changing or heightening how one sees color, form, things, people, nature and sometimes even life. In a basic way, art is cheapened as it becomes more costly. In his book *The Shock of the New,* *Time* magazine art critic Robert Hughes observed that art-investment propaganda had redefined art, "whose new task was simply to sit on the wall and get more expensive. By the end of the 1970s, we were getting to the point where everything that could be regarded, however distantly, as a work of art was primarily esteemed not for its ability to communicate meaning, or its use as historical evidence, or its power to generate aesthetic pleasure, but for its convertibility into cash."

Paradoxically, the best way to buy art to appreciate is probably to appreciate art. Unless you have some personal feeling for the artistic value of what you buy, you have no objective way of evaluating the wisdom and reliability of others' advice. Pioneering in relatively unexplored areas (where the greatest financial gains can sometimes be made) means relying most heavily on your own sense of artistic worth and your conviction that the rest of the world will ultimately confirm your vision. To invest well in art, one should probably not approach it as an investment at all, but simply follow the principles of intelligent collecting that are presented throughout this book. Buying, preserving and selling art with knowledge and care is the surest way to enjoy its lasting rewards, whether you collect for love, money or both.

APPENDIX

PROFESSIONAL ORGANIZATIONS

Art Dealers Association of America, 575 Madison Ave., New York, N.Y. 10022

The National Antique and Art Dealers Association of America, c/o A. Beshar & Co., 49 E. 53rd St., New York, N.Y. 10022

American Association of Dealers in Ancient, Oriental and Primitive Art, 159½ E. 94th St., New York, N.Y. 10028

Association of International Photography Art Dealers, Suite 2505, 60 E. 42nd St., New York, N.Y. 10165

American Association of Museums, 1055 Thomas Jefferson St., N.W., Washington, D.C. 20007

College Art Association, 16 E. 52nd St., New York, N.Y. 10022

The American Institute for Conservation of Historic and Artistic Works, Suite 725, 1511 K St., N.W., Washington, D.C. 20005

International Foundation for Art Research, 46 E. 70th St., New York, N.Y. 10021

American Society of Appraisers, P.O. Box 17265, Washington, D.C. 20041

Appraisers Association of America, 60 E. 42nd St., New York, N.Y. 10165

BROKERS SPECIALIZING IN FINE ARTS INSURANCE

Alexander & Alexander, 160 Water St., New York, N.Y. 10038 (contact Mortimer Silvey)

Huntington T. Block Insurance, 2101 L St., N.W., Washington, D.C. 20037 (contact Huntington Block)

Frenkel & Co., 156 William St., New York, N.Y. 10038 (contact Leo Frenkel)

Great Northern Brokerage Corp., 950 3rd Ave., New York, N.Y. 10022 (contact Norman Newman)

Frank B. Hall & Co., Wall Street Plaza, New York, N.Y. 10005 (contact Carmel Fauci)

Fred S. James & Co., 3435 Wilshire Blvd., Los Angeles, Calif. 90010 (contact Carl Allen)

Marsh & McLennan, 1221 Avenue of the Americas, New York, N.Y. 10020 (no single contact)

Republic Hogg Robinson of New York, 355 Lexington Ave., New York, N.Y. 10017 (contact Jeffrey Haber or Michael Fischman)

BIBLIOGRAPHY

GENERAL

The list that follows includes all books and articles mentioned in the text, in addition to many others that the author considers to be useful to collectors.

Art Law

DuBoff, Leonard D., *The Deskbook of Art Law,* Federal Publications, Washington, 1977

Duffy, Robert E., *Art Law: Representing Artists, Dealers, and Collectors,* Practising Law Institute, New York, 1977

Feldman, Franklin, and Weil, Stephen E., *Art Works: Law, Policy, Practice,* Practising Law Institute, New York, 1974

Hodes, Scott, *What Every Artist and Collector Should Know About the Law,* E. P. Dutton & Co., New York, 1974

Internal Revenue Service, "Valuation of Donated Property" (Publication 561)

Lerner, Ralph, chairman, *Representing Artists, Collectors, and Dealers,* Practising Law Institute, New York, 1981

Merryman, John Henry, and Elsen, Albert E., *Law, Ethics and the Visual Arts,* Matthew Bender & Co., New York, 1979

Nilson, Lisbet, "A Preview of the IRS Art Print Panel's Findings," *The ARTnewsletter,* September 15, 1981

Speiller, William, "The Favored Tax Treatment of Purchasers of Art," *Columbia Law Review,* March 1980

Authentication

Fakes and Forgeries, Minneapolis Institute of Arts, 1973

Goodrich, David L., *Art Fakes in America,* The Viking Press, New York, 1973

Hochfield, Sylvia, "The Mansoor Collection: An Insoluble Controversy?" *ARTnews,* Summer 1978

Horsley, Carter, "Metropolitan Reattributes 300 Paintings," *New York Times,* January 19, 1973

Rostron, Bryan, "Is Science Ahead of the Forger?" *New York Times,* August 19, 1979

Collecting Guides

Anderson, Alexandra, and Rickey, Carrie, with Trebay, Guy, "Up Against the Wall Street: An Investor's Guide to Galleries," *Village Voice,* October 15–21, 1980

Blodgett, Richard, *Photographs: A Collector's Guide,* Ballantine Books, New York, 1979

Buchsbaum, Ann, *Practical Guide to Print Collecting,* Van Nostrand Reinhold Co., New York, 1975

Collector's Handbook, Cincinnati Art Museum, 1978

Glueck, Grace, "Bargain Hunting at Rockefeller's New Store," *New York Times,* January 11, 1979

Ratcliff, Carter, "Making It in the Art World: A Climber's Guide," *New York,* November 27, 1978

Russell, John, "The City's Prints Scene: Quality Art at High Prices," *New York Times,* December 5, 1980

Russell, John, "A Connoisseur's Guide to the Fine Art of Print Collecting," *New York Times,* June 22, 1979

Russell, John, "A Tour of Los Angeles Galleries," *New York Times,* December 2, 1979

Shapiro, Cecile, and Mason, Lauris, *Fine Prints: Collecting, Buying and Selling,* Harper & Row, New York, 1976

Zigrosser, Carl, and Gaehde, Christa M., *A Guide to the Collecting and Care of Original Prints,* Crown Publishers, New York, 1965

Collectors and Collecting

Baker, Richard Brown, "Notes on the Formation of My Collection," *Art International,* September 20, 1961

Berges, Marshall, "Jennifer Jones & Norton Simon," *Los Angeles Times* "Home" magazine, December 15, 1974

du Plessix, Francine, "Collectors: Mary and Leigh Block," *Art in America,* September–October 1976

Gendel, Milton, " 'If One Hasn't Visited Count Panza's Villa, One Doesn't Know What Collecting Is All About' " *ARTnews,* December 1979

Getty, J. Paul, *The Joys of Collecting,* Hawthorn Books, New York, 1965

Hyams, Barry, *Hirshhorn: Medici from Brooklyn,* E. P. Dutton, New York, 1979

Levy, Alan, "Baron Thyssen's Old Masters: 'A Collection of Extraordinary Visual Intensity,' " *ARTnews,* November 1979

Rheims, Maurice, *The Glorious Obsession,* St. Martin's Press, New York, 1980

Saarinen, Aline B., *The Proud Possessors,* Random House, New York, 1958

Seligman, Germain, *Merchants of Art, 1880–1960: Eighty Years of Professional Collecting,* Appleton-Century-Crofts, New York 1961

Walker, John, *Self-Portrait with Donors: Confessions of an Art Collector,* Little, Brown and Co., Boston, 1974

Directories

American Art Directory, R. R. Bowker Co., New York (lists and provides information about art museums, schools, cultural organizations and periodicals)

The Art Index, Wilson, New York (lists art-related articles appearing in periodicals)

Burnham, Bonnie, *The Protection of Cultural Property: Handbook of National Legislations,* International Council of Museums, Paris, 1974

Collectors' Marketplace Directory, Artrepreneur, New York (lists New York dealers, auction houses and appraisers according to their specialties)

Glueck, Grace, "The Experts' Guide to the Experts," *ARTnews,* November 1978

Locus, Filsinger & Co., New York (a guide to which artists are represented by which New York galleries)

Locus Select, Filsinger & Co., New York (a national guide to which artists are represented by which galleries)

Official Museum Directory, American Association of Museums, Washington, and National Register Publishing Co., New York (lists and provides information about museums and cultural organizations)

Ticho, Suzy, *Directory of Artists Slide Registries,* American Council for the Arts, 1980

Who's Who in American Art, R. R. Bowker Co., New York

Maintaining a Collection

Consumer Reports, "How to Protect Your Valuables," August 1980

Dolloff, Francis W., and Perkinson, Roy L., *How to Care for Works of Art on Paper,* Museum of Fine Arts, Boston, 1979

The Gray Letter, "The Importance of Appraisals Is Increasing," August 3, 1981

Hochfield, Sylvia, "Conservation: The Need Is Urgent," *ARTnews,* February 1976

Johnson, E. Verner, and Horgan, Joanne C., *Museum Collection Storage,* UNESCO, Paris, 1979

Keck, Caroline K., *A Handbook on the Care of Paintings,* American Association for State and Local History, Nashville, 1965, revised edition 1976

Keck, Caroline K., *How to Take Care of Your Paintings,* Charles Scribner's Sons, New York, 1978

Keck, Caroline K., *Safeguarding Your Collection in Travel,* American Association for State and Local History, Nashville, 1970

King, James, "Security Equipment Survey," *Art Theft Archive Newsletter* (published by International Foundation for Art Research), May 1979

Mason, Donald L., *The Fine Art of Art Security,* Van Nostrand Reinhold Co., New York, 1979

Nauert, Patricia, and Black, Caroline M., *Fine Arts Insurance: A Handbook for Art Museums,* The Association of Art Museum Directors, distributed by American Association of Museums, Washington, 1979

Preservation of Photographs, Eastman Kodak Co., Rochester, 1979

Stolen Art Alert (formerly *Art Theft Archive Newsletter*), published ten times a year by the International Foundation for Art Research, New York

Tillotson, Robert G., *Museum Security,* International Council of Museums, Paris, 1977

Market Newsletters and Periodicals

Art & Auction, Daniel Zilkha, publisher, 250 W. 57th Street, New York, N.Y. 10019 (published ten times a year; previews and reviews of auctions, calendar of sales, reviews of art books and exhibitions, profiles of collectors and art professionals)

Art Investment Guide, Richard Hislop, editor, Art Sales Index Ltd., Pond House, Weybridge, Surrey, KT13, England (published three times a year; reports on major auctions, analysis of market trends)

The ARTnewsletter, Milton Esterow, editor and publisher, 122 E. 42nd Street, New York, N.Y. 10168 (published biweekly, except August; reports on major auctions, analysis of market trends, updates on news and legal developments affecting collectors)

The Gray Letter, Gray Boone, editor and publisher, P.O. Drawer 2, Tuscaloosa, Ala. 35402 (published weekly; reports on major auctions, analysis of market trends)

The International Art Market, Howard Katzander, editor, Art in America, 850 Third Avenue, New York, N.Y. 10022 (published eleven times a year; a compilation of price lists from recent auctions; some analysis of market trends)

The Print Collector's Newsletter, Jacqueline Brody, editor, 16 East 82nd Street, New York, N.Y. 10028 (published six times a year; print-related news and reviews, auction price lists)

Market Trends

Art as Investment, London Economist Intelligence Unit, London, 1979

Blodgett, Richard, "The Rip-Roaring, Record-Breaking Western Art Market," *ARTnews,* December 1979

Castelli, Leo, "Castelli Asserts His 'Right' to Set Prices," letter to the *New York Times,* November 9, 1975

DuBois, Peter C., "Critical Auctions: The Art Market This Month Faces Its Moment of Truth," *Barron's,* October 14, 1974

Ferretti, Fred, "Art and Money—Market Forecast: '74–'75," *Esquire,* November 1974

Frankel, Stephen Robert, "The Photography Market: A Decisive Moment?" *ARTnews,* January 1981

Glueck, Grace, "Art Dealers Revel in Boom from Amulets to Photographs," *New York Times,* December 6, 1979

Glueck, Grace, "How Do You Price Art Works? Let the Dealers Count the Ways," *New York Times,* January 20, 1976

Hughes, Robert, "Confusing Art with Bullion," *Time,* December 31, 1979

Ingrassia, Lawrence, "Inflation Leads Many Reluctantly to Switch from Saving to Buying," *Wall Street Journal,* July 25, 1979

Katzander, Howard, "Thoughts on the Art Market: A 20-20 Look at the Future," *The International Art Market,* April 1980

Knox, Sanka, "Prices Are Down at More Auctions," *New York Times,* October 26, 1974

Kramer, Hilton, "The Influence of Money on Taste," *New York Times,* June 18, 1978

Kramer, Hilton, "The New Vogue for Victorian Art," *New York Times Magazine,* February 4, 1979

Kuhn, Annette, "Post-War Collecting: The Emergence of Phase III," *Art in America,* September–October 1977

Mahon, Gigi, "Unveiling Sotheby's Art Index," *Barron's,* November 9, 1981

Maidenberg, H. J., "Investibles: Even a Bank Is Buying Art," *New York Times,* May 13, 1979

Nissen, Beth, "Cowboy Art: Where Deer and the Antelope Pay," *Wall Street Journal,* September 21, 1979

Ratcliff, Carter, "The Art Establishment: Rising Stars vs. the Machine," *New York,* November 27, 1978

Reif, Rita, "New York Challenges London in Art Sales," *New York Times,* July 14, 1980

Reitlinger, Gerald, *The Economics of Taste: The Art Market in the 1960s,* Barrie and Jenkins, London, 1970

Reitlinger, Gerald, *The Economics of Taste: The Rise and Fall of the Objets d'Art Market Since 1750,* Holt, Rinehart and Winston, New York, 1965

Reitlinger, Gerald, *The Economics of Taste: The Rise and Fall of the Picture Market, 1760–1960,* Holt, Rinehart and Winston, New York, 1964

Ricklefs, Roger, "Bye-Bye, Gogh-Gogh: Economic Woes Damp the Big Boom in Art," *Wall Street Journal,* October 25, 1974

Robards, Terry, "Painting and Antique Markets Grow Soft As Britons Invest in Easily Portable Items," *New York Times,* October 26, 1974

Rosenblum, Robert, "Art Ignored: The Other 20th Century," *Art Journal,* Summer 1980

Russell, John, "What Price Art? Today's Auction Boom Mixes Smart Money and Pounding Hearts," *New York Times,* May 31, 1980

Saltzman, Cynthia, "The Lively Market in Prints," *ARTnews,* September 1979

Price Guides

Annual Art Sales Index, Richard Hislop, editor, Art Sales Index Ltd., Pond House, Weybridge, Surrey, KT13, England (a comprehensive annual guide to international auction prices)

Auction Prices of American Artists, Richard Hislop, editor, Art Sales Index Ltd., Pond House, Weybridge, Surrey, KT13, England (a comprehensive annual guide)

Gordon's Print Price Annual, Martin Gordon, Inc., 25 East 83rd Street, New York, N.Y. 10028 (a comprehensive international guide to prices at print auctions)

International Auction Records, Editions Publisol, P.O. Box 339, Gracie Station, New York, N.Y. 10028 (a comprehensive annual guide to international auction prices)

Security and Protection

See the section "Maintaining a Collection."

Miscellaneous

Biblioteca d'Arte Rizzoli (*Tutta la Pittura di* [name of artist]), Rizzoli Editore, Milan (out of print)

Classici dell'Arte Rizzoli (*L'Opera Completa di* [name of artist]), Rizzoli Editore, Via A. Rizzoli, 2-20132 Milan, Italy (available at Rizzoli, 712 Fifth Avenue, New York, N.Y. 10019)

Conrad, Barnaby, III, "Profile: Berggruen," *Art/World,* November 15–December 13, 1978

Emmerich, André, "Ancient Art & Ethics," *The Art Gallery,* October–November 1978

Feron, James, "Rembrandt Brings $2.2 Million in Bid Mix-up," *New York Times,* March 20, 1965

Hughes, Robert, *The Shock of the New,* Knopf, New York, 1980

Kinkead, Gwen, "A Genteel War Heats Up the Art World," *Fortune,* November 20, 1978

Kramer, Hilton, "Johns's Work Doesn't Match His Fame," *New York Times,* December 18, 1977

Kramer, Hilton, "Picasso's Picassos in Minneapolis Show," *New York Times,* February 13, 1980

Kramer, Hilton, "Whitney Shows Warhol Works," *New York Times,* November 23, 1979

Reif, Rita, "Buying or Just Browsing, the Action Is at the Auction," *New York Times,* November 9, 1979

Reif, Rita, "A Turner Sells for Record $6.4 Million," *New York Times,* May 30, 1980

Saltzman, Cynthia, "Sotheby's Christie's Are in Costly Battle for U.S. Art Market," *Wall Street Journal,* July 7, 1981

Sanger, Elizabeth, "If Your Taste in Art Runs to the Bizarre, O.K. Harris Is OK," *Wall Street Journal,* August 18, 1978

Sotheby Parke Bernet Newsletter, "You Don't Have to Be Here to Bid," January–February 1980

Trucco, Terry, "The Bernat Sale," *The ARTnewsletter,* November 25, 1980

Trucco, Terry, "An Important Surrealist Cache," *The Artnewsletter,* March 3, 1981

KEY ART-HISTORY SOURCES

Except where otherwise noted, each of the following lists was compiled by one or more members of the appropriate curatorial department in the Metropolitan Museum of Art. I have eliminated those books that could not be found listed among the holdings of the Met's own library, one of the most extensive art-reference facilities in the country.

American Paintings and Sculpture

GENERAL SURVEYS:

Brown, Milton W., *American Art to 1900: Painting, Sculpture, Architecture*, Abrams, New York, 1977

Novak, Barbara, *American Painting of the Nineteenth Century: Realism, Idealism, and the American Experience*, Praeger, New York, 1969

Richardson, Edgar P., *Painting in America, from 1502 to the Present*, Crowell, New York, 1967

Wilmerding, John, *American Art* (Pelican History of Art series), Penguin, Harmondsworth, England, 1976

REFERENCE BOOKS:

Clement, Clara (Erskine), and Hutton, Laurence, *Artists of the Nineteenth Century and Their Works: A Handbook Containing 2050 Biographical Sketches*, Boston and New York, 1880

Cowdrey, Mary Bartlett, *American Academy of Fine Arts and American Art-Union, 1816–1852*, The New-York Historical Society, New York, 1943

Cowdrey, Mary Bartlett, *National Academy of Design Exhibition Record, 1826–1860*, The New-York Historical Society, New York, 1943

Fielding, Mantle, *Dictionary of American Painters, Sculptors, and Engravers* with an addendum compiled by James F. Carr containing corrections and additional material on Fielding's original entries, James F. Carr, New York, 1965

Groce, George C., and Wallace, David H., *The New-York Historical Society's Dictionary of Artists in America 1564–1860*, Yale University Press, New Haven, 1957

Naylor, Maria, ed., *The National Academy of Design Exhibition Record, 1861–1900*, Kennedy Galleries, New York, 1973

AMERICAN FOLK ART

(compiled by Nancy Druckman, specialist at Sotheby Parke Bernet, New York):

Bishop, Robert, *American Folk Sculpture*, Dutton, New York, 1974

Bishop, Robert, and Coblentz, Patricia, *A Gallery of American Weathervanes and Whirligigs*, Dutton, New York, 1981

Fales, Dean A., Jr., and Bishop, Robert, *American Painted Furniture*, Dutton, New York, 1972

Lipman, Jean, *American Folk Art in Wood, Metal and Stone,* Dover reprint, New York, 1972 (originally published by Pantheon, New York, 1948)

Lipman, Jean, *Techniques in American Folk Decoration,* Dover reprint, New York, 1972 (originally published by Oxford University Press, 1951)

Lipman, Jean, *Rufus Porter, Yankee Pioneer,* Clarkson Potter, New York, 1968

Lipman, Jean, and Armstrong, Thomas N., III, *American Folk Painters of Three Centuries,* Whitney Museum, New York, 1980

Lipman, Jean, and Winchester, Alice, *The Flowering of American Folk Art,* Whitney Museum, New York, 1974

Rumford, Beatrix T., general ed., *American Folk Portraits: Paintings and Drawings from the Abby Aldrich Rockefeller Folk Art Center,* Little, Brown, Boston, for the New York Graphic Society, 1981

Ancient Near Eastern Art

Frankfort, Henri, *Cylinder Seals,* Macmillan, London, 1939

Kenyon, Kathleen M., *Archaeology in the Holy Land,* Benn, London, 1960

Oates, David and Joan, *The Rise of Civilization,* Elsevier, Phaidon, Oxford, 1976

Orthmann, Winfried, *Der Alte Orient,* vol. 14, Propyläen Kunstgeschichte, Berlin, 1975

Porada, Edith, *The Art of Ancient Iran,* Crown, New York, 1965

Strommenger, Eva, *5000 Years of the Art of Mesopotamia,* Abrams, New York, 1964

Drawings

Stampfle, Felice, ed., *Master Drawings,* Master Drawings Association, New York (quarterly journal containing feature articles and reviews of books and exhibitions)

Egyptian Art

Cooney, John D., *Amarna Reliefs from Hermopolis in American Collections,* Brooklyn Museum, New York, 1965

Hayes, William Christopher, *The Sceptre of Egypt: A Background for the Study of the Egyptian Antiquities in the Metropolitan Museum of Art,* Harper in cooperation with the Metropolitan, New York, 1953–59

Smith, William Stevenson, *The Art and Architecture of Ancient Egypt* (Pelican History of Art series), Penguin, Baltimore, 1958

European Paintings

Classici dell'Arte Rizzoli series (*L'Opera Completa di* [name of artist]), Rizzoli Editore, Milan

Pevsner, Nikolaus, general ed., Pelican History of Art series, Penguin, New York (formerly Baltimore)

Blunt, Anthony, *Art and Architecture in France, 1500 to 1700* (Pelican History of Art series), Penguin, Baltimore, 1970

Hamilton, George Heard, *19th & 20th Century Art: Painting, Sculpture, Architecture,* Abrams, New York, 1970

Posner, Donald, and Held, Julius S., *17th and 18th Century Art: Baroque Painting, Sculpture, Architecture,* Prentice-Hall, Englewood Cliffs, N.J., 1972

Rosenberg, Jakob, *Dutch Art and Architecture: 1600 to 1800* (Pelican History of Art series), Penguin, Baltimore, 1972

Stechow, Wolfgang, *Dutch Landscape Painting of the 17th Century,* Phaidon, London, 1966

Far Eastern Art

CHINESE PAINTING

(compiled by the Cleveland Museum of Art and published in its News & Calendar, *January 1981):*

Cahill, James F., *Chinese Painting,* Skira, Lausanne, 1960

Cahill, James F., *Hills Beyond a River,* Weatherhill, New York, 1976

Cahill, James F., *Parting at the Shore,* Weatherhill, New York, 1978

Eight Dynasties of Chinese Painting, exhibition catalogue with essays by Wai-kam Ho, Sherman E. Lee, Laurence Sickman and Marc F. Wilson, Cleveland Museum of Art, 1980

Lee, Sherman E., *Chinese Landscape Painting,* Cleveland Museum of Art, 1962

Lee, Sherman E., *A History of Far Eastern Art,* Abrams, New York, 1973

Lee, Sherman E., and Ho, Wai-kam, *Chinese Art Under the Mongols,* Cleveland Museum of Art, 1968

Loehr, Max, *The Great Painters of China,* Phaidon, Oxford, 1980

Sickman, Laurence, and Soper, Alexander, *Art and Architecture in China* (Pelican History of Art series), Penguin, Baltimore, 1971

CHINESE CERAMICS:

Ayers, John G., *The Baur Collection* (four vols.), Collections Baur, Geneva, 1968

Ayers, John G., *The Seligman Collection of Oriental Art,* vol. 2: *Chinese and Korean Pottery and Porcelain,* L. Humphries for the Arts Council of Great Britain, 1964

Lion, Daisy (Goldschmidt), *Ming Porcelain,* Rizzoli, New York, 1978

Pope, John Alexander, *Chinese Porcelains from the Ardebil Shrine,* Freer Gallery of Art, Smithsonian Institution, Washington, 1956

Valenstein, Suzanne G., *A Handbook of Chinese Ceramics,* Metropolitan Museum of Art, New York, 1975

Wirgin, Jan C., *Sung Ceramic Designs,* Ph.D. thesis, Stockholm University, 1970

JAPANESE ART:

Stern, Harold P., *Birds, Beasts, Blossoms, and Bugs: The Nature of Japan,* Abrams, New York, 1976

Stern, Harold P., *Master Prints of Japan,* Abrams, New York, 1969

INDIAN AND SOUTHEAST ASIAN ART:

Boisselier, Jean, *The Heritage of Thai Sculpture,* Weatherhill, New York, 1975

Coomeraswamy, Ananda K., *History of Indian and Indonesian Art,* Munshiram Manoharlal, New Delhi, 1972

Craven, Roy C., *A Concise History of Indian Art,* Praeger, New York, 1976

Giteau, Madeleine, *Khmer Sculpture and the Angkor Civilization,* Abrams, New York, 1966

Goetz, Hermann, *India: Five Thousand Years of Indian Art,* Methuen, London, 1959

Kramrische, Stella, *The Art of India,* Phaidon, New York, 1954

Louis-Frédéric (pseud.), *The Art of India: Temples and Sculpture,* Abrams, New York, 1960

Münsterburg, Hugo, *Art of India and Southeast Asia,* Abrams, New York, 1970

Rowland, Benjamin, *The Art and Architecture of India* (Pelican History of Art series), Penguin, Baltimore, 1953

Sivaramamurti, Calambur, *The Art of India,* Abrams, New York, 1977

Greek and Roman Art

Andreae, Bernard, *The Art of Rome,* Abrams, New York, 1977

Beazley, J.D., and Ashmole, Bernard, *Greek Sculpture and Painting to the End of the Hellenistic Period,* Cambridge University Press, Cambridge, 1932

Richter, G.M.A., *A Handbook of Greek Art,* Phaidon, London, 1959

Robertson, Martin, *A History of Greek Art,* Cambridge University Press, Cambridge, 1975

Islamic Art

GENERAL:

Aslanapa, Oktay, *Turkish Art and Architecture,* Faber, London, 1971

Atil, Esin, *Art of the Arab World,* Freer Gallery of Art, Smithsonian Institution, Washington, 1975

Dimand, M.S., *A Handbook of Muhammadan Art,* Metropolitan Museum of Art, New York, 1958

Ettinghausen, Richard, *From Byzantium to Sasanian Iran and the Islamic World,* Brill, Leiden, 1972

Kühnel, Ernst, *Islamic Art and Architecture,* Cornell University Press, Ithaca, 1966

Otto-Dorn, Katharina, *Kunst des Islam,* Holle, Baden-Baden, 1965

Pope, Arthur Upham, ed., *A Survey of Persian Art from Prehistoric Times to the Present,* Meiji-Shobo, Tokyo, 1964–77

Sourdel-Thomine, Janine, *Die Kunst des Islam,* Propyläen Verlag, Berlin, 1973

Welch, S. Cary, *The Art of Mughal India: Painting and Precious Objects,* Abrams and Asia House Gallery, New York, 1963

ARCHITECTURE:

Hoag, John D., *Islamic Architecture,* Abrams, New York, 1976

CERAMICS:

Lane, Arthur,*Early Islamic Pottery,* Faber & Faber, London, 1947

Lane, Arthur, *Later Islamic Pottery,* Faber & Faber, London, 1957

GLASS:

Fukai, Shinji, *Persian Glass,* Weatherhill, New York, 1977

IVORY:

Beckwith, John, *Caskets from Cordoba,* Victoria and Albert Museum, London, 1960

METALWORK:

Barrett, Douglas E., *Islamic Metalwork in the British Museum,* British Museum, London, 1949

Fehérvári, Géza, *Islamic Metalwork of the 8th to the 15th Century in the Keir Collection,* Faber & Faber, London, 1976

PAINTING AND CALLIGRAPHY:

Arnold, Thomas W., *Painting in Islam: A Study of the Place of Pictorial Art in Muslim Culture,* Dover reprint, New York, 1965 (originally published by Oxford University Press, 1928)

Atasoy, Nurhan, and Cağman, Filiz, *Turkish Miniature Painting,* R. C. D. Culture Institute, Istanbul, 1974

Binyon, Robert Laurence; Wilkinson, J.V.S.; and Gray, Basil, *Persian Miniature Painting,* Oxford University Press, London, 1933

Ettinghausen, Richard, *Arab Painting,* Skira, Geneva, 1962 (distributed by World Publishing, Cleveland)

Lings, Martin, *The Quranic Art of Calligraphy and Illumination,* World of Islam Festival Trust, London, 1976

Robinson, Basil William, ed., *Islamic Painting and the Arts of the Book: Miniatures in the Keir Collection,* Faber & Faber, London, 1976

Schimmel, Annemarie, *Islamic Calligraphy,* Brill, Leiden, 1970

Medieval Art

Baxandall, Michael, *The Limewood Sculptors of Renaissance Germany,* Yale University Press, New Haven, 1980

Conant, Kenneth John, *Carolingian and Romanesque Architecture, 800–1200,* Penguin, Baltimore, 1966

Focillon, Henri, *The Art of the West in the Middle Ages* (2 vols.), Phaidon, New York, 1963

Gaborit-Chopin, Danielle, *Ivoires du Moyen Âge,* Office du Livre, Fribourg, Switzerland, 1978

Gauthier, Marie Madeleine, *Emaux du Moyen Âge Occidental,* Office du Livre, Fribourg, Switzerland, 1972

Hubert, J.; Porcher, J.; and Volbach, W.F., *Europe of the Invasions*, Braziller, New York, 1975

Lasko, Peter, *Ars Sacra, 800–1200*, Penguin, Baltimore, 1972

Mâle, Emile, *Religious Art in France: The Twelfth Century*, Princeton University Press, Princeton, 1978

Müller, Theodor, *Sculpture in the Netherlands, Germany, France, and Spain: 1400 to 1500*, Penguin, Baltimore, 1966

Pope-Hennessy, John, *An Introduction to Italian Sculpture*, Phaidon, New York, 1972

Sauerländer, Willibald, *Gothic Sculpture in France, 1140–1270*, Abrams, New York, 1972

Verdier, Philippe; Brieger, Peter; and Montpetit, Marie Farquhar, *Art and the Courts: France and England from 1259 to 1328*, National Gallery of Canada, Ottawa, 1972

von der Osten, Gert, and Vey, Horst, *Painting and Sculpture in Germany and the Netherlands: 1500 to 1600*, Penguin, Baltimore, 1969

Wixom, William D., *Treasures from Medieval France*, Cleveland Museum of Art, 1967

The Year 1200, Metropolitan Museum of Art, New York, 1975

Zarnecki, Jerzy, *Art of the Medieval World*, Abrams, New York, 1975

Photographs

Gernsheim, Helmut and Alison, *The History of Photography, 1685–1914*, McGraw-Hill, New York, 1969

Newhall, Beaumont, *The History of Photography from 1839 to the Present Day*, Museum of Modern Art, New York, 1964

Primitive Art

GENERAL:

Biebuyck, Daniel P., *Tradition and Creativity in Tribal Art*, University of California Press, Berkeley, 1969

Forge, Anthony, ed., *Primitive Art & Society*, Oxford University Press for the Wenner-Gren Foundation for Anthropological Research, London, 1973

Newton, Douglas, *Masterpieces of Primitive Art*, Knopf, New York, 1978

AFRICA:

Cornet, Joseph, *Art of Africa: Treasures from the Congo*, Praeger, New York, 1971

D'Azevedo, Warren L., ed., *The Traditional Artist in African Societies*, Indiana University Press, Bloomington, 1973

Elisofon, Eliot, and Fagg, William, *The Sculpture of Africa*, Praeger, New York, 1958

Laude, Jean, *African Art of the Dogon*, Brooklyn Museum with Viking, New York, 1973

Vogel, Susan, ed., *For Spirits and Kings: African Art from the Paul and Ruth Tishman Collection,* Metropolitan Museum of Art, New York, 1981

Willett, Frank, *African Art: An Introduction,* Praeger, New York, 1971

OCEANIA:

Cox, J. Halley, and Davenport, William H., *Hawaiian Sculpture,* University Press of Hawaii, Honolulu, 1974

Gathercole, Peter; Kaeppler, Adrienne L.; and Newton, Douglas, *The Art of the Pacific Islands,* National Gallery of Art, Washington, 1979

Guiart, Jean, *The Arts of the South Pacific,* Golden Press, New York, 1963

Linton, Ralph, and Wingert, Paul, in collaboration with René d'Harnoncourt, *Arts of the South Seas,* Museum of Modern Art, New York, 1946

Schmitz, Carl A., *Oceanic Art,* Abrams, New York, 1971

NORTH AMERICA:

Covarrubias, Miguel, *The Eagle, the Jaguar, and the Serpent: Indian Art of the Americas,* Knopf, New York, 1954

Douglas, Frederic H., and d'Harnoncourt, René, *Indian Art of the United States,* Museum of Modern Art, New York, 1941

Feder, Norman, *American Indian Art,* Abrams, New York, 1971

Fundaburk, Emma L., and Foreman, Mary D.F., *Sun Circles and Human Hands: The Southeastern Indians,* Luverne, Ala., 1957

Haberland, Wolfgang, *The Art of North America,* Crown, New York, 1964

Hawthorn, Audrey, *Art of the Kwakiutl Indians and Other Northwest Coast Tribes,* University of British Columbia, Vancouver, and University of Washington Press, Seattle, 1967

Willey, Gordon R., *An Introduction to American Archaeology* (3 vols.), Prentice-Hall, Englewood Cliffs, N.J., 1966–71

MIDDLE AMERICA:

Coe, Michael D., *The Maya,* Praeger, New York, 1966

Coe, Michael D., *Mexico,* Thames & Hudson, London, 1962

Covarrubias, Miguel, *Indian Art of Mexico and Central America,* Knopf, New York, 1966

Easby, Elizabeth, and Scott, John F., *Before Cortés,* Metropolitan Museum of Art, New York, 1970

Jones, Julie, *El Dorado: The Gold of Ancient Colombia, from El Museo del Oro, Banco de la República, Bogotá, Colombia,* Center for Inter-American Relations, New York, 1974

Kubler, George, *The Art and Architecture of Ancient America* (Pelican History of Art series), Penguin, Baltimore, 1975

Wauchope, Robert, ed., *Handbook of Middle American Indians* (16 vols.), University of Texas Press, Austin, 1964–73

Willey, Gordon, *Das Alte Amerika, mit Beiträgen von Ignacio Bernal, et al.,* Propyläen Verlag, Berlin, 1974

SOUTH AMERICA:

Bennett, Wendell C., *Ancient Arts of the Andes,* Museum of Modern Art, New York, 1954

d'Harcourt, Raoul, *Textiles of Ancient Peru and Their Techniques,* University of Washington Press, Seattle, 1962

Lapiner, Alan C., *Pre-Columbian Art of South America,* Abrams, New York, 1976

Steward, Julian H., ed., *Handbook of South American Indians* (7 vols.), U.S. Government Printing Office, Washington, 1946–59

Prints

Brunner, Felix, *A Handbook of Graphic Reproduction Processes,* Arthur Niggli, Teufen, Switzerland, 1962

Hind, A.M., *A History of Engraving and Etching from the 15th Century to the Year 1914,* Houghton Mifflin, Boston and New York, 1923

Hind, A.M., *An Introduction to a History of Woodcut* (2 vols.), Constable, London, 1935

Ivins, William, Jr., *Prints and Visual Communication,* Da Capo Press, New York, 1969

Mayor, A. Hyatt, *Prints and People: A Social History of Printed Pictures,* Metropolitan Museum of Art, New York, 1971

Mason, Lauris, and Ludman, Joan, *Print Reference Sources—A Select Bibliography, 18th–20th Centuries,* KTO Press, Millwood, N.Y., 1979

Twentieth-Century Art

Arnason, H.H., *History of Modern Art: Painting, Sculpture, Architecture,* Abrams, New York, 1968

Barr, Alfred H., Jr., ed., *Masters of Modern Art,* Museum of Modern Art and Simon & Schuster, New York, 1954

Barr, Alfred H., Jr., *What Is Modern Painting?* Museum of Modern Art, New York, 1943

Haftmann, Werner, *Painting in the 20th Century,* Praeger, New York, 1966

Rose, Barbara, *American Art Since 1900: A Critical History,* Praeger, New York, 1967

Rosenblum, Robert, *Cubism and 20th-Century Art,* Abrams, New York, 1961

Sandler, Irving, *The Triumph of American Painting: A History of Abstract Expressionism,* Praeger, New York, 1970

Schapiro, Meyer, *Modern Art: 19th and 20th Centuries,* Braziller, New York, 1978

INDEX

*Grateful acknowledgment is made to all those who have
given permission to use paintings and illustrations, as listed below:*

*Grateful acknowledgment is made to the following
for permission to reprint from previously published material:*

Art International: Excerpts from *Art International,* September 1961. Reprinted
with permission.

E. P. Dutton, Inc: Excerpts from *Merchants of Art, 1880–1960: Eighty Years of
Professional Collecting* by Germain Seligman. Copyright 1961 by Germain
Seligman. Reprinted by permission of E. P. Dutton, Inc.

Museum of Fine Arts, Boston: Excerpts from Francis W. Dolloff and Roy L.
Perkinson, *How to Care for Works of Art on Paper.* 3rd ed. Boston: Museum
of Fine Arts, 1979. Excerpts reprinted by permission of the publisher.

St. Martin's Press and Souvenir Press: Excerpts from *The Glorious Obsession* by
Maurice Rheims. Copyright © 1980 by Maurice Rheims, St. Martin's Press,
Inc., and Souvenir Press, Ltd.

Charles Scribner's Sons: Excerpts from Caroline Keck, *How to Take Care of Your
Paintings* (New York: Charles Scribner's Sons, 1978). Reprinted with the
permission of Charles Scribner's Sons.

Stolen Art Alert: Excerpts from "Security Equipment Survey," by James King,
published in *Art Theft Archive Newsletter,* May 1979.

An excerpt from *The Joys of Collecting* by J. Paul Getty, Hawthorn Books, 1965.

Lee Rosenbaum, who graduated magna cum laude *from Cornell University and has an M.S. degree from the Columbia University School of Journalism, has worked as a reporter (for the Binghamton* Evening Press*) and had articles published in many newspapers and magazines, including* The New York Times, *the New York* Daily News, New York *magazine, the* Wall Street Journal, *the* Village Voice, ART*news,* Art in America *and* Horizon. *Ms. Rosenbaum has served as associate editor of* ARTnews *and managing editor of* The ARTnewsletter, *an international biweekly report on the art market. From 1974 to 1978 she was editor of* Art Letter, *a national monthly for arts professionals. She is currently a contributing editor for* ARTnews. *Ms. Rosenbaum lives in New Jersey with her husband, Donald, and their son, Paul.*

A NOTE ON THE TYPE

The text of this book was set, via computer-driven cathode-ray tube, in a film version of a typeface called Baskerville. The face itself is a facsimile reproduction of types cast from molds made for John Baskerville (1706–1775) from his designs. Baskerville's original face was one of the forerunners of the type style known as "modern face" to printers—a "modern" of the period A.D. 1800.

Type composition by
Haddon Craftsmen, Scranton, Pennsylvania.
Printed and bound by
Murray Printing Company, Westford, Massachusetts.

Typography and binding design by
A. T. CHIANG